ADVANCE COMMENTS FOR *THE BOOK OF CO-CREATION*

R. Buckminster Fuller, inventor of the Geodesic Dome:

I am deeply moved by Barbara Marx Hubbard's *The Book of Co-Creation.* I confidently accredit her mystical experiences and her consequent viewpoint that everyone is a direct child of God. I do so because of a similar experience of my own. It was in February 1928 that I had this real and extraordinary experience, the only one in my life that was utterly mystical. I was walking on Michigan Avenue in Chicago when suddenly I found myself with my feet seemingly no longer touching the pavement. I found myself floating along at the center of a sparkling sphere. Then I heard a deep, loud and clear voice, such as I had never heard before, saying, "From now on you need never await temporal attestation to your thought. You think the truth." I find Barbara's interpretations of her experiences and her therefrom assumed self-disciplines to be inspired.

Elizabeth Campbell, former president, Association for Humanistic Psychology:

This work is revelation. New Testament scriptures come alive with new meaning. It is an inspiration to Christians as well as anyone who believes that human transformation is possible. This work provides a new message of hope, set in an evolutionary perspective, for our human species.

Gary Zukav, author of *The Seat of the Soul:*

I recommend *The Book of Co-Creation* to those who feel estranged from "Christian" activities and institutions, but who have found a Christ of ever-expanding generosity and love at the heart of their being.

Georg Feuerstein, Ph.D., author of *Structures of Consciousness:*

Every age reinterprets its inherited wisdom. Barbara Marx Hubbard's *Book of Co-Creation* renders this important service for the Christian tradition. Despite or perhaps because of the secular tone of our modern era, a dialogue with Christianity is fundamental to our self-understanding as Westerners. She shows how the essential core of the

Christian tradition contains a universal message that is singularly significant for our times, when we as individuals and as a species are called to jettison all egotistic ambitions and parochial concerns and to join the larger family of intelligent life in the cosmos. Barbara Marx Hubbard's vision for the human race is irrepressibly optimistic, and it offers us a viable alternative to the cynicism and apocalyptic pessimism infecting a growing number of people. Her book is a splendid manifesto for *Homo universalis,* the new Adam and New Eve who are joyous and responsible co-creators of the future.

John W. White, author of *The Meeting of Science and Spirit:*

The Book of Co-Creation is a beautifully stated/designed work. It deserves to be read widely. It also strikes me as having the potential for being set to music oratorio-fashion and becoming a contemporary Messiah. In any case, it ought to be illustrated by paintings from the masters of yesterday and today.

Rev. Marcia Sutton, minister, Church of Religious Science:

The Book of Co-Creation is a present day explanation of the heart of the sacred teachings. It takes us beyond the walls of the church. It must be translated through the culture not through the church. It will reach the Diaspora and bind us back again.

Dr. Thomas O. Paine, administrator of NASA during the Apollo program:

You are carrying forward the ecstatic philosophy of Teilhard de Chardin, emphasizing the uniqueness and unity of mankind, with our intellectual as well as physical links to the universe. You provide an answer to the question: "What is man, that thou art mindful of him?"

David Smith, director, Xavier University TV Center:

I had intense upwellings of emotion of profound joy that come from the peak experience of insight. I immediately recognized that I was listening to the words of Jesus. The words were not on the page but flowing directly to my heart. It was what I had been longing for most of my life. I view the text as a miracle. It is the next step in salvation history—the preparatory intervention of God for what is to come. It is a direct gift to humanity as a practical approach to understanding our journey. I cannot personally envision a more appropriate vessel for God's contemporary statement than Barbara Marx Hubbard.

Aspasia Voulis, artist:

Reading your book, with each page, the YES resonating through me is the cumulated YES of every creative person who has ever lived on this earth, healed by grace of all residue of hurt and misunderstanding—"the tears have been wiped away." It is a major work for the 21st century.

Archbishop Warren Prall Watters, D.D., director of Esoteric Studies, Church of Antioch:

Your book, as it stands, is a prologue to the growth and unfoldment of the New Order of Christian Worship proclaiming the new birth of Christ in the human heart. Your pertinent words in the book will surely help aspiring mankind to stand in spiritual being revealing God immanent.

Rama Vernon, president, Center for International Dialogue:

You are creating a road map for generations to come. And what you are giving now will go far beyond this earthly body.

Sidney Lanier, Episcopal priest, founder, American Place Theater, New York City, and A New American Place, San Francisco:

Your spiritual vision, substantiated by your writing and speaking, and culminating in *The Book of Co-Creation,* is a powerful religious impulse to impel our conscious evolution as a species. The book provides an opening for re-visioning the New Testament, the seed document of our Western culture. This is no small undertaking. It will raise the level of spiritual discourse, and promises to yield not only the meaning of our power, but also of our suffering. It is a foundation stone for a culture based on a responsible science and democracy.

You affirm by example, leading to the reclamation of the long repressed energy of women and feminine energy as a whole. The Ecozoic Age (Thomas Berry's phrase) demands the life-serving gifts of the feminine.Women must finally be present in the holy of holies of the temples, sharing with men the solemn responsibilities of convening and sacralizing culture.

T·H·E
REVELATION
OUR CRISIS IS A BIRTH

BY

BARBARA MARX HUBBARD

Published by
The Foundation for Conscious Evolution
336 Bon Air Center #384
Greenbrae, CA 94904
1-(800) 444-7030

Library of Congress Cataloging-in-Publication Data

Hubbard, Barbara Marx, 1929–
        The revelation: our crisis is a birth / by Barbara Marx Hubbard.--
1st ed.
        p. cm. — (The Book of co-creation)
        Includes bibliographical references and index.
        ISBN 0-9631032-1-0 : $25.00 — ISBN 0-9631032-0-2 (pbk.): $16.95
        1. Jesus Christ—New Age Movement Interpretations. 2. Creation. 3. Birth
(Philosophy) 4.Future in popular culture. I. Title.
II. Series: Hubbard, Barbara Marx, 1929– Book of co-creation.
BT304.93.H83 1993
232.9--dc20

                                                                93-19345
                                                                CIP

Copyright © 1993, Barbara Marx Hubbard

The Foundation for Conscious Evolution is dedicated to the awakening of
humanity's collective capacities.*The Revelation: Our Crisis Is a Birth* is published
by the Foundation as a part of the broad process of realizing the evolutionary
potential of humanity through a maturing science and spirituality.

Printed in USA
Second Edition

10 9 8 7 6 5 4 3 2 1

Cover design and illustration by Lightbourne Images
Author's photo by Nita Winter Photography

TO FOUNDERS OF A
NEW ORDER OF THE FUTURE

*A deep communion of pioneering souls
from every race, nation and religion,
who experience within themselves the
birth of the Universal Human.*

ACKNOWLEDGEMENT

The publication of this book and its associated outreach program was made possible through a generous grant from Laurance S. Rockefeller's Fund for the Enhancement of the Human Spirit.

TABLE OF CONTENTS

PROLOGUE

There are many of us scattered across the face of the Earth with a mysterious sense of the future and a profound attraction for the evolution of ourselves and our world. We are a future-oriented family of humanity who sense within ourselves the birth of the Universal Human. *The Revelation: Our Crisis Is a Birth* serves as a stimulator of our memory of the future. It is a call for this transcendent community—founders of a New Order of the Future—to gather and to support each other in fulfilling our destiny at this critical juncture in human history.

In the next thirty years we can destroy our world. With the very same powers—spiritual, social and scientific—we can evolve our world. Our mission is to serve as catalysts for a planetary awakening in our lifetime, to take a nonviolent path to the next stage of our evolution.

This book, and the larger *Book of Co-Creation* from which it comes, was inspired in 1980 by my direct experience of Christ. I was a futurist, public speaker and social innovator. I had studied the awesome story of creation, from the origin of the universe to us becoming conscious of evolution and responsible for guiding it on this planet. I had sensed that the human race was going through a "birth" to the next stage of our evolution. I knew we were at the threshold of a quantum jump through the activation of our collective capacities.

I had not, however, seen the relationship between our future and the life of Jesus. Then, quite unexpectedly, in a series of deep, personal encounters, I experienced the Christ as a living Presence guiding us through the great transition to universal life. He seemed to me to be our potential self, the Universal Human that we are to become. I was drawn to the New Testament, which inspired me to write a 1,500-page manuscript. In it the Christ voice calls to us in a tone of infinite compassion:

You, all of you who are desirous and ready, are the Way. Be a beacon of light unto yourselves. This tiny band, this brave congregation of souls attracted to the future of the world are my avant-garde—the New Order of the Future.

These are self-selected souls who have come to Earth to carry the miracle of the resurrection into action as the transformation of humanity from Homo sapiens *to* Homo universalis.

I call upon you to activate the capacities to save the world from self-destruction. I call upon you to undertake a mission comparable to the first disciples of Jesus. They were the first to carry the message of the reality of our potentials to the nations. You are to be the last to carry the message.

They lived at the beginning of the change. You live at the "end times," when the old shall pass away and the new shall appear.

This text is a call to action to new disciples of Christ to manifest their own capacity to do as I did, and more. This text is for the avant-garde of humanity who awaken with love in their hearts and joy in their spirit at the glory which shall be revealed in us.

I call upon Homo universalis, *those in whom the flame of expectation burns high, to set about the double task of self-transformation and the activation of the world's capacity to achieve the goal of its history.*

You are to become natural Christs. You are to communicate to the world its potentials to restore the Earth, free the people, and impregnate the universe with new life. You are to participate in the Instant of Co-operation, the Planetary Birth, the Second Coming.

It is with great joy and anticipation that I offer to you this work.

ABOUT THIS BOOK

The Revelation: Our Crisis Is a Birth is published by The Foundation for Conscious Evolution through a grant from Laurance S. Rockefeller's Fund for the Enhancement of the Human Spirit. It comes from a larger work, *The Book of Co-Creation*. The complete text, which includes commentary on the Gospels, Acts and Epistles, will be available (see order form at back of book). Section Two, *The Revelation: Our Crisis is a Birth*, on pages 83-296, culminates and epitomizes the larger manuscript.

This book consists of three sections:

Section 1, The Journey, tells the author's personal story, her lifelong quest to evolve, and her encounter with Christ and the New Testament.

Section 2, The Revelation: Our Crisis Is a Birth, is inspired by a Christlike voice that guides us through the original Revelation of St. John the Divine. It presents an alternative to Armageddon, the scenario of violence that currently shapes the spirituality of Western civilization. It reveals a gentle path to the next phase of evolution, a Planetary Birth Experience that can occur in our lifetime through the awakening of a critical mass of inspired individuals who make this their intention. It offers us a magnificent vision of our future, and attracts us forward toward its realization. *It is a first testament for the generation that has inherited godlike powers at the dawn of the universal age.*

Section 3, A Call to a New Order of the Future describes this New Order and invites the reader to help envision and co-create it. This section also offers a people's Planetary Birth Communion and other opportunities to participate, as well as resource materials for conscious evolution.

Conventions Used in this Book

All passages from the New Testament are quoted from the *21st Century King James Version.* This translation is a modernized edition of the original King James version. It was selected because it preserves the poetry of the King James version while substituting modern terms for certain archaic words.

Three typefaces are used in this book to distinguish its basic elements: **boldfaced passages** denote scripture, *italicized passages* represent the Higher Voices, and regular type represents the author's commentary.

T·H·E
JOURNEY

We are the seed of a fully human species. Our desire to grow is the pulse and power of evolution itself, motivating us to realize and fulfill our life purpose. Deep personal stories often reveal the pattern of the future human.

Each of us is an expression of the overall evolutionary journey. By tracing our individual stories, we discover our unique participatory role in the great transformation of our time.

My own personal story led me to the planetary story, which in turn led to my awareness of the universal potential of the human race and to my participation in a communion of pioneering souls attracted to the evolution of the world.

Everything that rises, converges. As we live our own stories fully, we discover our vocations of destiny, we attract to us our life partners, and we actualize our unique potential as vital members of the evolving world, at the time of its Quantum Transformation:

> Behold, I show you a mystery:
> We shall not all sleep;
> but we shall all be changed...

SCENE 1: THE QUESTION

All my life I have been a seeker for meaning. Born of a Jewish agnostic family in 1929, I received no spiritual training. I did not even know we were Jewish! My father never mentioned our past.

He was Louis Marx, a Horatio Alger type, raised in Brooklyn in poverty, risen to wealth as a toy manufacturer by the time he was thirty, sitting on top of the world in a triplex apartment on Fifth Avenue in New York City.

He was strong, vibrant, smelling of fine cigars, exuding power and excitement. Broadway openings. Trips to Europe. Gifts and toys—toys everywhere. He wanted nothing to do with the Old World. His was a world of new promise: if you worked hard, you could do **anything.** I grew up with an innate sense of hope. I was completely happy as a child, so naturally happy that I did not even notice it.

When I asked my father what religion we were, he answered, "You are an American."

"What does that mean?"

"It means **do your best,**" he replied.

At what? I wondered. His purpose was to make money. What was my purpose to be? I felt, even as a child, a call to serve a great and unknown cause.

When I asked him why he always worked so hard, he said, "I was tired of standing at the end of the line."

When I was twelve my mother became ill with breast cancer. We moved from New York to Scarsdale. A terrible gloom descended upon our house. I prayed to God for mother's recovery, offering my life for hers in a bargain with God—to no avail. After a painful and mutilating mastectomy she died. My father came home from the hospital and awoke us in the middle of the night. "Little mother is dead," he said. "There is nothing to do but cry." We all crowded onto his lap, four brokenhearted children and a devastated man, sobbing.

Suddenly I stiffened. A deep protest arose within me. I could not accept her death. It was intolerable. This horror is **not** inevitable! There must be something more. A fierce rage awakened in my soul at the injustice of innocent suffering. An aching void contracted my heart, hurting like an ancient wound. I wandered around the Scarsdale mansion, lonely, crying, seeking for what I did not know, trying to take care of my younger brother and sisters. This was the beginning of my quest to understand the future of humanity.

Three years later, when I was fifteen, the United States dropped the atomic bomb on Japan. I remember vividly the shock...and then the questions arose which have magnetized my attention and directed my life from that day forward:

> **What is the meaning of our power?** What is the **purpose** of science and democracy? Are we headed toward destruction? Or are we moving toward meaningless affluence, which had already struck the rich in the developed world?

Neither seemed right. Neither corresponded to the magnetic attraction for the future that pulled at my solar plexus, calling for something more, something new. Again the question, what is new? What are we aiming for that is desirable? I saw that if we continued to "work hard" in the direction we were going, we could destroy everything!

Although I did not articulate it this way at the time, I started on a search for an image of the future commensurate with our capacities and our aspirations. My innate sense of hope as an American was infused with the feeling that we were moving toward something great, unprecedented, wonderful...yet what could it be?

I admired my father tremendously. Yet I could not be what he was. I was a member of the next generation of Americans. What was I to do my best at? I certainly could not do my best at more of the same if that was going to destroy the world.

The answer must be in a book. Someone must know! So I began to read with a deep hunger for meaning. I had to find out what our power is for. The answer to this question was, for me, the Holy Grail.

I read like a child starving for life. I remember sitting in bed with books piled all around me, falling on the floor, covering the night table. First, the world philosophies. What do they say about the future? Very little indeed. Either they look backward toward a golden age; or are stoical, accepting nature as is; or repetitive, expecting nothing new under the sun; or existential, asserting that there is no intrinsic meaning, only what you make up; or absurdist/nihilistic, based on the inevitable increase of entropy and the heat death of the universe.

None of these philosophies resonated with the intuitive hope, the magnetic sense that something great is coming in the future.

In 1948, I wrote in my journal:

> It's Christmas, but I feel none of the mystery, the peace or the warmth that comes to one of Christ's birthday...There is a constant pull in the middle of my stomach...I've achieved nothing, yet those same eyes have seen visions of untold glory. There is a key to my desires, which I hold but can't use...I'm like a magnet feeling the attraction of another magnet, yet held apart. Either I will respond to it or die...

I turned to the world religions, looking for one thing: the image of the future equal to our collective capacities. Much more interesting! They all "predicted" transformation. Especially the Judeo-Christian vision, which suggested a time would come in history when, as St. Paul said, "We shall not all sleep; but we shall all be changed...in the twinkling of an eye, at the last trumpet. For the trumpet shall sound, and the dead shall be raised incorruptible, and we shall be changed....the sufferings of this present time are not worthy to be compared with the glory which shall be revealed in us...and there shall be no more death, neither sorrow, nor crying, neither shall there be any more pain; for the former things are passed away."

There! The magnetic pull was for that. Every fiber of my being was excited. That must be the meaning of our power. But what is that? And how do you get from Scarsdale, New York, to the New Jerusalem?

I tried to make the mystical leap of faith from here to there, but my rational mind would not go. I failed, falling into a metaphysical abyss, between secular reality and spiritual faith.

In desperation, I joined the local Episcopal Church. I'll always remember the unsuspecting priest—affable, pallid, correct, traditional. "How shall we all be changed?" I asked him. "Is the resurrection, the ascension and the promise that we will do the works that Christ did true? Is there any **reality** to this? I want to go the Whole Way with it if it's true."

The priest looked embarrassed. I had the feeling that he did not really believe any of it.

He preached that God was good, while we were helpless and guilty.

I wanted to rise up and say, "No! It's not true. We must be great. God would not have created us helpless." But I did not dare. Besides, when I prayed I heard no voices, saw no signs. Only silence. I despaired and left the Church.

The next step in my quest was academia. I went to Bryn Mawr College with my burning question: What is the meaning of our power? There I could not even **ask** the question. Every subject was in separate boxes: mathematics, English, science, the philosophy of religion. There was no subject called "The Future of Humanity." I spent most of my time alone, reading philosophy.

I wrote in my journal during my freshman year:

> How can people live and not know why they are living? What is the purpose of life, beyond things? My difficulty is that I cannot find a way to get experientially to the ultimate reality. There is no method to connect that ultimate reality with the personal need for purpose....All my life I have absorbed and absorbed—never once given. By using myself as a catalytic agent I hope to give pattern and form to the mass of sensations which have impressed themselves upon my brain. The power of intelligence is the power to connect, relate and integrate impressions. We are all surrounded by facts and truths, but in order that we understand them, we must put them into a configuration.

By this time my brother and father thought that something was wrong with me. I was always in my room reading. They thought I must be very unpopular. So my brother, Louis, who was at Princeton, sent a stream of attractive young men to "take me out." (She needs a man! She should get married and have children. That will make her happy.) Of course, I asked each of the suitors **the** question: What is the meaning of our power? And I also asked them: What is **your** purpose? Quite understandably, they had something totally different in mind than I did!

I was at a metaphysical impasse. I could not find the way forward.

THE ARTIST

At age eighteen, I took my junior year abroad in Paris, at the Sorbonne and the Ecole des Sciences Politiques, an elite school for French civil servants. One day I separated from the group of girls I travelled with, for the first time going all alone to have lunch. It was a cold November afternoon. Wood fires filled the damp Paris air with a delicious aroma.

The tempting scent of roasting food attracted me to a little restaurant called Chez Rosalie. There were only two empty places, opposite each other in the crowded room, thick with the smoke of Gaulois cigarettes. In a few minutes the door opened, and a tall, young American entered. He had a large aristocratic head with thick, curly dark hair and full lips...very handsome, I thought. His eye caught mine. There was nowhere he could sit but opposite me! I smiled secretly...I felt attracted to him. I pushed my bread crumbs about on the wooden table and sipped my wine, hardly daring to look up. Finally, I raised my eyes to his and asked him if he'd like some of my wine. He said yes. We began to talk. I asked him my perennial question.

He spoke slowly, deliberately, his grey blue eyes holding me in a powerful gaze. He drew his breath in and answered as though he had been holding this jet stream of an idea for eons and was finally letting it out: "I am an artist. My purpose is to create a new image of man commensurate with our capacities to shape the future."

Instantaneously the idea flashed through my mind, "I'm going to marry you." (And I did!)

That afternoon we sat in the little café while the owner swept up around us, smiling sweetly, knowing as the French do, that we were falling in love. Earl Hubbard told me that when a culture loses its story of where it is going, it breaks down. Only when a society has a shared story that gives hope can it be great. For example, when the Homeric legends were written down, the Greeks then had a story out of which the Golden Age was born. And when the Gospels were written down, Western civilization had its story. In our time, he said, there is no shared story that gives hope to us all. The Gospels, as usually interpreted, are narrow, unscientific and exclusive. Materialistic scientism's story of universal heat death, and its assertion that there is no design, meaning or direction in the process of creation, makes all human aspiration for higher life a hopeless illusion. Humans have no greater purpose than the other animals. In fact, we are so destructive that we may well (and perhaps should) become extinct before we destroy the world. Modern society has no shared story that fits current knowledge and gives us hope.

Earl said that the last great image of the human being was created in the Renaissance, in Michelangelo's sculpture of David, the noble nude body, assured, humble, at once human and divine.

"Imagine a rapid film sequence," he said. "Start with the statue of David—now see the gradual break-up of the image into points of light in the paintings of Manet, Monet and Pissaro. Now the image breaks up in Picasso, watch it disintegrate and disappear in Jackson Pollock's great splattered streaks of light...Where are we? We're gone!"

He said he had to return to America, for it was our turn on the stage of history. "This is our indelible moment," he said. It was in this new world that an artist would discover the new image of man. I knew in that instant I would join him on this quest.

Yet as we were preparing for the wedding I began to feel fear. I was being drawn away from my purpose, into some new identity, lost in materiality. Earl wanted a home and children. He wanted me to cook and clean and care for him. He asked me what kind of stove I would like! I was horrified. I didn't want any stove! I smiled as though it were wonderful, but my heart was sinking. I wanted to go back to Paris. I wanted to get a job in

Washington. I wanted to be a great person. But I had no model of the woman I would like to be. I thought something was wrong with me.

We were married at the majestic St. Thomas's Church in New York City. Even as my father and I walked toward the altar, I felt as if I were moving inexorably toward a head-on automobile crash. Although I could see it coming, I felt helpless to do anything about it.

I loved my husband deeply, yet right from the beginning I had no desire to be anyone's wife. It felt weird to be "Mrs. Earl Hubbard." What happened to Barbara Marx? What happened to the questing, passionate girl seeking a great cause?

In 1952 my father took me to see his friend, President Dwight Eisenhower. I was shown into the Oval Office and was electrified by the brilliant and charismatic gaze of the new president. "What can I do for you, young lady?" he asked pleasantly.

I looked into his intense blue eyes and said, "Mr. President, I have a question for you."

"Yes?"

"What is the purpose of our power?" I asked.

He appeared startled. He closed his eyes for a few seconds, shook his head and said slowly, "I don't know."

It flashed through my mind, "We'd better find out."

The church didn't know. The university didn't know. The most powerful political leader in the entire world had no idea. The United States, now the mightiest country in history, had no sense of direction. Our vast technological-military-industrial power was focussed on defense and consumption.

DEPRESSION

We had moved to a small artist's studio in Lime Rock, Connecticut, in the foothills of the Berkshire mountains. I became a homemaker. It was the 1950s. I lived in a beautiful New England environment, with clean air, clean water, but no purpose. Instead of pursuing my question, I immediately began to have babies...one, two, three, four, five! I joined the League of Women Voters, the car pool, the play group, the debating society, feeling drained, disoriented, exhausted.

I loved the miracle of giving birth—the labor pains, the delivery, nursing, caring for the new life. I adored my children. In fact they gave me my greatest joy, the only respite I had from the aching void. Yet as soon as each child was weaned, my question deepened, as did my feeling of depression. If I did not even know my purpose, how could I be a good mother? I loved my husband and children with all my heart, but my life's purpose was unknown, unengaged, unrealized. I was a lost soul trapped in the material world, reproducing my species with no sense of purpose.

It was an old-fashioned marriage. Earl believed a woman's place was in the home, supporting her husband and children. I devoutedly played that role, wanting to please him. I took care of the children, cleaned the house, cooked the meals, and wrote in my journal. This was before the emergence of any of the "movements," particularly the woman's movement. One day, as I was thinking of people I admired, I could not think of a single woman, except perhaps Marie Curie and Eleanor Roosevelt. My heroes were Pericles, Lincoln, Churchill.

Earl was painting seven days a week with fierce intensity. I wanted to die. I wrote in my journal, which had become my lifeline:

> How can I trust myself when it seems I am always wrong? Does the higher meaning I'm after exist at all? Whatever wrongness exists in me is in so deep and down so far that it **is** me. If I'm wrong, it's my very nature to be wrong. There's nothing I can do to change who I am. I have no alternative being to turn into. I must live it out as Barbara, then die.
>
> It is the fall of 1957, six years after marriage. I have come to the end of my endurance. No matter who I am with— Earl, my father, even my own children—I feel as though I were separated from them by this invisible shroud. I am able to converse, but not to initiate conversation. If they stop talking, I stop talking. I feel panicky. I search my brain for something to say, to assert myself, to feel alive at least, but incredibly, I can find nothing. Emptiness. I'm frightened. I smile and act as if this is the way I am supposed to be, this stone

woman. I have no understanding of what's happening to me. I only know that the enormity of my failure overwhelms any tiny gesture I make to rescue myself.

THE LIGHT DAWNS: THREE EVOLUTIONARIES

Gradually, in the 1960s, as I entered my thirties, I found my way to the light, to the new shared story. Three great modern thinkers provided me with the logic of hope. They laid the foundation for a new vision of our future that is equal to our power and aspiration. They provided clues to the mystery of the meaning of our power.

First came Abraham H. Maslow's *Toward a Psychology of Being*. It saved my life. He said that once our deficiency needs are relatively easily met, our growth needs for a richer sense of beingness, for chosen work of intrinsic value, become imperative, as necessary as food is to the hungry. If we don't grow at that stage, we get psychologically ill. It is normal to desire more than comfort. He also pointed out that all self-actualizing people feel related to a transcendent or transpersonal order beyond mere personal self-fulfillment.

I realized that the human being is so constituted that we are **driven** to actualize our potential beyond maintaining material survival or comfort. In this "beyond" lies our greatness. Our potential has barely been tapped. Most people, for most of the time, have had maximum numbers of children, worked eighteen hours a day to survive, and died young. Now, our generation will have fewer children, live much longer lives, and succumb to illness if we don't find our life's purpose.

As long as Western society has no further goal than material well-being, even if all people were to reach that state they would still feel incomplete until they also found their chosen life purpose.

I understood my problem was growth potential unused, because I did not know what to work for. I had not found my vocation. I was underdeveloped, not sick! My alienation was a divine discontent, driving me toward the next level of growth. I was determined to learn how to be "normal," joyful, natural in the 20th century. I sought to find my life purpose.

Through Maslow I discovered the first answer to my perennial question: **The meaning of our power, our affluence and technologies, is to free us to find our creative vocation and to actualize our potential through meaningful, chosen work.**

The second life-saver was Teilhard de Chardin's *Phenomenon of Man.* An epiphany! Teilhard described a continuing, evolving pattern in the process of nature which leads to greater whole systems with higher consciousness and freedom. From molecule, to cell, to animal to human and now to us on planet Earth...the process is still going on. We are approaching a time when the whole world will link up in one interfeeling organism.

Teilhard called this advent "Omega," the "Christification of the Earth." Each of us, being members of the one body, will be collectively lifted up in consciousness. This is a natural occurence, and can be expected to happen in real, historical time.

Not only does the individual have unused growth potential, so does the world, so does our species, so does the universe! Something new is coming. The magnetic attraction was right. I could trust my intuition.

"Behold, I show you a mystery; We shall not all sleep; but we shall all be changed." Is this mystical intuition of forthcoming great change an actual evolutionary forecast? Might this change be a **natural** evolutionary step, occurring in real time once the planet is sufficiently evolved for us all to be connected up as one body? Is our extended nervous system, the electronic and mass media—television, radio, computers (and now faxes)—laying the basis for this change?

I began to get "hot." The mystery seemed to be unveiling itself to my wondering eyes.

A second answer emerged: **The meaning of our power is to connect the world into one living, interacting organism of far greater capacity than the sum of our separate parts. Science and technology are a vital part of the noösphere, the thinking layer of the Earth. Through the mass media we are being linked into a single, vast body that is about to become collectively self-aware!**

For me ideas are not abstract concepts. They are living, breathing **beings** that transform our lives. I realized that the image of reality we hold is the most important idea we have. For as we think about reality, so we feel, act and create. I literally began to be flooded with excitement, like a detective in a mystery story who has just found a great clue.

The third discovery was R. Buckminster (Bucky) Fuller. In his little book, *Utopia or Oblivion,* he said that the human mind is designed to know the design of nature. The universe is not going down to increased disorder; it is instead building up toward ever higher order because it is increasing in intelligence—through us!

Intelligence, proclaimed Fuller, is not physical, it is metaphysical: we cannot know less, only more. We are rapidly learning how to do ever more and more with ever less and less. Our technology is becoming ephemeralized, miniaturized, and aesthetic, like nature's technologies: photosynthesis, DNA, the human brain.

We now have the technology, resources and know-how, Fuller said, to make of this world a 100 percent physical success. We can begin our work as citizens of local universe, which is to educate ourselves to our full potential. We can become self-evolving, self-regenerating and eventually continuous humans, transcending the mammalian life cycle. The growing edge of technology is giving us the power to transform ourselves as well as our world.

I was thrilled with this tremendous affirmation of my intuition that something new and great is coming: **The individual human has enormous untapped potential. The planet itself is evolving toward a quantum leap, wherein all of its members will experience themselves as part of one body. We have the ability to overcome physical lack, and even to change our physical nature—our body/mind systems. These great evolutionary goals are the meaning of our power.**

THE INNER VOICE AWAKENS

One day I took a walk, overwhelmed with gratitude. I said out loud to the universe: "Thank you, thank you, **thank you!**" Then I heard the inner words, which seemed to flow from the heart of the cosmos directly into my heart: *"Thank you, Barbara!"*

I felt ecstasy, joy, beatitude. The pain that I had felt since my mother's death healed in that instant. Instead I felt warmth, mother's love, yet at a far different scale. There is a **relationship** between me and IT. I am not alone. I am not abandoned. I am part of this cosmos. My desire is Its expression. Its expression is my desire. I and It are connected! My aspirations to be more, to do more, were not the false and wishful thinking of an ignorant and stupidly hopeful, naive woman. **They were the direction of evolution itself!** The aching void was, at least in that moment, filled. This was the "good news" that my restless mind had so desperately sought.

Now that I knew this, what should I do? What will happen when the world discovers all this? Will everyone feel as I do? Am I crazy...or is this true? I began actively to seek out my vocation of destiny, sensing that I was to be an "advocate for humanity."

It was clear to me that our species has no vision of its collective potential. While we are continually being told everything that is wrong with us, and made painfully aware of our failures, who is offering us a vision of our possibilities? Yet without a vision, our species will surely perish.

Then in 1962 John Glenn penetrated our blue biosphere into outer space. I had a sense of our species at the moment of physical transformation. Not only is our consciousness expanding as the mystics have proclaimed for ages...so also, our bodies are transcending Earth-boundedness. When I saw the rocket rise on television the words FREEDOM! BIRTH! exploded in my mind. I found myself trembling, crying, as though "I" were being born. We could become a universal species! That was part of the purpose of our power, our technolgies, our sciences. They provided us with the skills to carry us beyond the womb of our mother Earth into a universe in which there are undoubtedly billions of life-systems comparable to our own. The Western world has been developing the technologies of transcendence commensurate with our visions of transcendence.

It was like being alive when the fish flopped out upon the dry land: a critical evolutionary event, and this time we are here! I saw, however, that most people were lacking an evolutionary perspective and could not understand the meaning of the space program.

I began to move beyond my role as a wife and mother of five. In my reaching out, I met Jonas Salk, the great biologist. He is a radiant, magnetic man, a poet of biological wisdom, a prophet of the coming evolutionary change. I had written to one of Jonas' board members, Jerry Piel, head of *The Scientific American.* I proposed a Theater of Man to be established at the Salk Institute. It should be the place to dramatize the evolutionary destiny of the human race, I wrote. He showed the letter to Jonas.

One day the phone rang. It was Jonas. "You have expressed my dream," he said. "You have stated my vision far more clearly than I could...we must be two peas in the same pod! May I take you out to lunch?"

The very sound of his voice activated my whole being. I knew my life would never be the same again. Several days later he drove up. It was a glorious September day. The trees glittered golden and yellow, the freshly mown lawn smelled sweet, the apple trees were laden with red, shining fruit, glowing in the heat of the noonday sun.

He opened the door and looked into my eyes. "This must be Eden," he said, smiling at me. "Yes," I answered, "and I must be Eve."

As we drove to New York I told him all the things that were "wrong" with me: my love of the future, my desire to evolve, my feeling of connectedness with all being. He smiled and said, "Barbara, there's nothing wrong with you. You combine the characteristics needed by evolution now! You are a bivalent bonding mechanism—you have hooks on two ends. You are just what's needed, and I will introduce you to some others I have found."

I cried with happiness in the car, pretending to have a bad case of hay fever. The "ugly duckling" I feared myself to be was a swan! My life was suddenly meaningful: I was an essential participant in the universe!

Teilhard once described this experience. He said, "You have only to take two people in a gathering, endowed with this mysterious sense of the future. They will gravitate instinctively toward one another; they will know one another...no racial or social barrier seems to be effective against this force of attraction..."

Jonas said he had spent a quarter of a century finding such "mutants." He would introduce me to those he had found. And so he did. Al Rosenfeld, science editor of *Life Magazine,* Dr. Joel Elkes, head of the

Department of Neuropharmacology of Johns Hopkins University, Louis Kahn, the architect...each meeting was a revelation, an affirmation so deep that I began to feel genuinely transformed. For those of us who have this mysterious sense of the future it is absolutely essential to meet others who share our passion. Our evolutionary potential is activated by the contact.

I was joyful, radiant, filled with a vitality. I felt as though my very cells were being rejuvenated. I wrote in my journal:

> This Christmas of 1964 is the best of my life, not because I've achieved my ideals but because the problem of identity has disappeared. I can never again say I am nothing, for as all people are, I, too, am the inheritor of the evolution of the ages. In my genes are the generations. Every cell in my body identifies me with the great and terrible adventure of inanimate-to-animate-to-human, and every desire of my being sets me passionately to work to further the rise of humaneness out of humanity. I am what was and what will be. If I am nothing, life is nothing; that it cannot be—and be.

A New Image of Humanity

Meanwhile, Earl was developing a new artistic image. First he eliminated the body. "Our physical bodies are no longer our instruments of action," he said. "Our physical functions are being assumed by our extended bodies, our new machines—our rockets, our telescopes, our satellites. Our personal body is becoming our 'house of thought.'"

As the body was disappearing in Earl's paintings, the background was opening out toward the universe that we had seen during John Glenn's space flight. The background became velvet black, the color of the universe, and the face became a glowing starlight, the synthesis of all color. It represented individual awareness.

"From the new perspective of space," Earl said, "humans become humankind: one body on Earth, reaching out to make contact with other life."

This image of the face as starlight against the universe of black imprinted itself deeply into my being. It awakened an emotional receptivity, an expectation of something about to happen. Our quest, the purpose of our marriage was being realized. This was a new image of man...except I posed for it...it was womankind in the universe that I saw!

I felt a tremendous inner tension. The intellectual ideas had burned themselves into my heart, my body, my soul. The hundreds of hours of reading, questioning and discovering were preparing me to experience, indeed to **embody,** that which I had understood.

SCENE 2: THE PLANETARY BIRTH EXPERIENCE

On a fateful afternoon in February 1966, I was taking my usual daily walk. It was a freezing day. The trees stood black and brittle against the winter sky. There was no sign of life anywhere. I wrapped my scarf around my face to protect myself from the bitter cold and walked with my head down to avoid the wind.

I had been reading Reinhold Neibuhr on the subject of community. He had quoted St. Paul's famous statement: "For as the body is one, and hath many members, and all the members of that one body, being many, are one body, so also is Christ." As I contemplated that idea, I felt a deep frustration.

The early Christians had a story to tell: a child was born....Everyone could understand this story, from kings to peasants. Unexpectedly a new question burst forth in my mind. I spoke it out loud. Lifting my voice to the ice-white sky, I demanded to know:

"What is **our** story? What in our age is comparable to the birth
  of Christ?"

I knew it must be one story for all of humankind, for we are all members of one planetary body.

I lapsed into a daydreamlike state, walking on the path around the top of the hill, in deep concentration and receptivity. My thoughts quieted down. I was poised from within, to catch the slightest hint of revelation.

Suddenly my mind's eye penetrated beyond the blue cocoon of Earth, lifting me up into the utter blackness of outer space. From there I witnessed the entire sweep of Earth's history, as though I were viewing a technicolor movie.

I witnessed the Earth as a living body, just as the astronauts did. It was alive! Then I experienced a kinesthetic imprint of the planetary organism. I felt myself to be a cell in that body. Earth was gasping for breath, struggling to coordinate itself as a whole. The pain of its whole body was being communicated through the mass media, the nervous system of the world. I felt everybody's pain as my own...for we are one body.

THE PLANETARY SMILE

Then the movie sped up. I saw something new. A flash of extraordinary light more radiant than the sun surrounded the planet. Instantly, all of us were attracted to the light. We forgot our pain, and at that moment of shared attention, empathy began to course through our planetary body. Wave upon wave of love flowed through all people. A magnetic field of love aligned us. We were caressed, uplifted in this field of light. We felt our inner light rising. Mass healings occurred. People flooded out of their houses, offices and buildings, meeting each other in ever-growing gatherings, embracing, loving one another. It was like a thousand Berlin Walls coming down at once...all over the world.

A beat began to pulse through the planet. The air cleared, the waters purified. Food coursed through the whole system, reaching all of our members. The mass media throbbed with light, carrying stories of our transformations while itself being transformed in the process.

Rockets rose majestically, carrying the seed of Earth life into the universe. The Earth coordinated herself as one body.

With each wave of harmony, the glowing light that surrounded us intensified. We were being coordinated by an invisible design. The light became brighter and seemed to fuse with the light that is within us. Each of us was a point of light, growing brighter as we joined with other points of light. As we connected on Earth, millions of distant points of lifelike light also appeared in the surrounding universe. And as we harmonized, they became even more visible and were drawn to us...life to life, light to light. We were attracting beings comparable to ourselves.

I heard a tone, a vibration that oriented us in one direction. The entire human race was magnetized by that sound. The animal kingdom was gentled. The lion did lie down with the lamb. The glowing light around our planet seemed to be intelligent, loving, familiar. It was about to speak with us directly. We were straining to understand, yet were too immature to fully recognize the meaning of the sound.

Then I heard the inner words clearly:

*Our story is a birth. It is the birth of humankind as one body. What Christ and all great beings came to Earth to reveal is true. We **are** one body, born into this universe. GO TELL THE STORY OF OUR BIRTH...**Barbara!***

My vocation! To tell the story of our birth! My prayers had been answered. I had found my path, I knew why I was alive. The search for the cause had been found. "Oh, thank God, thank God, thank God. Our story is a birth!"

In response to those words, which had seemed to come from deep within the universe, billions of us opened our collective eyes and smiled. **It was a planetary smile**—like the first smile of a newborn baby, when her nervous system links up and, seeing her mother, her tiny face relaxes into an amazing, radiant smile. Somehow she knows her mother, even though she has never seen a human being. And just as that baby knows her mother, humankind knows the light. Even if we have never seen it clearly, each of us has, in a secret place in each of our hearts, experienced the light that has been seen by all mystics. Now, for the first time we were seeing it together. Ecstatic joy rippled through the planetary body...and through me as one of its billions of members.

I saw that it was true. We are being born. Our defense systems, our economies, our communication systems, our cultures are all linking, despite our differences. We are going to be one body, whether we like ourselves or not! The same process that joined atom to atom, molecule to molecule, and cell to cell, is now joining us. We are the generation born when the whole planetary body is being born.

The world crisis suddenly made sense...our condition is dangerous but natural. Of course we must stop our unrestrained growth in the womb of Earth; we must handle our toxic waste, shift to renewable energies, restore our Mother and begin to explore the universe beyond our home. We simply have to grow up! We've never seen another planet go through its birth process. Maybe we're normal!

"Behold, I show you a mystery: We shall not all sleep; but we shall all be changed." Omega! **The planetary birth is a real event in cosmic time.**

This experience was an expanded reality experience of something that is **really happening to us now!** When we take the perspective of ourselves as a universal species and speed up time to see the pattern in the process of evolution, it all becomes obvious.

THE EVOLUTIONARY SPIRAL

With that the technicolor movie resumed. The whole story of our birth unfolded, like a speeded-up film of the growth of a plant from bulb to bloom. I witnessed the life of our planet, from the quantum instant of its conception to the quantum instant of our collective awakening, of our birth as one body.

I felt myself tumbling through an evolutionary spiral. Each great quantum transformation was a turn on the spiral—a radical leap to a new order of being. "I," the macrocosmic, universal I, the "I" that is "we," the "I" in each of us that was, is, and ever will be, experienced the whole story of creation as **our** story.

I felt the spiral unfold: the creation of the universe, the formation of the Earth, the appearance of single-celled life, of animal life and of human life. Then we began to approach our own turn on the spiral. I saw the early religions in India, Egypt, Greece, Israel—from Buddha to Christ—as harbingers of the next stage of evolution. They demonstrated to us that **we are** higher beings, founders of the future. I saw the emergence of science as the great tool for understanding how nature works, so that we can evolve consciously with her. I saw democracy as the great liberator of human potential. I saw the explosion of the atomic bomb as the beginning of our collective labor pains. It was the signal that the Cosmic Child, humanity, could either kill itself by remaining in self-centered consciousness, or instead emancipate itself for universal life.

The next turn on the spiral began, revealing the "synergy" of which Bucky Fuller wrote. The separate parts of humanity are coming together to form a whole that is greater than and unpredictable from the sum of its parts. Synergy feels like love, loving one another as ourselves. We **are**, in fact, one body! Our capacities as a whole are infinitely greater than when we are separate tribes and nations. Once our consciousness shifts from feeling separated to knowing that we are all members of one body, our vast technological genius begins to serve the growth of ourselves as one planet. And that consciousness shift **can** happen in the twinkling of an eye!

Once our consciousness shifts collectively of course we can restore the Earth, we can feed all people, we can emancipate unique potential. We can! We can! We can! We have the capacities to do it **already,** as Bucky said, we just don't know that we can. The Cosmic Child can live. Our birth is natural. Yet we must **know** that we are being born, not dying, else we will not fully activate our new capacities before it is too late.

I saw the rockets as nature's seed pods of Earth-life bursting into the universe. I saw our mass media—our planetary nervous system—link up and report our growth, awakening all of humankind's members to their parts in the process of growth.

I realized that in the very same decade when we were learning to preserve our Earth and limit growth here, we were also stepping off the planet to begin the establishment of new worlds in space. At the same time we were also beginning to learn the language of DNA, the genetic code that designs bodies for this Earth.

We are becoming universal humans! We will have to change our bodies to live beyond this Earth for which they were designed. New bodies will be essential in a radically new environment. Nature always creates new bodies for new consciousness, in order to transcend new frontiers: the fish, the bird, the hominids, *Homo sapiens*...and next, *Homo universalis.* We, too, shall evolve new bodies for new worlds, only this time it will be through **conscious** rather than unconscious evolution.

Astronautics, genetics, cybernetics and nanotechnology (the ability to construct at the atomic level) are natural capacities of a universal species that is moving from its terrestrial to its universal phase. Furthermore, these powers are far too great to be contained by a biosphere, or in self-centered consciousness. They are **meant** for cosmic consciousness and universal action. For us to stay in this stage would be like a baby trying to remain in the birth canal. It would kill us all.

Oh, my God! I thought, this whole process is really the birth of a universal species. It is not a metaphor, it is an actuality. What we call "evolution" is actually an organic process that creates beings capable of evolving consciously. **We are becoming conscious evolutionaries!**

I saw humanity, at the next turn of the spiral, gaining the powers of co-evolution and co-creation, just as all our religions told us we would. ("Co-creation" means conscious co-operation with the process, direction and purpose of evolution—the implicate order of the cosmos: God.)

I saw, perhaps most fundamentally of all, that the vast effort of humanity to "be fruitful and multiply" would have to be curtailed in our generation. One more doubling of the world population will destroy our life support system. Our Mother will not support us if we continue to grow in numbers! We must stop. Where is this powerful prime energy to go? In a flash I saw it!

The energy of **pro**creation was to be emancipated for **co**-creation, for chosen work, for vocation. The sexual drive to reproduce the species would be transformed into the suprasexual drive to evolve the species. We would desire to join, not only our genes but our genius, to evolve ourselves and our world. Sexuality and suprasexuality would merge in one great orgasmic effort to evolve!

What had happened in my own life, the search for meaningful work, was a natural extension of sexual energy. Imagine when the whole world turns on to its creative drive!

The so-called "population crisis" is a crisis of our planetary birth. The limits to growth on Earth shift us from procreation to co-creation. Creativity will be emancipated *en masse*. The passionate love of chosen work which Maslow discovered in all self-actualizing people is the next stage of sexuality. That's why it's going to happen! And we are going to love it as much as we love sex!

All of these thoughts flashed through my mind in a single gestalt, an integration of everything I knew. It was a kinesthetic experience of a natural set of events that is happening right now.

Then the technicolor movie stopped. It had lasted a few minutes at most. I stood alone upon the hill. Tears of joy were frozen upon my face, my heart was bursting with joy. Ask and it shall be given. Knock and doors will open. There was no outward sign of what had happened. Yet I knew it was real. It's happening now. I had seen with universal eyes. I ran home, the cold air searing my lungs and my face, to tell my children and my husband that I had to "go forth and tell the story of our birth."

I rushed out to Earl's study to tell him, feeling suddenly shy. What should I say? I blurted it out with terrific enthusiasm. Instantly I felt his pain. He looked crushed. "Barbara, I thought I was going to make you happy," he said, sadly. "But I see you want to do it for yourself." I embraced him to comfort him, to tell him I loved and needed him. But I knew in my heart that I had to express myself, as well as support him. I could not be secondary any longer.

CONSCIOUS EVOLUTION

The flame of expectation rose to a burning intensity, motivating me to seek an expanded vocation, an evolutionary connection between my need for personal growth and the needs of a world in transition. My second life began, a chosen life. I felt free within myself, for I had a purpose related to the evolution of the world. I worked with a powerful joy to understand the Story of Creation at the dawn of the Universal Age.

I read cosmology, geology, biology, paleontology, anthropology, history, religion, current events and futuristic books to trace the outline of the story. I saw the evolutionary spiral as the spine upon which to hang all knowledge. Through studying cosmo-genesis, bio-genesis and homo-genesis we would learn "conscious evolution," deducing guidelines by which to co-design a positive future.

Conscious evolution is the "meta-discipline" of our age, a discipline in which every field and function of human endeavor re-cognizes itself as an aspect of a universal process that moves toward greater complexity, freedom and order. Reality is, in Bucky Fuller's phrase, "a verb, not a noun."

I wrote a "Center Letter" to a thousand persons, whose names I collected from books, magazines and friends, people like Lewis Mumford and

Father Thomas Merton, asking them what they thought was the next step for a positive future. I invited Abe Maslow to lunch. He was another soul mate, a brother. He shared with me his "eupsychian network," his list of over three hundred people who were leaders in the young human potential movement. He deeply encouraged me. "Barbara," he said, with that gentle twinkly look, "never let the bastards get you down." He was fighting the "reductionists" in his field, the guardians of the prevailing view that we are "nothing but" the consequence of our biochemical drives. They were attacking him, as they were Jonas. (Later, as he was dying of a heart ailment, he scribbled me a note from the hospital: "Barbara, you represent life. Keep going.")

I wrote to everyone in Maslow's network, asking for their positive views on our future. Many responded and I published their responses. The Center Letter spread. People in Africa carried it on bicycles. It went behind the Iron Curtain. I received letters from all over the world. Whomever I liked, I invited to lunch. Within six months I was connected to leaders of the emerging world.

My young teenaged daughter, Woodleigh, said, "Mom, you have transformed from a cave-age lady to a space-age lady in one year." This was the truth. When we discover our life purpose we are changed. We enter a new life cycle. We are no longer aging and dying, we are growing and evolving.

It is an interesting fact that I have not been really sick enough to spend even one day in bed since the Planetary Birth Experience. (I capitalize it because I believe it is a real event that may come in our lifetime.) I used to get colds, sore throats, stomach upsets frequently. Since that day in 1966, if I feel an illness coming on, I have merely to **think** of the experience and I feel connected to the Whole Planetary Body. Energy floods my system... and I am healed!

I began "breakfast dialogues" with Earl. He was brilliant, an artist with words. I would ask him questions about the meaning of space, of freedom, of the United States. He answered with vivid images and ideas. We began to shape the evolutionary philosophy that would guide my life. I took notes. I taped it. I typed it. I edited a book for him entitled *The Search Is On.* I organized an exhibition for him at the Huntington Hartford Gallery of Modern Art entitled "The Challenge Is Freedom," with words and paintings. I loved his words. We sat for hours every morning. It was genuine co-creation. My love for him deepened as my life expanded.

Yet I now had my own friends. I was fully engaged in my own creative life, publishing the Center Letter, talking for hours on the phone with Jonas, seeking out new writers and thinkers and meeting them for lunch. Lancelot Law Whyte, who had written *The Next Development of Man*, and I became close friends, discussing philsophy far into the night. I found I could communicate these ideas so that people were touched in their inner knowing, awakened and enlivened by what I said.

During this process, despite our deepening relationship, my husband and I grew apart. I tried to readjust our relationship to be two equals working together. But everything I was doing felt to him like a rejection. He had a different picture of marriage. From his point of view, I had stopped being his "wife" when I developed a life of my own. This sounds archaic now, since the woman's movement, but then we had no guidelines to transform our relationship midstream.

Together we had conceived and raised five beautiful children. And we had given birth to "a new image of man commensurate with our capacity to shape the future," as we had said at the Chez Rosalie eighteen years earlier. Yet the growth in me was implacable and irresistible. I no longer knew how to hold my marriage together now that I had found my vocation. I was caught on the cusp of the old relationship between men and women, and the new.

Of course, the drive for creative self-expression can be balanced with relationship if the two partners are conscious from the beginning that they are to be equals. But my husband and I did not understand how to make this shift at that time.

With anguish in my heart, I told my beloved children, with whom I had the deepest relationship, that their mother was a pioneer, making a new place for them. My nine-year-old son, Wade, said to me, "Mother, we know you love us, you are doing what mothers are supposed to do. You are creating the future."

Now, in 1993, I can say, with gratitude and relief, that what seemed like a grave failure may actually have been a liberation for both Earl and me. Most important, the effect of my life on my children has been surprisingly positive. The five children and four grandchildren have become extraordinarily loving with one another. My daughter Alexandra, who is a whale researcher, said, "Mom, we are like a whale pod." By some grace, the children love one another and me with an unconditional, totally supportive love. They have all followed their own "vocation of destiny."

When I was fifty they gave me a birthday party. "What did I do well as a mother, and what did I do badly?" I asked them. Their answer was, "What you did well was to believe in your own dream and do it the whole way. What you did badly was you didn't know how to say 'no' to us. We could have used more guidance."

Somehow by having surrendered to my own deepest calling, while expressing my love for them, I had given them an example which they have followed and from which they are now reaping the rewards. Even though separation, and then the divorce, was surely painful to them, each of them has a deep sense of purpose and is following a unique chosen life. They have had to earn their own way, for I could not support them as my father had supported me. I feared that I had been a poor mother, but the fact is, they benefitted from my example. They know in their thirties and forties that their lives have just begun.

Back then in the 1960s I did not know how it would turn out. But as Robert Frost said, "My life was a risk...and I took it." Having secured my love for my children as best I could and sought forgiveness from my husband, I moved into the larger world to fulfill my vocation.

SCENE 3: THE MISSION—GO TELL THE STORY

I believed the space program was a vital evolutionary step, not that it was the only important step. But it was being misunderstood and maligned by so many brilliant people, I thought I had to do something. With Lady Malcolm Douglas-Hamilton, who had organized "Bundles for Britain," I organized a meeting called "Victory in Space" in New York City. We invited astronauts, aerospace exectives, space scientists, people like Werner von Braun, Krafft Ehricke, Neil Armstrong. One of my invitations landed on the desk of Air Force Lt. Col. John J. Whiteside, chief officer for information in New York City. He called to find out about the event, and naturally, I invited him to lunch. (By this time I had an apartment in New York.) I opened the door and saw a rough, sexy, smart, witty man. He had no idea what he was getting into! He was a believing, yet renegade, Southern Baptist who loved whiskey, women and song! He had been a coal miner in Southern Illinois, then had risen up through the ranks of the air force to its key position with the mass media. He had an office on Fifth Avenue, a driver and all the perks of the military life. He told me, shaking his head, that his job was to "sell" the C-5, the F-111 and Vietnam War to the mass media.

Then he described how he had pioneered in live coverage of the space program. Nobody had wanted to cover it live. NASA feared there might be an accident. The mass media thought it was too expensive. But he pressed for it and won.

"You know what you were doing, John," I said. "You were covering the birth of humanity...live!" I told him about my experience of seeing John Glenn go into space and described my Planetary Birth Experience.

It was amazing, the effect those words had. He literally caught his breath. "Oh my God," he said, "I always knew there was some deeper reason, some greater meaning to what we were doing. It was as though we were covering the birth of Christ by reporting the labor problems at the inn and the cost of the straw in the manger!"

He ordered dozens of copies of *The Search Is On,* and helped us organize "Victory in Space."

Thus began the process of trying to get the mass media to let us "tell the story of our birth."

John thought he could get the support of the media, because the heads of the major networks—guardians of the gates of the planetary nervous system—were among his best friends.

He took me to one network chief after another. We'd enter his office, John would chat a few minutes, then say, "Barbara, tell him the story."

I remember sitting in the office of Robert Wussler of CBS News overlooking New York City, one of the most powerful control centers of mass media in the world. They select the news that we see. Bob was urbane, sophisticated, slightly cynical. He looked at me with amusement as I eagerly and innocently shared this vision with him. My heart sank. It was like an early disciple of Christ trying to tell a pagan Roman general about the resurrection!

He loved John and didn't want to hurt my feelings, but in no uncertain terms, he told us he could not find a place for it on the media...there was no category for such "news."

It seemed to me that the media had a communicable disease! I called it "disempathitis of the nervous system." They report mostly on violence and put us to sleep. They are relatively "dead" on empathy, insensitive to human development and growth, unaware of new potentials. They are biased toward destruction and dissent, claiming these to be more "real" than the "new" news of our emerging potentials.

SOCIAL ARCHITECTURE FOR CONSCIOUS EVOLUTION

After many such failures, we decided to communicate the message in our own way. John suggested I ask my sister Jacqueline if we could live in her Washington D.C. mansion, Greystone. It was being lent to relatives when her husband moved from clerking for Supreme Court Justice Harlan, to teaching law at Stanford University in California. She said yes.

Greystone was a mysteriously beautiful old house with grey flagstones, a grape arbor, a tennis court. It was tucked deep in Rock Creek Park beyond the reach of the traffic and noise of the city. We moved in and set up The New Worlds Training and Education Center. We became an oasis of the future in the nation's capital...alive with visitors, members of Congress, researchers, students. In 1970 we formed The Committee for the Future to bring the positive options into the public arena for discussion and action.

We tried to tell the story in terms that people could understand. We are being born into the universe. We are not in a closed system. The limits to growth are a birth phase. Soon we will be able to restore this Earth and develop new environments in space.

What does this mean for our economic system, our educational system, for defense, for art, for religion, for human development? We talked to people in every category. Many finally said that they understood, but that other people wouldn't. Labor leaders said they got it, but business never would. Business said they understood, but you would never get govern-ment to go along. Government officials said they would like to do it, but the people wouldn't want it.

One day John drew a wheel and said, "Let's put everybody who dis-agrees with one another in this wheel and ask him or her to let us know what would happen if the United States developed a new goal of building new worlds on Earth, new worlds in space. What would happen if we set up a thirty-year Earth-Space Human Development Process to actually DO IT?"

We invented a remarkable process called SYNCON (for **synergistic convergence**). It took place in a large wheel-shaped environment divided in sections for different task forces representing key functions in the social body such as environment, business, health and defense.

At the "growing edge" of the wheel were smaller task forces for people in the biological, information, space, physical and psychological fields who are developing new capacities for the human race. Around the wheel artists designed environments, sculptures, events to represent to us ourselves as a whole. At the very edge of the circle was a little task force called

"Unexplained Phenomena" where people who had unexplained experiences such as UFO's, healing, and paranormal capacities could go.

The process was for members of each group to state their goals, needs and resources, then for all groups to listen to one another's goals, and to match needs with resources in the attempt to make the whole system work for everyone. At the growing edge the researchers and scientists told the people of their new capacities. At the end all the walls came down in a symbolic ceremony signifying that we are all members of one body whose capacities are far greater than we imagine when we are separate and fighting with one another.

The first event was held at Southern Illinois University, where John had gone to college and where his son, J.P., was then enrolled. On SYNCON eve John was already at the university. When I arrived I found John in the student ball room. I was thrilled. The students had built a cosmic wheel. It looked like a flying saucer. In the center was the "Coordinating Hub." There was a little spiral staircase, like a social DNA, that went up to a balcony where anyone could look down upon the body as whole.

At the first SYNCON we had leaders from every field: Jean Houston; Ambassador Lazar Moisov, Yugoslavian head of the U.N. Security Council; Norman Cousins; Nobel Prize–winner Glenn Seaborg; astronaut Edgar Mitchell; Carl Madden, chief economist of the U.S. Chamber of Commerce. Also hippies, black power leaders, white southerners, radical students, welfare mothers.

Social synergy buzzed through the group, drawing together former adversaries. People discovered that they could get what they sought far better through co-operation than conflict. As the task forces came up with their goals, needs and resources, they took down the walls between sectors. At the end, all of the walls came down in a musical ceremony.

All heaven broke loose! Former radicals embraced conservative economists, Nobel prize-winning scientists conversed with psychics. Technical experts, black power leaders, southern conservatives and welfare mothers intermingled.

In each sector of the wheel was a TV camera and a monitor so participants could both see what was happening in the other sectors and be recorded themselves. It was an internal nervous system.

Every evening John produced the New Worlds Evening News. He recorded on television every new agreement to emerge from each formerly conflicting area, and played it back every night. He said that unless people see it on the news they do not believe that it happened. By putting ourselves on the news as news makers, we were maturing the electronic nervous system. People were fascinated. They watched the New World News over and over again.

The SYNCON process was a tiny microcosm of "synergistic democracy," or "synocracy," wherein the separate parts discover how to grow as co-operating members of one living body. It was a social love affair, a fabulous demonstration of the next stage of self-government. We did twenty-five such events, from Washington D.C to the inner city of Los Angeles, where we involved gang leaders who were vying to kill each other on the streets. The process worked every time. We were prototyping the Planetary Birth Experience of actually being members of one body. Synergy—the emergence of greater capacity from the activity of co-operating parts—is the way that nature works.

In the early 1970s we began to frame a long-range goal for the United States: Building New Worlds on Earth, and New Worlds in Space. The objectives of this goal were to restore the Earth, free people from hunger and poverty, emancipate human potential and begin to develop the vast regions of outer space and the human spirit. We tested it out in all the SYNCONs. It worked every time. Such a long-range goal would help every sector of society.

Yet I was also becoming exhausted. Something was missing. The "center did not hold." We experienced tremendous social highs, but did not know how to sustain them. Neither John nor I was entrepreneurial. I was paying for everything, and rapidly depleting my inheritance. There was not enough money to go around. My family was worried about me.

Even deeper than my own problems was the depressing realization that all human endeavor, no matter how magnificent, seemed incomplete and doomed to failure due to the fatal flaw of self-centeredness, the illusion of separatedness. No matter what power we gained, how could we change our nature? A New Worlds goal in the current human stage of consciousness would undoubtedly be misued—power corrupts and absolute power corrupts absolutely. We were talking about the human race gaining godlike powers and using them for the good. Is this possible given our current mind-set? How do we change human nature itself? What was the missing link? What trigger would activate our potential for the good?

In 1977 I began to meditate, going to the hill behind my home in Washington D.C. each morning. I learned to say the Lord's Prayer in deep concentration. I started to hear regularly an inner voice. I recorded its message in my journal:

> *Now is your moment of greatest faith. You have separated yourself from psychological dependencies. You are beginning to establish your own relationships. Good! Now—you have not yet achieved cosmic tranquility. You are still anxious. I want you to continue your initiatives. But they alone will not suffice. Now is the greatest leap of faith for you. Have utter faith in my design. Achieve deep peace. Be prepared for a great force to enter your life to do this work. It cannot enter till you have achieved deep peace. Your reward for peace, which can only be achieved by faith, is contact with the great force and the other forces waiting in the wings.*
>
> *Barbara, stop struggling.* **I must find one of my children who is not struggling.** *I cannot reveal to you even the mechanical steps you must take, until you are at peace. Keep your attention on me at all times. Practice continually tuning in. Whenever you feel anxiety, go back to God's school. Remember that you are an agent of the Creative Intention, experimenting for God. There is a design, but it is flexible.*

I had no name for this voice. But I loved it with all my heart and soul. In its presence, my whole being surrendered. Whenever I heard it, I was deeply relieved and joyful, and set about to follow its guidance minute by minute.

When John asked me what I really wanted to do I said, "I want to tell the story." Having been rebuffed by the mass media, I had stopped trying, and had become instead a "social architect." Now my true vocation was reactivated.

THE THEATER FOR THE FUTURE

John and I decided to put on a "Theater for the Future: Previews of Coming Attractions." He asked me to list every idea I wanted to communicate. I got an enormous sheet of paper, and wrote down over a hundred ideas, starting with the origin of the universe, the evolution of Earth, life, animal life, human life and now ourselves undergoing a crisis of birth. He put images and music to these ideas, producing a beautiful, computerized, multimedia production, which I performed from the halls of NASA to the Georgia State legislature...wherever I was asked.

At the Theater's finale, playing Pachelbel's Canon in D, with the image of billions of galaxies glittering in the background, I shared from the depth of my being the Planetary Birth Experience. When I spoke the words, I reactivated in myself the actual experience that had happened in 1966. The words became flesh in me as I spoke, "We are one body...We are being born...We are higher life...We are an immortal species...The second couple reaches the second tree—the Tree of Life, the Tree of the Gods, the Tree of the healing of the nations. Whole being to whole being we now unite for the evolution of the human race..."

The meaning of our new crises is to activate our new capacities.

The purpose of our new powers is to give birth to universal life...and we knew it all the time.

EARTH-BOUND HISTORY IS OVER. UNIVERSAL HISTORY HAS BEGUN.

Deep empathy arose between me and the audience. I was not simply telling about the future. We were experiencing ourselves as universal beings at the next stage of evolution, now.

These evenings had a profound effect on my biochemical system. Although I was speaking on behalf of the human species in the future, my nervous system was taking it personally right now. After each performance, I would notice a strange phenomenon. My body heated up. I was filled with inner radiation. A blue light would pulse in my third eye. I became clairvoyant. I could tell what people were thinking. I could speak to a disease or pain in someone's body and feel its response. These affirmations were evolving me!

CHANGE OF LIFE: A MYSTERIOUS PASSAGE

By the winter of 1979, just as I was about to turn fifty, the next great step in my mysterious quest began to unfold.

I realized that I was crossing a strange and wondrous threshold into a new life cycle. In my meditations my body had told me for some months that it wanted to change.

One day, while I was cleaning up the basement, an inner voice surprised me by asking, "Do you want to die?"

I paused and realized that a fateful choice was about to be made on the inner plane. I was about to make a "decision" as to whether I had more work to do here, or was finished and could die. (I was going through menopause. Nature was finished with my reproductive phase.)

I asked myself the question out loud: "Do you want to die?" The answer came clearly. "No, I have more to do. My work is not finished. In fact, it has barely begun."

I went back to my task of organizing the basement. I heard another question, "Do you want to get cancer, or do you want to rejuvenate?"

This was a real surprise. I had no idea that I had such a choice. "I want to rejuvenate," I said, out loud, startling myself. "But I don't know how."

The answer came: *Create an environment of total inner peace. Guard your thoughts with a sword of steel. Let no negativity or anxiety enter your being. I will do the rest. Your body **knows** how to rejuvenate. There is a co-creative system, just as there is a procreative system. Your co-creative system is about to turn on. This is what the inner radiation means. Create inner peace, and have faith in your capacity to become a universal human, a Christlike being. Prepare for the marriage of Christ and Eve. Prepare for the wedding of the self-centered, creature human that you have been, with the God-centered, creative human that you potentially are.*

I sensed that if I gave in to the voice of death for even an instant and agreed with it, my body would go right into its next level of mammalian programming, to find the best way to kill me.

I recalled from my studies of evolution that sexual reproduction and scheduled death of individual parents had been "invented" at the time of multicellular life. Single cells had divided to reproduce. They were semi-immortal. They did not die, but rather they wore out. With sex and death came the origin of the species and the populating of the Earth with all forms of life. Was the next step in the life cycle—beyond sexual reproduction and unchosen death—now emerging just as we were learning that we must reduce population growth here, and move into the universe? In that new environment wouldn't we have to live for millennia to travel among the stars? I felt intuitively that this was true.

And so, the voice for life consciously asserted itself and said: "I choose to go on. My work is not done here. I chose to come here to work for the transformation to universal life, and I will not go home until we have achieved this task."

The Marriage of Christ and Eve

I felt that two stages of development were crossing paths within my being: the mammalian life-cycle and the universal life-cycle.

We know the power of imagery on health. Was it possible, I wondered, that envisioning ourselves as the next stage with empathy and total motivation can trigger the hormonal/adrenalin system to produce a bodily transformation similar to puberty and reproduction on the sexual level?

I had been contemplating the virgin birth. It is written in the Gospels that Christ was born without sexual intercourse and had the capacity to resurrect his body after physical death. And he said, "There is no marrying in heaven."

Is this actually how it is done at the next stage of evolution: Conscious reproduction of new bodies that are capable of continuity of consciousness? Are we moving beyond sexual reproduction and preprogrammed death?

In order for "Eve" to marry Christ, one's body must be prepared to transform, to regenerate itself. (Eve as used here does not just represent woman, but rather Eve-consciousness, the phase of self-centered *Homo sapiens* that both sexes have experienced since the dawn of humanity. I identify with Eve as a creature-human who is seeking reunion with God.)

If we are approaching a new "normalcy," normalizing in ourselves what Christ could do, as the next stage in our evolution, then do we have the innate ability, as a proto-universal species, to "become mothers to ourselves," giving birth to ourselves as fully evolved humans?

Is this androgyny?

Is co-creative suprasexuality meant to regenerate our bodies, so that we can live up to our motivation to become universal beings? Is this the ultimate meaning of all our research into aging and disease?

These are the questions I asked myself as I was feeling some deep change taking place in me.

On Christmas of 1979 the mystery unfolded. I had a startling revelation which I recorded in my journal:

> **The benign presence I sensed in my planetary birth experience was the Christ.** The light that surrounded the Earth and awakened us collectively was the Christ-light. The light that arose within us was the Christ-light that dwells in every one of us!

The Christ "act"—to do the work that he did—is a new kind of resurrection and transformation at the dawn of the next stage of evolution.

The marriage of Christ and Eve happens at the Second Coming. It is in real time, like his birth. It is an event in history.

I realized that I was living through a slow-motion epiphany. My mind-body was supercharged with excitement. The higher voice and my own conscious mind began to weave together. It was sometimes difficult for me to tell which voice was speaking: Barbara's voice or the higher voice.

I relaxed my figuring-it-out mind, to allow my deeper knowing to speak. When the stream of ideas began I was filled with awe, wonder, release and joy. I realized there is always a vast and powerful stream of consciousness in our minds, which we can tap into at will, and that holds within it the intelligence of the Creation, of which we are conscious parts.

SCENE 4: THE CHRIST EXPERIENCE

I went to Santa Barbara to write a book on the future of humanity. I rented a little house, to be all alone for the first time in my life. John stayed in Washington.

I was hyper-stimulated from doing the Theater for the Future. My mind-body system was tremulous with the desire for a higher order, a new synthesis. I knew that the meaning of our power was universal life. I knew that our collective story is a birth. But still, who are we as human individuals? Earl's original question about a new image of humans commensurate with our power was still unanswered. His own image of a disembodied face the color of starlight was not enough for me.

What does it feel like, what does it look like to be at the next stage of our evolution? What is the future human **like?** This was my question.

I developed "writer's block." So many ideas were pressuring to come forth through the narrow opening of my rational mind. In surrender I called my sister in Palo Alto. "Jacqueline," I said, "let's take a day off together. Let's have some fun in Santa Barbara. Will you come down to spend a day with me?" She gladly agreed, and so we set out one morning for a day of sisterly companionship.

MOUNT CALVARY MONASTERY

We drove up the hills of Santa Barbara toward Cold Canyon. The day was intoxicatingly pure, brilliant, clear, bright, clean, light, glowing. The vegetation was alive after ten days of rain.

The trail we found was overgrown, so we decided to go on toward the Botanical Gardens.

We followed a winding road up the mountain. On our left was the sea, glittering and shimmering in the sun. On our right were the mountains framed by the utterly ultra-blue sky.

The air felt like heavy sweet water upon the face.

We climbed and climbed. Suddenly I saw a little weathered wooden sign: "Mount Calvary Monastery."

"Let's go see it," I said to Jacqueline, suddenly feeling a mysterious attraction.

We began an even steeper climb. Excitement rose within me. My body felt the inner radiation—that electric field which has so disoriented me.

"Jacqueline, I feel as though I've been here before. I know this place. I've got to spend some time here. Something's going to happen here."

We saw the little monastery upon Mount Calvary in Santa Barbara. On either side of the beautiful wooden door a man and a woman were painted in gold upon the stucco walls. Jesus and Mary? Adam and Eve? Christ and Eve?

I sat upon the stone wall, looking at the great arc of the shining sea, the mountainous Earth arisen, and then, mystically, magically, miraculously, hang-gliders—human butterflies—appeared, afloat above the monastery at Mount Calvary in an ecstacy of freedom and weightlessness. Mass metamorphosis! We **shall** all be changed!

All at once an idea flashed through my mind, electrifying my whole body with inner radiation.

"Jacqueline," I said, "the resurrection was **real.** He did it! And so will all of us who are willing to do as he did, all who are willing to follow the commandment of love."

I suddenly realized that the man Jesus was a future human, an evolutionary template. His demonstration lodged in us the expectation of a personal future in a transformed body, in a transformed world in a universe of many mansions. The capacities to do as he did have been activated by the expectation.

Now is the fullness of time. The Planetary Birth is the time on the planet when individual members can transform their consciousness and activate their capacity to rejuvenate their bodies. Eventually we will be able to build a body like Jesus' new resurrected body, through scientific and spiritual maturation—a body that is totally responsive to godlike intention.

Tears came into my eyes. I put my arm around Jacqueline's shoulder. "I've got to go into the monastery," I said.

I rang the bell. I cracked the door to see an elegant large foyer, with Spanish chairs, red cushions and a polished wooden floor.

A young priest with red hair came to the door dressed in a white monk's robe.

"Hello," I said. "May I know what place this is?"

"This is a monastery—a retreat house."

"Could someone like me come here? My name is Barbara Hubbard. I'm a futurist on a spiritual quest."

"Sure, I'm just having lunch, could you come back in ten minutes?"

I nodded, smiling at his casual manner, in contrast to the awesome anticipation I felt.

I returned. He answered the door, ready and smiling. "My name is Adam," he said, shaking my hand.

I laughed. The symbols were incredible:

Mount Calvary: the place of the crucifixion.

The hang-gliders: the resurrected multitude, the new norm, the butterflies emerging from caterpillars.

Santa Barbara: the spiritual Barbara that I am here to become.

Adam: the present world.

"This is an Episcopal monastery," he said.

"Oh, no," I laughed again. "I tried to find God through an Episcopal church in Scarsdale years ago...but it didn't work."

"No kidding," he said, as he showed me through the exquisite dining room.

"I would like to come here for a retreat. Do you think that is possible?"

"That's fine, we're having a silent retreat next weekend." He took me to his desk and gave me the schedule.

"February 1-3: Quiet weekend: A nondirected weekend of silence open to everyone, to renew inner peace and meet the Lord in the monastic round of Offices, Eucharist, quiet and nonverbal fellowship."

"I'll be there," I said.

He put my name down.

Several days later I checked in for the silent retreat. Early in the morning, as I was sitting beneath a little wooden cross upon the top of the hill, overlooking the world below, the inner voice guided me as I wrote in my journal:

Saturday, February 2, 1980:

Mount Calvary

Santa Barbara

California

U.S.

Solar System

Milky Way

Universe

God

Today is the day when the marriage of Christ and Eve is consummated. Today is the day of your union. Today is the day of grace and joy when the evolving human marries the evolved human. Eve, the evolving human, marries Christ, the evolved human, the universal human, the human in God's image.

To marry Christ, Eve must become whole. She can no longer separate herself from others, her reason from her intuition, her feminine from her masculine, her good from her evil, her high from her low. To marry Christ, Eve must become one.

Eve becomes One Whole Being. She can take every step by her own desire and will, except this last step. To marry Christ, she must be asked, be invited. The grace of Christ's love must descend upon her and lift her up beyond her will, her desire, her capacity.

Readiness is her task.

Salvation is Christ's task.

Then the "voice," which until now had seemed to be my own "Higher Self," became elevated and was transformed into an even Higher Voice, the Christ voice. I felt an electrifying presence of light, a field that lifted me up. The words began:

My resurrection was a signal of all of yours. Why do you suppose I submitted to the calumny of Calvary but to demonstrate that the physical body can and must be transformed?

The resurrection was an early attraction signal to the human race of what can be done through love of each person as a member of one's own body and of God above all else.

The intensity of that love, the power of that connectedness is the key to the resurrection, now known as the transformation.

The resurrection was a future forecast of an approaching new norm.

The transformation of Homo sapiens *to* Homo universalis *is the acting out of that forecast by the human species.*

What I did alone, now all can do who choose to love God above all else and their neighbor as themselves. That great commandment of pure love combined with the knowledge of God's processes of creation gained by science in the past two thousand years is the formula for victory.

Mount Calvary two thousand years ago was a signal of resurrection through death of this body.

Mount Calvary now becomes a signal of the transformation of this body through the union of love and knowledge.

You, all of you who wish to partake of the next step, must do as I did by the means which your God-given minds have lovingly developed. You may add to your spiritual power your new technologies of transcendence, your extended brain-mind bodies, incorporated in your rockets, computers and precious machines. These are God-given tools for you to use now.

I had to make my example by super-human means, to set the pattern for evolving humans to use as a beacon of light.

You are not super-human but fully human. Your unfinished species is ready to evolve. The time has come on Earth for this quantum change to occur in many of you.

The change is demonstrable not metaphoric. It can be seen, felt, tasted, touched as was my glorified body when I resurrected and appeared to the disciples—when I let Thomas touch my hands and feel the wounds with his own hands. Seeing is believing. That is why I appeared in a new body. That is why some of you must do the same, not by being crucified but by being uplifted bodily in your early vehicles of universal life.

You must unite with all on Earth who are attracted to self-transcendence. You must also go outward into the universe, physically, in space-craft. Joining with all of humanity through your media, you will love everyone as members of one body. By seeing yourselves on television as one body in the act of loving yourselves as one body, millions who are prepared will realize at one instant in time a demonstrable change.

Energy is building up in millions of bodies now for this normalized act of transcendence.

You already know me—all of you who desire to evolve, all of you who desire to live in the New Jerusalem, all of you who are believers.

I, Jesus, the man, was able to manifest Christ consciousness in one lifetime, and exert it to transform my physical body. This capacity is the beginning of the next phase. It is literally child's play for a universal being, as easy as it is for you to learn a language at the age of two or three, an impossible task for an animal.

What I have done, you shall do, and more. You can be my links to humanity. Just as I am humanity's link to God, you and others who are so attracted to the evolution of the world are human links to the trans-human state that is mine. I cannot "return" until enough of you are attracted and linked.

I will give you all the help I can without destroying your initiative, independence, sanity and humanity.

You are not to become martyrs, saints or crazy fools. You are to become evolved humans, normal, good—models for others that are

reachable. When I came two thousand years ago, I had to perform mir-
acles including the resurrection, which appeared to be supernatural,
but were only natural at the next level of Spirit power.

Now it is a fusing of spiritual intention to serve the will of God,
which is our own, with scientific awareness of how the universal laws
operate, that will normalize the miracles and make them accessible to
all people of good will.

I was electrified. It was an omnipresent Being that I felt from within as
the resurrected Christ. I did not see a vision. I felt a Presence. I lived for
hours in a new state of being. I had only to think of him, and the Presence
was present. It was both within me, and beyond me, it was my Self and yet
far more than myself. There was a relationship between me and the
Presence. I loved that Being with all my heart, soul, mind and body and
was lifted up by the Presence into a field of love.

A NEW ORDER OF THE FUTURE

One day, after communion, I went to sit in the little garden next to the
large wrought iron cross. The bees buzzed throughout the flowers.
Hummingbirds hung in midair. Oranges glinted in the light. The Presence
surrounded, penetrated, infused me with itself, and continued to communicate an inner stream of ideas. I wrote in my journal:

NOW you understand—it is your own maturing that is the key.
Take the perspective of a more mature species, what you will be like
when the human race grows up, stops fighting and starts using its full
capacities harmoniously. As each person has a higher, wiser self, so does
the species-as-a-whole.

Be members of a more mature species now. You have the powers of
Christ NOW. This is what I came to Earth to reveal. You can do what I
do and even more shall you do.

Take this seriously. It is true. I cannot come again until the world
realizes and acts upon its own power for the good.

Your maturity—all the volunteers giving their total being—is the
key now. Stop being children. Start being like me. Yours are the powers,

yours the glory, yours the triumph. As you align your will with God's will, loving God above all else and your neighbor as yourself, you will become free.

You, all of you who are desirous and ready, are the Way. Be a beacon of light unto yourselves.

This tiny band, this brave congregation of souls attracted to the future of the world are my avant-garde—the New Order of the Future.

These are the self-selected souls who have come to Earth to carry the miracle of the resurrection into action as the transformation of human-ity from Homo sapiens *to* Homo universalis.

The words came with a rhythm of their own as fast as I could record them. I was literally scribbling at lightning speed as the monks of the Order of the Holy Cross walked by me in the garden, smiling pleasantly. I wondered what they'd think of all this. Is it blasphemous to believe in the reality of the promise in the light of our new capacities?

The ideas continued:

The text of the New Order of the Future is the Story of Creation.

The first chapter is revealed in the religions of the world, especially the Judeo-Christian which foresaw the future most clearly. Its vision as stated by Paul, is true.

"Behold I show you a mystery: we shall not all sleep; but we shall all be changed." Revelation shall be unfolded in evolution through the marriage of faith and knowledge in each of you.

The second chapter of the Story of Creation is being discovered by the sciences of humanity.

The maturing human intellect is rediscovering its connection to the creation as it perceives that the material world is an abstraction of the nervous system. The ultimate reality is not matter but patterned, inten-tional energy...God.

The maturing human intellect is catching a glimpse of God's proce-sess so that we can co-operate consciously with the Creator. We are entering the first phase of conscious evolution for which the Order of the Future is formed.

The maturing human intellect, now confronted with the mystery of the creation with a greater knowingness than ever before, must humbly and joyfully consecrate itself to working with the creation to achieve the next level of consciousness, freedom and order in this world and in the universe beyond.

The third chapter in the Story of Creation is written by the participants in the drama, the actors in the passion play.

The text is pre-scripted, pre-patterned, pre-potential but not pre-determined.

The articles of faith are:

> *There is a Designing Intelligence in the universe.*
> *We are the creations of that Intelligence.*
> *We are ready to become co-creative with the Intelligence to act out the next chapter in the history of the world.*
> *We recognize in all humility that we are an infinitesimal part of an infinite universe.*
> *We are capable, even in our infancy, of resonating with that Infinity to an ever more precise degree.*

My hand became cramped I was writing so fast. The flood gates of my mind had opened. It was as if an unseen intelligence was infiltrating the memory bank of my brain, selecting ideas that had been stored through years of experience. I organized nothing. I thought of nothing. I simply followed the stream of ideas. Then came another unexpected thought:

Now, Barbara, read through the New Testament for the vision of the future. You have neglected Christ. You found the clues in God's process of creation but were struck down by emptiness in your heart till you were required to seek the love that passeth all understanding. Now, returning to the Episcopal monastery that you rejected in your youth, you have discovered that the pattern has also been revealed in the Bible. Most specifically, you recognized that THE RESURRECTION IS REAL. Now go to the Bible and pick out the predictive passages. Study the Bible as you have studied the Story of Creation as revealed in the

Book of Nature. You found God through the works of nature. You found Christ through your need for unconditional love.

SCENE 5: ENCOUNTERING THE NEW TESTAMENT

I went into the monastery to find a Bible. Back in the garden I opened it at a passage from First Corinthians:

For since by man came death, by Man came also the resurrection of the dead.

1 CORINTHIANS 15:21

I wrote this response in my journal:

With man came the awareness of death and the effort to overcome it. All of human history can be interpreted as the effort to overcome the limits of mammalian existence; eating, sleeping, reproducing and dying. Through tools, language, religion and art, and today through science, industry, technology and the conscious activation of our human potential, we strive to overcome the limits of the material world.

Our generation, born at the time when humankind-as-a-whole is born from Earthbound to universal life, is the first to have the capacities to act out the resurrection as the transformation.

Soon I recognized that all passages in the Bible are predictive. It is the gospel of our future.

Every morning at the monastery, I arose at dawn and received the Communion feeling the Presence, incorporating It. Then I moved to the little stone bench in the sun in the garden at Mount Calvary. There I sat, surrounded by honeysuckle and hummingbirds. I would open my Bible with deep anticipation, allowing my attention to be drawn to specific passages, continuing with the writings of Paul:

And so it is written: "The first man Adam was made a living soul." The last Adam was made a life-giving Spirit.

I Corinthians 15:45

The first human was endowed with a consciousness of the Creator buried deep within the psyche. Human beings have always known that they are more than a perishable body. From the dawn of human consciousness they have recognized death as a transition to a new life; they prayed for the departed; they strove to be prepared to go beyond the narrow confines of the material world as perceived by the five mammalian senses: sight, taste, touch, hearing and smelling. The living soul of the first Adam, that which makes the early human more than an animal, carried the human race from its beginning to its present precipice of power.

Now is the beginning of the Second Adam, who is endowed with a life-giving Spirit. The Second Adam has a new body, which resonates at a higher frequency, naturally overcoming the last enemy, death. The transition from this life to the next is made in a new way as we graduate from the Epoch of the First Adam to the Epoch of the Second Adam.

The transition is made, not by disintegration, but by conscious integration of the intention of the individual with God. The Second Adam is a chosen state. Only those who intend to be transformed, are. It is a pure, free choice. No one who chooses not to join his or her will with God's can become a life-giving Spirit. Intention is the key. Thus is the Kingdom protected from the unwilling, from those who do not intend to do the will of God.

All is well. All is choice. In the end there is no coercion, only free will, aligning freely with the will of God. The former things are not remembered. The past has passed away. The first Adam has done his work, which was to prepare the way for the life-giving Spirit. The living souls of the first Adam, whose bodies have disintegrated in the graves of Earth, are reclothed with new bodies at the time of the transformation, their pioneering service to the future honored through the halls of Heaven. All is well. Not a hair, not a feather is uncounted. The will to live on is the key to the Kingdom of life. As we will, so shall it be when our will and God's are one.

In response to each biblical passage I simply asked: How did this happen? What does it mean for us now? I used the life of Jesus and the New Testament as an evolutionary map of our potential, and thereby saw the meaning of our new powers: They are the evolving capacities required for our fulfillment of his promise that those who believe they can do the work he did will, in fact, have life-everlasting.

> Behold, I show you a mystery: We shall not all sleep; but we shall all be changed in a moment, in the twinkling of an eye, at the last trumpet. For the trumpet shall sound, and the dead shall be raised incorruptible, and we shall be changed. For this corruptible must put on incorruption, and this mortal must put on immortality. So when this corruptible shall have put on incorruption, and this mortal shall have put on immortality, then shall be brought to pass the saying that is written: "Death is swallowed up in victory. O death, where is thy sting? O grave, where is thy victory?"
>
> *I CORINTHIANS 15:51-55*

Behold, the mystery will soon be revealed. The time of transformation is at hand. The twinkling of an eye, the trumpet's last blare, come for the person when the planet has reached its limits and is ready like an egg to give birth to its child.

We humans, the bodily children of Earth, will become universal as we carry Earth's body into the universe. In that environment, mammalian bodies will soon perish. The new bodies will be formed by the intention to survive and grow in the new environments of a universe of infinite variety, magnificence and surprises.

Oh, humanity, what your eyes are about to behold will fill your breaking hearts with joy.

You who are saddened by the infantile condition of the human race, take heed. Lift up your hearts, raise your eyes, throw back your heads and sing praises for the day that is coming.

You have always known you are one body, now you see you are.

You have always intuited that you were immortal, now you know you are.

You have always known you were universal, now you voyage to the stars.

You have always known you were beloved, and now you feel the love.

You have always known you were unfinished, now you are evolving before your own eyes.

The movie of creation is speeding up, to let you see the pattern of the future unfold before your eyes.

In the twinkling of an eye you see the next step of creation. The film accelerates. The static frames blend, you see God's hand at work vividly for the first time.

As you move off Earth-time onto cosmic time the invisible hand of God is revealed by the speeding up of the picture.

There were gradations of voices, from my own deeper knowing, to a higher intelligence, to what seemed like a Christ voice, electrifying and personal.

As my Bible commentary proceeded, I realized that I was being uplifted into a new pattern of thought. My futuristic intuitions were being affirmed and reinforced by Scripture. I began to experience an inner evolution. I felt the Christ presence as a living, intimate reality, which is available to each of us at all times. I could sense the Christ voice whenever I focussed my attention upon it.

I began to record in my journal the words that it directed at me personally:

Dear Barbara, as you take these words down know you are one of my dearly beloved daughters, one of those women who are now emerging everywhere for whom I have been waiting until the fullness of time.

Such women as you are becoming whole. In your wholeness you will free the men who love you to become whole, and the children who love you to become whole, and the parents who love you to become whole.

In your wholeness all of you will heal the world and make it ready to participate in the building of the New Jerusalem.

Apply everything in your writings to yourself. You must become what you say is possible. You must demonstrate the psychological state of universal consciousness as a new norm. That is the first purpose of your writings.

What is the second purpose of these writings?

The second purpose of these writings is to call for the completion of the good news concerning the transformation of the world. To prepare the self-elected for the full glory of the Kingdom. To knit the strands into a whole by providing a self-organizing matrix for the word and the acts through the television nervous system of the world. As soon as you—all who know your potentials—can tell this vision on television, you will have begun your real work in the world.

What shall I do about the periods of depression and disconnection?

Have faith that they will pass. Use them as practice periods to orient your magnetic needle of attention toward God in times of stress. This is an essential skill.

It seems that I've hit a consciousness barrier. I go so far—and seem almost there—at the place of connectedness, and I fall back down. It is an increasingly painful place to be. Can you help me?

Yes, I can. Use those moments as exercises of attention. Focus your concentration consciously on me, and you will experience yourself capable on your own of returning to the center of connectedness.

It is essential that all of you become self-authorized, that is, capable of connecting to your Higher Self, and through your Higher Self to me at all times, without the help of external signs or gestures of affirmation of any kind from anywhere. There are many long dark nights of the soul as you leave the comforts of the self-conscious world to reach the joys of alignment with the whole.

Your process is gradual. Your mission is to be able to trace your steps and reveal your path to others by showing the steps you took. If you leap too fast, you will not know what happened. You are an evolutionary, not a mystic. You have evolutionary consciousness, not mystical consciousness. The movie of creation is not speeded up to infinity to reach the white light. It is speeded up only fast enough for you to see the patterns and act upon them consciously, sharing with all who are so attracted.

This is a new stage of consciousness for humanity that you are growing toward, suitable for this age of response-ability. Everything you have been saying is true. Now you must apply it to yourself. There are no short cuts to the resurrection. Be a beacon of light unto yourself. Love everyone. Forgive all attack. Stop attacking yourself. Release your attention to focus on me.

If you are to become a beacon of light you must simply constantly remember to place the magnetic needle of your attention on God. This attraction will gradually cause all distractions to lose their hold on you.

The Christ voice spoke further of a "New Order of the Future" that would emerge from the collective practice of these instructions:

This Order for the Future is designed to hasten the maturing of my people. It is not an order of worship. It is an order of partnership. I sit on the right hand of God. So must you. I cannot come to you unless you grow up to be my equal.

Gather unto yourself this tiny band, this congregation who are beacons of light unto themselves, so that the light in each of you can raise the light in all and illuminate the world with the recognition that
We are one body
born into this universe
seeking greater awareness
of our Creative Intention.

Are there any special steps you would like us to take to hasten our spiritual maturation?

Yes. Meditate on the resurrected Christ and know that I am your goal. You are to be like me. You cannot save the human race unless you demonstrate that you can save yourselves. The need for hope is deep. No temporary overcoming of ego's problems in the world, no temporary balance of powers or healing of wounds will suffice.

Your hope lies deeper than the removal of problems. Your hope springs from the transforming of yourselves.

Put the circle of white light around you. Empty your mind of all thoughts you do not think with me. Bring the energy of pure love into your body and, in a state of deep peace, let me activate your mind-bodies at the next level.

My stay at Mount Calvary Monastery was coming to a close...the retreat in which I was to "meet the Lord."

I was deeply grateful for the monastery. It brought to me the symbols of the past, which had been conceived, nurtured and passed on for nearly two thousand years. They are symbols especially concerning our personal relationship to God. For Jesus represents that personal relationship. He is that toward which we are evolving and through which each of us can know our Creator more directly as he did.

I was learning to love these symbols and images, which I rejected in my first attempt to join the Episcopal Church in Scarsdale in 1946. Then I could not tolerate the emphasis on guilt, pain, suffering and sin. Where, I asked, was the celebration of our power, goodness, glory and future?

I discovered our splendor through the revelation of God's Cosmic Story—the evolution of the universe that has created us, humankind, one body, now being born into the universe, seeking to know our Creator more intimately and immediately than through the narrow slit of self-consciousness.

But I lacked the personal contact with the Creator. I was too infinitesimal, God too infinite.

Thus I came to seek Jesus.

What a marvelous picture it had been here at the Mount Calvary Monastery. The last two days I was the only woman and the only guest, with seven monks robed in white. Every morning they performed the communion ceremony, since it was Easter week. Seven monks of the Order of the Holy Cross and one futurist. Seven gorgeously dressed monks, in robes of silver, gold, crimson and white at the break of day, in the little chapel overlooking the mountains and the sea of Santa Barbara...and one fifty-year-old stranger in blue corduroy pants and running shoes.

We celebrated together the "mystery of our faith" that Christ was born of the Virgin Mary, died on the cross, rose the third day and ascended into heaven where he sits at the right hand of God the Father. We shall do as he did; we shall die to this body of flesh and blood, be born anew into new, incorruptible bodies. We shall ascend beyond this planet, and become partners with God in conscious co-creation of this world and worlds beyond.

My emphasis was on the resurrection and the ascension. Theirs was on the forgiveness of sins, the suffering and the death on the cross. We represented two vast ages—premillennium and postmillennium.

This distinction was underlined by one of my encounters at the monastery. When I arrived on the last Friday of my visit, a priest greeted me, and asked me what I had been doing.

"I've been writing a futurist's interpretation of the New Testament," I said. "I've been studying the resurrection of Jesus as a real event, and imagining our collective capacities to do as he did, eventually not dying, producing in abundance, ascending into outer space. I'm focussing on the resurrection."

"What about the crucifixion?" he said, scowling at me.

"There would be no meaning to the crucifixion without the resurrection," I said.

"There are lots of crucifixions without resurrections," he replied.

I contracted and felt rebuffed. There seemed to be a barrier between me and them. I wanted to be part of a community—but was there one that actually **believed** that we would do what Jesus said we would? Would a "New Order of the Future" be accepted by the Church?

I realized that the living, resurrected Christ is the evolutionary potential of the human race, drawing us **forward** toward our fulfillment.

The revelation became clear. In my Planetary Birth Experience I had a powerful sense of "other life," a benign, loving Presence, felt as intelligent light, that was longing to communicate with us as much as we were longing to communicate with "It."

Whenever I really probe my own deepest motivation and expectation, it is for that CONTACT, not as an individual experience, but as a shared planetary experience.

At the time of the Planetary Birth Experience in 1966, I fell in love with that unknown, unidentified Presence. Nevertheless, I put it out of my conscious mind. It was too far ahead of me. I could not understand it.

The quality of that Presence was the same I rediscovered in my study of the Gospels. That's why it was so familiar to me. I felt I knew Jesus more intimately than I knew myself. He is more real. He is me-in-the-future. He is everything I want to be.

The quality of the Presence at the time of the Planetary Birth Experience—a kinesthetic, precognitive flash—was one of overwhelming magnetic **love** and desire to speak with us, to encourage us to grow up, to join him.

This Presence corresponded to the experience of the "magnet" at the core of my solar plexus which I felt so many years ago. It was of that magnetic pull I wrote: "It's killing me. Either I will respond to it and achieve my desire...or die."

But what was my desire? And how was I to achieve it if I did not know it, I wondered. Then I saw the answer.

The Presence was the Christ—pulling the Christ within me to be like him, to know him, to be him. It was my potential being attracted to him. It was my own future, our own future, reaching into the present, pulling us forward.

After the Planetary Birth Experience I learned to talk about that magnetic pull as the "evolutionary attraction," moving us to fulfill the evolutionary design—which is to become Universal Humanity. And it is, but it was all impersonal.

Now, since my understanding that Jesus' resurrection was real, I can relate the two experiences, both collectively and personally.

Universal Humanity is us-in-the-future, collectively. It is the next step of human evolution.

Jesus, as the resurrected Christ, is an individual example of us-in-the-future. He demonstrated to us what we are naturally to become. He sowed the seed in our minds, and triggered the scientific and democratic revolutions of modern society, which provide the needed capacities, when developed to their **next** stage, to achieve collectively, a Christ action—a real transformation of those members of our species who have eyes to see and ears to hear.

I, as a member of the human race reaching puberty at the time of the atomic bomb (the sign that the Great Transition had begun), picked up his signal without knowing whose it was. I dedicated my life to discovering the reality of that magnetic attraction toward the future. I could not find it in scientific materialism, which saw the universe going down to a heat death. Nor could I find it in fundamentalist Christianity, which ignored the potentials of our scientific/technological capacities. Nor could I find it in liberal humanism, which ignored the Creator and our transcending future.

Every time in my life when I tried to realize this aspiration in action, the action seemed insufficient, and I aborted it, hence my deep fear of failure. I have "failed" at every worldly thing I've ever done, because I stopped doing it.

Everything I could think of doing was too **limited** as an acting out of this experience, because this experience is not wholly of this world.

As Jesus said to Pontius Pilate: "My Kingdom is not of this world. If My Kingdom were of this world, then would My servants fight, that I should not be delivered to the Jews. But now is My Kingdom not from hence." (John 18:36).

The experience has to do with the transformation of the world, not its reformation.

CO-CREATIVE WOMAN

I returned to my little house in Santa Barbara. At first I was afraid that the writing would stop when I was not at the monastery. But I found I could do it anywhere. I had been calling John on the phone, reading this to him. As a traditional Southern Baptist, he was amazed, then he was thrilled. "Barbara," he said, "I'm a soldier, I'll never be a co-creator, I've done too much that I know isn't right...but this, I tell you, I'd stake my life on it. It's true."

I began to feel myself evolve **as a woman.** Far from degenerating and dying at menopause, it was obvious I was regenerating and evolving into an expanding life cycle.

I sensed that not only would we dissolve patriarchy—we would evolve into holy unions of equal co-creators guided by the deep feminine attraction for new life.

The Bible writing continued:

> But I would have you know that the head of every man is Christ, and the head of the woman is the man, and the head of Christ is God...For a man indeed ought not to cover his head, inasmuch as he is the image and glory of God; but the woman is the glory of the man. For the man is not of the woman, but the woman of the man. Neither was the man created for the woman, but the woman for the man.
>
> *I CORINTHIANS 11:3, 7-9*

Paul set the tone for two thousand years of domination of man over woman.

The two thousand years are over.

The domination is ended.

It may have had meaning during the time of the preservation of the seed of the expectation of life-everlasting.

During that time the instruments and institutions of transformation were exquisitely designed, mainly by the masculine conceptual mind. Science and democracy were matured by the dominant masculine consciousness, as it gained understanding of the material world in preparation for the transformation from terrestrial to universal life, in preparation for acting out the resurrection through collective human capacity.

We had to have science and democracy to take the next step of evolution, in which the sacred individual gains co-creative power as joint-heir with Christ.

Science—the understanding of the material world, or God's processes of creation—and democracy, the emancipation of individual creativity through the guarantee of inalienable rights, have been magnificent achievements in the last two thousand years, which enable us to take the step from the creature/human condition.

Women have been largely occupied in the procreation, nurturing and educating of the young.

Now, the situation is rapidly changing. We are at the point where the first phase of science and democracy has been completed. Dominion over nature produced by science must become co-creation with nature. Individual creativity, liberated by democracy, must become synergistic co-operation within a more complex whole—the emergence of a new order of freely participating individuals, enlarging the definition of self-interest to include the larger body of humankind.

Women are now to arise from the role of procreation to take leadership in a new partnership with men for the co-creation of universal life.

Only the fusion of feminine consciousness with the masculine will produce whole beings in which emotional maturity is attained and love infuses power until they are one and the same.

The feminine energy, therefore, refocuses itself to take the initiative in guiding science and democracy toward synergistic co-operation in the building of new worlds on Earth, new worlds in space.

Women are not to consider themselves only healers of the wounds of the past, or restorers of the ravages of the modernized world. We are also arousers of the technologies of transcendence, to carry the seed of life into the cosmos so that a universal species may be born out of the peoples of Earth. Ours is the task of suprasexual arousal of the co-creative capacities of the human genius—male and female.

Women are leaders, pioneers, innovators, guided by their attraction for more life.

We lead by our attraction for the next step of evolution.

A new "Eve" arises at points of quantum transformation. She arose at the time of the leap from animal to human consciousness. She ate of the fruit of the Tree of the Knowledge of Good and Evil. The experience of separation began. Her desire for knowledge aroused the masculine intellect, and the dominion of the male began. We learned how the material world works.

Now, Eve rises again as we leap from self-centered to co-creative, universal consciousness. We are about to eat of the fruit of the Tree of Life, and become godlike. Woman's desire for Christ-being, for godlike inheritance, for partnership with God, through the maturation of intellect in service of pure love, must **attract the energies of the world** to a new level of creativity.

Right now the male capacities are dammed up by the limits that their success has created. The limits to growth in a finite world are constricting the creativity of the masculine mind. There men stand with their great machines of transcendence: the rockets, the computers, the instruments of microbiology and microtechnology. Scientists, astronauts, explorers, inventors, creators of all races, creeds and colors are stymied by lack of vision of what the power of the world is for.

This magnificent masculine genius is being told that the purpose of the power is only the stewardship of Earth, the conservation of its resources, and the comfort of its billions of bodies.

The masculine genius for creation is not yet being told that its purpose is also the creation of universal life.

This is the attractive role of the Second Eves.

THE RADICAL TRUTH

I realized from the Scriptures that my deepest, secret longing for personal transformation was not some strange aberration of a far-out futurist, but the very ancient central truth that billions of people throughout the world **already** have believed for two thousand years. Nothing in current scenarios of the future could equal the radical promise of the Bible for our total evolution. This thought was beautifully stated in this reponse to Galatians:

> **I do not frustrate the grace of God; for if righteousness come by the Law, then Christ is dead in vain.**
>
> GALATIANS 2:21

Consider the universe in all its splendor. Contemplate the billions of galaxies. Imagine the creation of this whole realm of reality. Focus upon the intelligence manifested in the exquisite organization and design of every entity, from sub-atomic particles to the human brain. Recognize that in you is the essence of that intelligence. View yourself as a being just opening your eyes to the fact of your personal participation in the evolution of the universe—a creative member of the ongoing creation.

Ask yourself how much you consciously know about how and why the creation works. Think how limited the social laws you submit to are in relation to the process of creation of the universe. Imagine that Christ is that aspect of yourself which knows the laws of creation—not social laws, but God's operating principles. Now, seek contact with those principles by grace—that is, by the fact that those principles are alive and are reaching toward you even as you are reaching toward them. Surrender. Do not frustrate "the grace of God"—the Divine attraction for you—by prejudging how righteousness may be acted out by you.

Believe for an instant that the whole universe is alive and attracted to you as you are attracted to it. Let the magnetism of that mutual attraction flood your nervous system with the force that binds atoms to atoms, molecules to molecules, cells to cells.

> *Break the bonds of self-consciousness by allowing the electricity of Creative Intelligence to flash through you consciously. Take the blinders off: Be blinded for an instant, as Paul was on the road to Damascus; let your inner eyes become accustomed to the light; then act in a state of grace—a state of attraction to and harmony with the whole creation.*

THE MEANING OF OUR POWER

As I wrote each morning, my heart expanded, my spirit soared. I knew I had crossed the great divide from one state of consciousness to the next. I had found the answers asked so long ago at the dropping of the atomic bomb. My intuition of something great and new coming had been affirmed.

The meaning of our power is to surrender the illusion that we are doing this alone. It is to intend with all our hearts, souls and bodies to become Universal Humans. It is to reorient our great social and scientific capacities in alignment with Christ consciousness to transform this Earth from a place of pain and sorrow to a Kingdom of Heaven.

Soon my stay in Santa Barbara was over. I packed up my precious journals and flew back to Greystone in Washington, D.C. I was reborn. I continued in the same routine, arising early every morning and writing. From Paul I turned to Matthew, and proceeded through the whole New Testament—the Gospels, Acts, Epistles. This outpouring culminated in the commentary on *The Revelation to John*. This final writing epitomizes and highlights the entire fifteen-hundred-page manuscript. In it the Christ voice takes over and offers us a new scenario of a gentle Second Coming, a natural birth of ourselves as a universal species co-creative with God.

It is with deep excitement that I present in the following pages the writings inspired by the Book of Revelation. It is given to connect and empower those for whom its message rings true.

T·H·E

REVELATION

OUR CRISIS IS A BIRTH

This text is written for the co-creators of new worlds, the builders of a new Heaven and a new Earth. It is written for those now on Earth in whom the flame of expectation burns, who wish to become like Christ, to do as he did and even more.

This is a moment of cosmic choice for the people of Earth. We have been given the power to build new worlds, or to destroy our own world. We stand at the threshold of Universal Humanity...or at the brink of Armageddon.

We see beyond us the New Jerusalem, the vision of ourselves in the future, which Christ came on Earth to reveal. We also see the abyss between here and there.

The New Jerusalem is the next stage of evolution. It is a community of natural Christs, co-operating with each other and God, endowed with the capacity to overcome hunger, planet-boundedness, death and separation from the universal community of life in the many mansions of this infinite Creation.

The Revelation to John described the violent path to the New Jerusalem; it is the way of a planet whose inhabitants refuse to give up their selfish life.

In this text we discover a loving path to the New Jerusalem. It is a path for a planet whose people choose to use their power, in all its splendor, for the transformation of the whole body of humankind.

The choice is given to our generation. There are alternatives to the tribulations. There are graceful births toward universal life. This text is a description of the fulfillment of Christ's life in the light of what we have learned through intellect and individuality, through science and democracy, since he came to Earth nearly two thousand years ago. It is written for new disciples of Christ who seek to work together for the Planetary Birth, a peaceful Second Coming of the Christ within and beyond—the birth of Universal Humanity.

NOTE: All passages from the New Testament are quoted from the *21st Century King James Version*. Three typefaces are used in this book to distinguish its basis elements: **boldfaced passages** denote scripture, *italicized passages* represent the Higher Voices and regular type represents the author's commentary

The Revelation of Jesus Christ, which God gave unto Him to show unto His servants things which must shortly come to pass. And He sent and made it known by His angel unto His servant John, who bore record of the Word of God and of the testimony of Jesus Christ, and of all things that he saw. Blessed is he who readeth, and those who hear the words of this prophecy, and keep those things which are written therein; for the time is at hand.

REVELATION 1:1-3

Blessed are you alive on planet Earth who are electing to be guides through the tribulations that are now beginning.

The word of prophecy has been heard by all the nations. The end of this phase has begun. This text is written for those of you who are prepared to lead your brothers and sisters out of "the valley of the shadow of death," just as Moses led the Jews out of the land of Egypt.

Your Exodus is from the creature/human condition. Your Promised Land is the New Jerusalem. Your image of humans is the natural Christ. Your process of transformation is the tribulations and the judgment, which will separate the whole-centered from the self-centered. Those of you who are preparing to act as guides across the "river of the Water of Life" to the other side, read on.

John, to the seven churches which are in Asia: Grace be unto you and peace from Him who is, and who was, and who is to come, and from the seven Spirits who are before His throne.

REVELATION 1:4

To the scattered people of Earth who intend to become fully human: You are the new church that is now gathering in my name. You who intend to follow my way the Whole Way, hail!

Grace be unto you. You shall be enabled by the process of evolution to transcend your own limits. You cannot do it by human will and desire alone. You are to be empowered by the force that creates the universe.

Peace also be unto you. You are to develop total peace based on total faith, deeper than your intellects can yet fathom. This inner peace is a prerequisite for would-be guides through the coming last days. Without inner peace, you cannot hear the Voice for God speaking within you.

Practice overcoming all fear.

> And from Jesus Christ, who is the faithful witness, and is the first-born of the dead, and the prince over the kings of the earth. Unto Him who loved us, and washed us from our sins in His own blood, and hath made us kings and priests unto God and His Father, to Him be glory and dominion for ever and ever. Amen.
>
> REVELATION 1:5-6

I, who have made you kings and priests, am now to make you co-creators. Women and men are no longer to separate for my sake, but to unite for my sake, whole being with whole being, so that you can become the second fruits of the dead—a generation that moves beyond degeneration to regeneration. I was the first begotten of the dead. You, dearly beloveds, are to be the next begotten of the dead.

I overcame the mammalian life cycle. So shall you.

> "I am Alpha and Omega, the Beginning and the Ending," saith the Lord, who is, and who was, and who is to come, the Almighty.
>
> REVELATION 1:8

I, Jesus Christ, am a state of being that pre-existed the evolution of the world, and is now pre-potential in the world that is passing away. I, Jesus Christ, am a personification of God, which all beings can also become.

Each of you is created in the image of God, as I was. Each of you can be a co-creator with God, as I am. Each of you can be joint-heir with me, evolving from Alpha toward Omega, toward the time of the Universal Pentecost when all consciousness throughout the universe is connected in celebration of the union of each with all. The Planetary Pentecost, which you are now approaching, is the first step toward the Universal Pentecost which is to occur ages and ages hence.

> I, John, who also am your brother and companion in tribulation and in the Kingdom and patience of Jesus Christ, was on the isle called Patmos, for the Word of God and for the testimony of Jesus Christ.
>
>

REVELATION 1:9

I, the transcriber of *The Book of Co-Creation,* who am also your sister and companion in tribulation, am here among others to send forth the word of Jesus Christ to the members of his body who wish to be the eyes and ears of the transformation now under way. This word is for those who wish to see and hear the way to evolve, in order to do it themselves as a demonstration for all others to see.

This text is written as a guide for those who wish to become the eyes and ears of the whole body of Christ—the church of the future, those who see ahead, the discoverers of my Design so that it may unfold perfectly without defect.

Be perfect. Be whole. Be prepared. Be joyful, dearly beloved, and proceed to become the image of God, like me, Jesus, your model, your template, your potential, your future self.

> I was in the Spirit on the Lord's Day, and I heard behind me a great voice as of a trumpet, saying, "I am Alpha and Omega, the First and the Last," and, "What thou seest, write in a book and send it unto the seven churches which are in Asia: unto Ephesus, and unto Smyrna, and unto Pergamos, and unto Thyatira, and unto Sardis, and unto Philadelphia, and unto Laodicea."
>
>

REVELATION 1:10-11

I was in a state of deep searching in the New England fields when I asked the question: What in our age is comparable to the birth of Christ? What is our story?

Suddenly my mind's eye penetrated the blue cocoon of Earth as if focused from the blackness of outer space.

I witnessed our planet as one body, struggling to coordinate as a whole.

I felt the pain everywhere.

I gasped for breath as the pollution choked the biosphere.

I cried out in hunger as the food ran out.

I called out in agony for the suffering of those who are diseased.

Then, I reached beyond the planet for new life. With that reach I saw the Earth coordinate; I saw the members of the body politic connect, link, and suddenly love one another as they saw with the same eyes and heard with the same ears that they are members of one, whole, good body.

I experienced the presence of a being that infused the entire planet with love.

We groped with infants' tongues to speak with the Presence who loved us, but we did not know the language.

I heard the words:

Our story is a birth. It is the birth of humankind. Go forth and tell the story. Humankind has been born into the universe.

Tell the story to all people who have eyes to see and ears to hear and who desire to participate consciously in the process of creation.

I do report these words for those who are now desirous of becoming conscious participants in our birth from self-centered terrestrial consciousness to whole-centered universal consciousness.

The script is revealed in the story of evolution and in the birth, teachings, death, resurrection and ascension of Jesus Christ.

We are now discovering the script of the story of creation. We are actors in the play.

We are now living out our own unique interpretation of a script that is being played in multitudes of ways throughout this universe without end.

> And I turned to see the voice that spoke with me. And being turned, I saw seven golden candlesticks; and in the midst of the seven candlesticks One like unto the Son of Man, clothed with a garment down to His feet and girded about His breast with a golden girdle.
>
> *Revelation 1:12-13*

▲

And I set forth to tell the story of the birth. But I did not know that the Presence I had experienced was Jesus Christ. He did not tell me then. How would I know? I was an unbeliever. I was seeking meaning without God. I was seeking to evolve without the model of Jesus to guide me.

I had discovered the Pattern in the process but I had not discovered the Patterner. I had discovered the potential in the process for universal life, but had not yet imagined that this potential is in me and in you.

I thought it was in others yet to be born, ages and ages hence. And so I had set forth to tell the story without Jesus as a model, without God as our Creator, and without the consciousness of the Holy Spirit as an inner guide. I was a blind pioneer, driven by desire to become fully human.

> His head and His hair were white like wool, as white as snow, and His eyes were as a flame of fire; and His feet like unto fine brass, as though they burned in a furnace, and His voice as the sound of many waters. And He had in His right hand seven stars, and out of His mouth went a sharp two-edged sword, and His countenance shone as the sun shineth in his strength. And when I saw Him, I fell at His feet as dead. And He laid His right hand upon me, saying unto me, "Fear not; I am the First and the Last. I am He that liveth, and was dead; and behold, I am alive for evermore, Amen, and have the keys of hell and of death."
>
> REVELATION 1:14-18

Imagine yourselves at the next stage of human evolution with all your capacities operating harmoniously.

You-in-the-future will be as different from yourselves-in-the-present as you today are different from early Homo sapiens, *several hundred thousand years ago.*

Imagine how your early ancestors would describe you if you visited them in their caves, arriving in your jets, flashing your images on portable television screens, talking to your colleagues on the moon. It would be almost indescribable. They would think of you as spirits, as gods to be feared and placated.

If you tried to speak to them, to reassure them, you would have difficulty narrowing your vocabulary sufficiently to suit their limited experience of their own latent potential. It would be hard for them to believe that they had the capacity to do as you do—and even more.

Yet, it is so. When John saw the "One like unto the Son of Man," he was awed. Imagine what you will be like when you, too, are fully evolved!

Your body will not decay. It will shine with the radiance of the total love you feel for God and all beings.

Your eyes will be lit with the fire of joy that you are the blessed Son or Daughter of God, co-creative on a universal scale.

Your feet will be like fine brass. You will glow with a biomagnetic field through which you will materialize and dematerialize, ascend and descend, from one vibratory plane to another. You will glitter and coruscate with the radiance generated by the intensity of your coherent thought in alignment with God.

Your voice will have the sound of many waters. It will flow effortlessly with the profound oratory of perfect meaning and truth in every word. You will know what to say at all times as your mind is linked with the mind of God. Remember the most eloquent moment of your life. Multiply it by the intelligence of God and imagine how you will sound when you have inherited godlike powers!

You will hold the stars of Heaven in your hands. Even now you reach with a baby's hand toward the moon. Like a child still bound to your crib, you reach beyond the rails toward a bright object nearby. This is just the beginning. Soon you will leave your cradle and stand, a giant upon the Earth, with your feet firmly rooted in the clay of this world and your arms reaching to touch the stars in the galaxy surrounding your planetary system. You will be in touch with the universe. You will be godlike men and women.

Out of your mouth will come words of perfect discernment: Yes, this is consonant with God's will; No, that is not consonant with God's will. Your voice will be a two-edged sword. You will constantly cut away that which is off the mark. You will be able to align your will with the will of God at all times. Your power to create and destroy will come from God.

Your countenance will be as glorious as the sun, shining with the strength given to you by your heirship as a Son or Daugther of God. As Jesus was transfigured, so you will be transfigured when you recognize that you are the direct children of God.

When John saw this great being, he fell at his feet as dead. The shock was almost more than he could bear. Now, dearly beloved, you live two thousand years after John. You have democratized through technology many of the miracles which higher beings performed. You can travel by image with the speed of light; you can heal; you can leave this Earth alive and return; you can produce food out of the thin air; you can destroy cities and build cities; you are learning to change your bodies.

Therefore, you need not be shocked when you see Jesus the second time. You are already becoming accustomed to some of the powers of co-creation.

Your nervous systems must be prepared to accept the shock of seeing yourself-in-the-future in its full potential. Your self-confidence must be high enough to accept your inheritance. Confidence means "to trust with." You are trusting me, as you would an elder brother who has already plunged from the high diving board, when he beckons you onward saying: "Follow me. You can do it, too."

Do not be afraid, dearly beloved. I have come to Earth to demonstrate your potential. I took on a mortal body like yours to demonstrate your potential to build a new body. I did not suffer on the cross and rise again on the third day to show you what I could do, but what **you** *can do.* **Yours** *is the power.* **Yours** *is the glory. That is my message to you!*

Fear not. I am the first and the last. I am he that liveth, and was dead. I demonstrate to you that death can be overcome. I am the first and the last because I am eternal. I have no beginning and no end. I manifest in time but I am not of time. I am eternal and evolving. And so, you are eternal and evolving.

The eternal you is beyond time. You are with God. You are of God. You are in God always, and God is always in you.

When you decide to enter the arena of time, you materialize in a body to do the work of the world. While you are in a body doing the work of the world, your mind-body forgets from whence it came. But your Higher Self never forgets. It always knows its eternal connection with God.

At the next stage of evolution, you will cease forgetting who you are. When you take on a consciously-created body like my resurrected body, you will be aware **always** that you and God are one.

It is very difficult to keep your attention on that fact when you feel bound in an animal body as at present, dearly beloved. That was my own most difficult challenge—to keep my attention focused on my true identity while in a body whose five senses are constantly signaling separation, vulnerability and death.

You will have the "keys of hell and of death" as you have the keys of Heaven and eternal life. The crux—always—is choice. At the next stage of evolution, life is a constant choice. If you falter in your choice to live as a Son or Daughter of God, you experience disconnection from the force. At the Christ-stage of existence you cannot forget who you are—and continue to live at that stage.

You will no longer be sustained by an autonomic nervous system and organic functions of which your conscious mind is totally ignorant.

You will not be ignorant of anything. All will be conscious. Every cell in your new body will be consciously communicating with you. You will be in charge of your body consciously, maintaining it, discarding it or evolving it into new forms to meet new environments beyond planet Earth. All will be chosen, all will be willed, by the joint will of you and your Creator as one. Amen.

> **"Write the things which thou hast seen, and the things which are, and the things which shall be hereafter."**
>
> REVELATION 1:19

Write the things which you have seen in the past, dearly beloved, and write the things which you have seen in your vision of the future, so that your brothers and sisters can act in the present to fulfill their destiny as heirs of God.

Write of their potentials. Let them know how good they are. Tell them that God loves them. Tell them that I love them. Tell them that they are to love *themselves as much as they love me. Tell them to recognize the God within themselves, and to follow that light through the darkness of the tribulations to the dawn of the Universal Age, when only the God-conscious continue to exist, and everyone is like Christ.*

> **"The mystery of the seven stars which thou sawest in My right hand, and the seven golden candlesticks: the seven stars are the angels of the seven churches, and the seven candlesticks which thou sawest, are the seven churches."**
>
> REVELATION 1:20

What is the church now? The church is the consciousness within all individuals that they are natural Christs. The church is the body of believers who are conscious of being me.

The existing church is resurrected from the seed to the flower as I was resurrected from the dead to the ever-living. The evolving church is the consciousness that you can do as I do and even more. The evolving church is the body of your corporate action to realize your potential to become me, the Christ who already exists within you as your Potential Self.

This church is forming like my first church, which was established upon the rock of awareness of one man, Peter, that I am Christ, the Son of God.

The second church is forming in the light of the combined awareness of all those who know that they are, like Christ, Sons and Daughters of God.

We are entering the Universal Age. Earthbound history is concluding. Universal history has begun.

The meaning of your crises is to activate your potentials to be me.

The purpose of your power is universal life, to be co-creators with God and joint-heirs with me.

> **"Unto the angel of the church of Ephesus write: 'These things saith He that holdeth the seven stars in His right hand, who walketh in the midst of the seven golden candlesticks: I know thy works and thy labor and thy patience, and how thou canst not bear them that are evil, and how thou hast tried them who say they are apostles and are not, and hast found them liars; and hast borne,**

and hast patience, and for My name's sake hast labored and hast not fainted. Nevertheless, I have something against thee, because thou hast left thy first love. Remember therefore from whence thou art fallen, and repent and do the works as at first; or else I will come unto thee quickly and will remove thy candlestick out of his place, except thou repent.'"

REVELATION 2:1-5

The evolving church is the belief and the passionate intention to be like Christ. It exists in the individual who so believes and intends, and in the congregation of believers and intenders. It is known as the "mystical body of Christ."

This body of Christ, the corporate consciousness of those human beings who are aware that Christ is within each of them as well as beyond each of them, must now be made whole again. The church of Ephesus represents those believers who have corrupted the church's first love by expending its energy in condemning those who are evil, deceitful and hypocritical, and who may lie about their faith. The churches of condemnation have forgotten their first love, and their reason for being, which is to proclaim that humanity is already saved by my demonstration of human potential, if they will but follow me and do as I did.

The churches of condemnation spend more time criticizing than they do co-creating. Their ministers do not apply my message to themselves. They do not demonstrate the Christ-capacities of co-creation. They do not personally intend to do as I do and even more. How, then, can they guide their flocks?

The churches of condemnation cannot bring redemption until they redeem themselves, by re-attuning to their first love. Their first love is the expectation that the end is at hand, that the New Order of the Ages has begun, that the time is here when we shall not all sleep but shall all be changed as I come again, arisen as the Christ within you.

Revive your expectation in the reality of this promise, O churches of condemnation. Revitalize your faith in yourselves and desist from criticizing the faithless. Your faith will awaken the flame of expectation—the deep intuition that you are to become like me—in the hearts of millions. Be a beacon of light unto yourselves, O pastors of the church of God.

If you do not do the "first works" based on your "first love," it is not I who will "remove thy candlestick." You will have removed it yourself. For when the light of faith in the reality of the promise goes out in you, you are no longer a light to others. You are in the dark. You must pray for the light to rekindle in you before you can once again enlighten others.

It is not enough to tell people to be good and to love each other. I did not die on the cross and resurrect myself merely to demonstrate human love alone. My greater demonstration was that human love is the path toward suprahuman life—that if you put the Kingdom first and love your neighbor as yourself, you will have ever-evolving life.

O people of the church of God, reaffirm your own faith in the Kingdom. Reexamine what is meant by "Heaven." Take another look at the vision of the New Jerusalem. Shift your weary glance from the secular city to the City of God, and envision yourselves as builders of that city.

You are guides through the tribulations, leading the builders of the City of God through the disorder of the modern world, toward the New Order of the Ages, in which the intellect will be in perfect alignment with the Intention of the Creation.

O people of God, you must first become like me—healers, lovers, transformed beings. Put the Kingdom first, and all will be given to you.

> **"He that hath an ear, let him hear what the Spirit saith unto the churches. To him that overcometh will I give to eat of the Tree of Life, which is in the midst of the Paradise of God."**
>
> REVELATION 2:7

*O people of God, O churches of Christ, O believers in the promise, hear this: Those who act upon the promise **now** will inherit the powers of God. To you who overcome your limits of self-centeredness and become God-centered, I will deliver the fulfillment of the aspiration of the ages.*

O you who believe that you can do as I do, the Tree of Life is yours. Generations ago the first man and woman broke out of the creature/human condition. They ate of the fruit of the Tree of the Knowledge of Good and Evil, and felt separate from the Creator. They gained their own capacities for co-creation through the development of individuality and intellect. They were prevented from access to the Tree of Life, to the knowledge of how the invisible technologies operate, for they were still in a state of separate, self-centered consciousness, too childish to inherit the Kingdom.

Now, the human race is maturing. Although you are still not fully ready, because of your self-centeredness, the time has come when the risk of transformation must be taken. Yours is the generation to inherit the keys of the Kingdom. Yours is the generation to whom it is being given to know how to transform. Your scientific knowledge and individual capacity must flower now or die in the bud. Now is the season for the flowering of Christlike humans.

He that hath an ear—those of you who are hearing an inner voice and following its guidance—listen constantly, beginning right now. For the word is going forth to those whose ears can hear, that you are to prepare to experience the mystery which shall be revealed by the activation of your Potential Self, the Christ within.

That activation within, fused with your emerging technologies of astronautics, genetics, cybernetics and noetics, will bring to flower a garden of Christlike humans in this generation, to be loving beacons of light enabling all others who so desire to do the same.

The "church" that shall be uplifted before the tribulations intensify is not those who are preserving the seed, but those who are sprouting the flower.

This church is the **consciousness** *that you and I are one. Those who absolutely know this will go the next step in this lifetime. You are the generation born when humankind is born into the fullness of its expression. You are the generation of the awakening of the Universal Human, en masse, for all to see, while there is still time for all to choose to be Christlike.*

I am the way. God consciousness is the only way. I said it once, and I now say it again. Let those with eyes to see and ears to hear know that in all those who overcome their self-imposed limitations, I will awaken the capacity to be Universal Humans, co-creative humans, heirs of God. You whose ears hear my voice now will be enabled to act as emancipators of your generation—lib-

erators, as I was, not from some temporal tyranny, but from the tyranny of the creature/human condition.

The meaning of your new capacities gained through science and democracy is universal life. Not a reformed world but a transformed life, a New Heaven and a New Earth. Let all who desire to be natural Christs follow me now.

The way is within you. Listen. Listen. Listen. I am here for all to hear, right now.

> "And unto the angel of the church of Smyrna write: 'These things saith the First and the Last, who was dead and is alive: I know thy works and tribulation and poverty (but thou art rich), and I know the blasphemy of them that say they are Jews and are not, but are the synagogue of Satan. Fear none of those things which thou shalt suffer. Behold, the devil shall cast some of you into prison, that ye may be tried, and ye shall have tribulation ten days. Be thou faithful unto death, and I will give thee a crown of Life.' He that hath an ear, let him hear what the Spirit saith unto the churches. He that overcometh shall not be hurt by the second death."
>
> REVELATION 2:8-11

The church in Smyrna represents those believers who are persecuted for their faith.

Believers in your potential to be me, listen now. You have nothing to fear. Eternal life is already yours. An irreversible process has begun in you, which can no more be turned off than the mechanism of puberty. You will go the Whole Way to become co-creative. You may be killed, but you shall not die. You shall be resurrected, as I was. If you are called upon to suffer and die during the tribulations, you must keep in mind at all times that the suffering of the present cannot compare with the glory which shall be revealed in you. Yours the glory, yours the power, O believers in your potential to be Christlike humans.

"And to the angel of the church in Pergamos write: 'These things saith He, who hath the sharp sword with two edges: I know thy works and where thou dwellest, even where Satan's seat is; and that thou holdest fast My name and hast not denied My faith, even in those days wherein Antipas was My faithful martyr, who was slain among you, where Satan dwelleth. But I have a few things against thee, because thou hast there them that hold the doctrine of Balaam, who taught Balak to cast a stumbling block before the Children of Israel, to eat things sacrificed unto idols, and to commit fornication....Repent, or else I will come unto thee quickly, and will fight against them with the sword of My mouth.' He that hath an ear, let him hear what the Spirit saith unto the churches. To him that over-cometh will I give to eat of the hidden manna, and will give him a white stone, and on the stone a new name written, which no man knoweth except he that receiveth it."

REVELATION 2:12-14, 16-17

The message to the churches is as old as the churches, for the human condition has not fundamentally changed in the last two thousand years—though it is closer to changing than ever before, since the time of Quantum Transformation is at hand.

There are hundreds of ways of going off the mark. There is only one way of hitting the mark.

The church of Pergamos represents those believers who are seduced by overemphasis on the flesh, sensuality, on bodily needs and bodily delights.

*It is the **over**-emphasis that is wrong. I did not come to deny the body but to fulfill it.*

You do not fulfill your body by focusing on its present condition. You fulfill your body by focusing on its growing edge capabilities: its capacities for wellness, for sensitivity to divine intention, for regeneration, for transfiguration, for testing its outer limits—and overcoming them.

Oversensuality reinforces the hold of the creature/human nature over your higher capabilities. It is an unfortunate self-limitation to your own emancipation.

Yet, do not suppress your sensuality. Rather, use it as an energy to catapult yourself into the suprasexual desire for co-creation with God.

You are becoming your Christlike selves. Sexuality is extending toward suprasexuality. As you have fewer children and live longer lives, procreativity is becoming co-creativity.

There is no sacrifice in Heaven, trust me, dearly beloved. Sexual union is a magnificent first step. Now you may climb to joys you have never dreamed of. You may lift to pleasures beyond the fantasy of the most sensual dreamer on Earth. The ecstasy of sexual union is a prelude to the even greater joy of uniting minds.

You were not born to be celibate. You were born to be natural Christs. You will be uplifted by enacting creative desires in empathetic union with the universal community of godlike beings.

Consciously ask your sensual nature to extend its desire to include the union of aspiration and ideas, to create acts for God in the world.

Empathize. Have suprasexual intercourse, joining with one another to liberate the potential in each rather than to possess each other. Love, honor and emancipate each other to ever greater acts of co-creation.

Be faithful to your potential, not to your past. Be fruitful and originate works for the future.

O believers-in-your-potential-to-be-me, do not deny your sexuality; attract it to its complete fulfillment: permanent union with God to co-create life ever-evolving.

"And unto the angel of the church in Thyatira write: 'These things saith the Son of God, who hath His eyes like unto a flame of fire, and His feet are like fine brass: I know thy works, and charity and service, and faith and thy patience, and that thy last works be more than the first. Notwithstanding, I have a few things against thee, because thou dost permit that woman Jezebel, who calleth herself a prophetess, to teach and to seduce My servants to commit fornication, and to eat things sacrificed unto idols. And I gave her space to repent of her fornication, and she repented not. Behold, I will cast her into a bed, and them that commit adultery with her into great tribulation, except they repent of their deeds. And I will kill her children with death, and all the churches shall know that I am He who searcheth the thoughts and hearts; and I will give unto every one of you according to your works.' "

REVELATION 2:18-23

The church in Thyatira represents those believers who have succumbed to the arts of divination.

There are many false prophets practicing occult arts, who interpret signs without understanding the significance of my intent. They catch glimpses of truth but falsify the whole through incompletion of vision.

To be like me, follow me, and take no other seductive side paths to posterity.

I have provided everything you need. If you follow my demonstration by demonstrating that you can do as I did, everything shall be given to you.

If children are to inherit the Kingdom of their parents, should they go wandering into the city looking for a mindless job? No, they should place all their attention on being prepared for the power which they shall receive in the fullness of time.

Dearly beloved, your Creator has given you everything you need. Now you give all in return—which is you behaving in God's image—a young god, a joint-heir with Christ.

"And unto the angel of the church in Sardis write: 'These things saith He that hath the seven Spirits of God and the seven stars: I know thy works, and that thou hast a name that thou livest, but thou art dead. Be watchful and strengthen the things which remain, that are ready to die, for I have not found thy works perfect before God.' "

REVELATION 3:1-2

The church in Sardis represents those believers in whom the flame of expectation has almost gone out. They maintain the ritual of religion but no longer experience the joy of union with God. They are almost dead.

Those of you who once loved me, and who have become worn down by misdirected attention to the world, revive your dying hearts, arouse your flame of hope, let the needle of your attention be magnetized to the promise I have made to you.

> " 'Thou hast a few names even in Sardis, who have not defiled their garments; and they shall walk with Me in white, for they are worthy. He that overcometh, the same shall be clothed in white raiment; and I will not blot out his name from the Book of Life, but I will confess his name before My Father and before His angels.' "
>
> REVELATION 3:4-5

What is the Book of Life?

It is the databank of the characteristics required for reproduction, renewal and resurrection. It is the documentation of the evolutionary selection process, the record of those characteristics which have further evolutionary potential.

The Book of Life is the place where your works are recorded, your thoughts registered and your acts noted.

At the time of the Quantum Instant there will be a judgment of the quick and the dead. That is, there will be an evolutionary selection process based on your qualifications for co-creative power.

Only those who have elected to use their powers well in their lifetime will be resurrected and reincorporated with genetic code and memories intact. Their bodies will be rematerialized. This is a universal law: Only the good evolves—"good" meaning that which is capable of aligning with the whole emerging system, by attuning to its overall design.

A Quantum Transformation is the time of selection of what evolves from what devolves. The species known as self-centered humanity will become extinct. The species known as whole-centered humanity will evolve.

The goal of evolution is the emergence of beings in the image of the Creator. God is creating godlike beings through the evolution of worlds in the universe without end. Amen.

> "And to the angel of the church in Philadelphia write: 'These things saith He that is holy, He that is true, He that hath the key of David, He that openeth and no man shutteth, and shutteth and no man openeth: I know thy works. Behold, I have set before thee an open door, and no man can shut it. For thou hast a little strength, and hast kept My Word, and hast not denied My name.' "
>
> REVELATION 3:7-8

The church in Philadelphia represents those who have preserved the spirit of brotherly love. Thank you, dearly beloved. You have an open door to the world. No one can prevail against the power of pure love. You, in a state of brotherly love, have been empowered by that love to resist all blocks to your work. You have the door to everything. All doors will be opened to those who love each other for my sake rather than for the sake of the comfort of the world.

Some churches have limited themselves to secular compassion, forgetting transcendent compassion. Secular compassion is the desire to make everyone comfortable by fulfilling the deficiency needs of all people for food, shelter, esteem, security and community. This is necessary, but not sufficient, for human nature is not satisfied by comfort alone. Comfort and well-being as an end goal are bound to fail, for the moment they are achieved the comforted again become uncomfortable. Our requirements for creative function and transcendent meaning push against the self-centered consciousness of the comfortable, causing nameless pain.

This pain is me signaling the creature/human child to become a full human, a natural Christ. The pain is me signaling you to grow to fulfill your potential rather than to rest as a dying human, clinging on to life for one brief instant in time.

The church of brotherly love has kept my word and has not denied my name. It has practiced transcendent compassion as well as secular compas-

sion. Transcendent compassion extends love to the person's potential to become a natural Christ, wherein all true comfort lies.

Transcendent compassion heals the wounds of the present by lifting attention to what can be, thereby stimulating the joy of growth, creativity and connecting with others for the sake of a positive goal beyond the capability of anyone to achieve alone.

Only transcendent compassion will comfort the sick, heal the wounded and empower the godly to become heirs of God.

Only through a generation of heirs of God, empowered with co-creative capacities and transcendent love, can the world be saved.

These are my people who are founding the New Order of the Future, who are building upon the church of brotherly love the church of transcending love. This love lifts the congregation from creature/human comfort to fully human life ever-evolving in my universe without end.

Only through co-creators can the pain of the hungry, wounded and sick be finally assuaged. The world has gone too far into need for its requirements to be met solely by secular compassion oriented to fulfilling deficiencies.

For every mouth fed, three more are hungry. For every body saved from a disease, six more are reproduced who are sick. For every house built, the biosphere is yet more overloaded.

More of the same will not suffice, dearly beloved.

The time of the Quantum Transformation is at hand.

I require those who can comprehend the whole hierarchy of human needs, from the need for food to the need to become godly. I require those who can act upon the whole hierarchy at once as I did when feeding the multitudes with bread and fish while filling their minds with the idea of life beyond the animal body.

While we are in the animal body we are bound to care for its requirements—never as an end unto itself but always as a means to gain the capacity to go beyond the limits of the mortal flesh by stimulating the growth of a new body—like mine.

The church of the future is the state of transcendent love which sends forth its emissaries to:

replenish the Earth;
free Earth's people from poverty;
emancipate individual potential;
build new worlds in space;
and generate new godly bodies to inhabit those new worlds,
carrying the seed of life to fulfillment as the flowering
of godlike humans co-creating a New Earth,
and a New Heaven.

> " 'Behold, I will make them of the synagogue of Satan, who say they are Jews and are not, but do lie—behold, I will make them to come and worship at thy feet, and to know that I have loved thee.' "
>
> REVELATION 3: 9

I will make those who have renounced their own potential to become god-like—by maintaining the old law of an eye for an eye rather than the new law of love and forgiveness—come to you, dearly beloved, who love God above all else, your neighbor as yourself and yourself as me.

There shall be a great rejoicing among Jews and Gentiles as we approach the Quantum Transformation. They will not unite by ecumenical conferences or institutional coalitions. They will join as individuals who are attracted to the potential of humanity for universal life as heirs of God.

This is the Jewish vision of the future personified, not as the single savior Jesus, but as a generation of humans determined to trust God's promise enough to go the Whole Way; a generation without the arrogance to set false limits on God's creatures; a generation who will lead us through the tribulations to the New Jerusalem.

> " 'Because thou hast kept My word to be patient, I also will keep thee from the hour of temptation, which shall come upon all the world to try them that dwell upon the earth. Behold, I come quickly; hold that fast which thou hast, that no man take thy crown. He that overcometh will I make a pillar in the temple of My God, and he shall

go out no more; and I will write upon him the name of My God, and the name of the city of my God, which is New Jerusalem, which cometh down out of Heaven from My God, and I will write upon him My new name.' "

REVELATION 3:10-12

Dearly beloved of the church of brotherly love, to you it has been given to be the first generation to overcome the creature/human condition. Love is the way.

When the Quantum Instant triggers the Quantum Transformation the world will be thrown into crisis. Yet you shall not be in crisis. You shall be in love. You will not be tempted to succumb to despair, though all around you other people may be despairing.

Hold fast that which you have; your love of God, neighbor and yourself as Christ. Keep your attention on the next step—the Kingdom of God—and step by step you will lead the children of God out of the valley of the shadow of death to the mountain at Calvary, where the cross will be taken down and the New Jerusalem will be built up.

I will make of you a pillar in the temple of my God. You shall never have to return to the self-centered stage of human existence. You will never again have to undergo the process of birth, forgetting who you are, and struggling as a helpless mammalian infant to know God.

Never again shall you have to return to the human condition. Henceforth you shall evolve consciously, aware at all times that you and God are one forever.

I will write upon you my new name, which is not the Master Jesus who went to the cross but the risen Christ who arose from the dead, ascended into heaven, and sits at the right hand of God.

I died so that you may live as Christ.

Hold fast to that belief so that no man take thy crown. You will not be crowned, you will not be enlightened, you will not be transformed, except that you believe it is so.

Your faith shall make you free—this is your choice.

Freedom is real.

That is the law.

"He that hath an ear, let him hear what the Spirit saith unto the churches!"

REVELATION 3:13

Remember, the church is the congregation of believers in me. It is the field of action of the believers doing as I did, and even more.

Members of the existing churches, hear this: You have preserved the seed through two thousand years of winter. Thank God.

Now the spring has come. The seed you have preserved is growing. Out of the creature/human is springing up the creator/human. The Sons and Daughters of God are aborning by the millions. A generation of Christlike humans is emerging before your eyes.

This is a tremendous triumph for those who have preserved the seed.

Dearly beloved of the existing churches, do not reject the saviors of the world, the natural Christs who are springing up among you, as well as among peoples who, though they have not been institutionalized as Christians, yet hold God consciousness in their attention at all times.

Free them to go naked into the world, unadorned by the armor of institutions, or the labels of the past. Free them to do as I did and even more. Free them to say as I did to the priests of my day: Love God, neighbor and yourself as Christ, and all shall be given to you.

Do not crucify them as you crucified me, O existing churches of the world.

He that hath an ear, let him hear what the Spirit saith unto the churches.

"And unto the angel of the church of the Laodiceans write: 'These things saith the Amen, the faithful and true witness, the beginning of the creation of God: I know thy works, that thou art neither cold nor hot. I would thou wert cold or hot. So then because thou art lukewarm, and neither cold nor hot, I will spew thee out of My mouth.' "

REVELATION 3:14-16

You who are neither cold nor hot are to be pitied, dearly beloved.

The cold have never heard the word of life-everlasting, and are innocent of the choice. Their time has not yet come.

▲

The hot have heard the word and are passionately intent on the consummation of their union with me, their Higher Self, their godlike being.

The lukewarm have heard and have responded half-heartedly. Their condition is deadly, for their hope has irreversibly begun to trigger their mechanisms of transcendence. Their spirit yearns for total union. Their intellects call out for knowledge of God; their bodies desire to become incorruptible heirs of God. And yet they hesitate to commit to the fulfillment of their deepest need. Their misery is nameless, a constant anxiety destroying their joy, making them sick, causing them to hate the life they lead.

The lukewarm have chosen the impossible task of being safe in the birth canal—half born. They have chosen not to live on, even though they know they can. Their character is not strong enough to evolve. I mourn, and yet we must move on.

> " 'Because thou sayest, "I am rich and have increased my goods and have need of nothing," and knowest not that thou art wretched and miserable, and poor and blind and naked, I counsel thee to buy from Me gold refined in the fire, that thou mayest be rich, and white raiment, that thou mayest be clothed and that the shame of thy nakedness may not appear, and anoint thine eyes with eye salve, that thou mayest see. As many as I love, I rebuke and chasten; be zealous therefore, and repent.' "
>
> REVELATION 3:17-19

If you assume that you are comfortable and have no need to grow toward your natural Christhood, you may suffer far more than those who are struggling consciously with the pain of growth.

Whether or not you are aware of your own potential to go beyond the creature/human condition, that potential is growing within, pressing upon your system for recognition. If you do not respond, you become subtly sick, ill with ailments brought on by suppressed growth potential, a primary cause of disease, violence, alienation and abuse.

*I counsel you to respond to the aspiration within you—unsettle your life, if need be. Temper your emotions in the fire of transcendence so that you may use its energy to work with your Higher Self, not against it. **Everything that***

rises converges. *You will fulfill your heart's desire if you aspire for union with God.*

Only those who are willing to work upon their own limits—self-correcting, self-liberating and self-developing—will evolve. I love those who desire to be like me. My rebukes, dearly beloved, are like the words of a teacher to the greatest students on planet Earth. It is for your own good that I make demands on you to grow to full stature. If no such demands are being made on you from your Inner Voice, you will be unprepared when the Quantum Instant comes. You will not know what to do. You will be as children who, not knowing how to swim, are suddenly thrown into the waters.

Purify. Prepare. Learn to forgive your human self and nurture the Higher Self to the point where it becomes totally you. There are then no separate parts to break apart, to disconnect, to be corrupted. If thine eye be single—your attention focused on wholeness—then you will be whole. Practice resolving all inner conflict by asking your body, your emotions, your ego, your creative function, to join together to fulfill the will of your Higher Self, which is at one with the will of God. To fulfill the highest aspect of your being is to fulfill your whole being.

The motive behind desire is not what it seems. You may think you want a person to love you, a particular job, a reward, recognition, fame, wealth, power. If you achieve this desire, you will instantly discover that another desire magnetizes you, and you are struggling again—as Buddha, my brother, taught centuries ago.

There is a desire beneath all surface desire. It is this primary desire that you must uncover and fulfill. When in deepest silence, ask yourself: What is my deepest desire? You will inevitably discover one answer, and one alone.

Your deepest desire is to unite your will with God's will. Your deepest desire is union with God. Your deepest desire is to be like me, who is at one with God. Your deepest desire is to to be a co-creator in the image of God.

No other desire will fulfill your potential. All other desires are symptoms of the fundamental desire for union with God.

" 'Behold, I stand at the door and knock; if any man hear My voice and open the door, I will come in to him, and will sup with him, and he with Me. To him that overcometh, will I grant to sit with Me on My throne, even as I also overcame and am set down with my Father on His throne.' "

REVELATION 3:20-21

In each of you I am. To each of you I call. Within each of you I await your response to my call. I am your inner voice, that still, small voice within that activates you to be what you can be, and which heals you from your wounds of self-criticism and self-denial.

It is you who must open the door. I knock. You open. If you open your door of awareness and invite me into your consciousness, I will eat with you and you with me. I will take communion with you as I did at the last supper with my disciples. For you are now also my disciples.

"He that hath an ear, let him hear what the Spirit saith unto the churches!"

REVELATION 3:22

You who believe in your potential to be me are the self-elected church of the future. Yours is the greatest responsibility, for yours is the greatest awareness. You know the long-range growth potentials that are natural for a planetary species at the time of cosmic birth. You know that the meaning of your new crises is to activate your new capacities. You know that the meaning of your new powers is universal life. You know what has to be done by the self-elect. O believers in your potential to be me, awaken and unite your efforts across the world. I will do the rest.

I knock. You open the door.

After this I looked, and behold, a door was opened in Heaven; and the first voice which I heard was as it were of a trumpet talking with me, which said, "Come up hither, and I will show thee things which must be hereafter."

REVELATION 4:1

How could John know what would happen in the future? How can we know?

How does a child know he will grow up to be an adult capable of reproducing other beings like himself, capable of transcending the limits of infancy to become a person who can travel with the speed of light by image around this Earth and into the universe without end?

Children know these things because they know their parents, their siblings, their friends who are already doing them. John knew what was to come because he was also granted the privilege of seeing beings more matured than he.

You will know your future just as John did, by encountering beings who have evolved beyond the creature/human state, from creature to co-creator.

This does not mean that you will know precisely what will unfold for you, any more than children knowing they can grow up to be parents will know what kind of parents they will be.

You will know your potential future by encountering those who have already fully realized their potential to be heirs of God, co-creators, continuous beings in a universe without end. Dearly beloved, you are now in the position of infants just born, whose eyes are not yet open.

As a planetary species you are newborn. You have just established your electronic planetary nervous system. You have just penetrated your biosphere and are learning to live in outer space. You are just now becoming aware that you can no longer live solely on the terrestrial resources of your Mother Earth, but must co-create your own universal resources. You are in shock, traumatized by birth.

It is obvious—so obvious. The way you will know what is coming next is to encounter those who have already matured in the universal phase of development. They are multitudinous. They love you. They need you. They care for you.

Your task is to wake up! Open your collective eyes and see that you are not alone. Unblock your womb-stopped ears and hear together for the first time the music of the spheres. Coordinate your corporate body and reach for the stars. This reach will connect cells to cells, until you unite enough to share the experience of the Universal Christ, your elder brother, your guide through this brief stage of transition from Earthbound to universal life.

Now you see through a glass darkly. Soon you will see face to face.

Now you are in pain. Then you will be in joy. Now you fear that you cannot manage a complex planetary system. Soon you will know that the planetary system is guided by a cosmic template, just as your body is guided by a biological template coded in your genes, your DNA.

Now you fear that you cannot feed, house and clothe the suffering communities within your planetary body. Then you will know that you live in an abundant universe, in which you can co-create resources by the power of thought.

Now you see that you are polluting your biosphere in the effort to meet the requirements of people for freedom and abundance. Then you shall discover that your planet is your mother, your home base, to be cared for as you grow up to explore and create new worlds. A New Heaven and a New Earth shall you create.

Come up hither, and I will show thee things which must be hereafter. Be willing to lift your imagination enough to see that which you have never seen before. Recognize that you have been gestating in the womb of Earth, building your universal capacities. Now you are born.

Open your minds.

Wipe away your tears.

Prepare to see yourselves in the future—that which you already potentially are right now.

A door in Heaven is opening for those who have eyes to see. The door is the passageway from self-centered to whole-centered consciousness. "Heaven" is you at your next stage, you as a co-creator in the image of God.

What you are now discovering in the Book of Revelation is yourselves revealed. The purpose of this revelation is to encourage you to grow naturally, to relieve you from fear of your power, to give you a vision of your self so beautiful that you will happily turn your attention from the pain of birth to the glory that is being revealed through you who are to become universal beings.

> And immediately I was in the Spirit; and behold, a throne was set in Heaven, and One sat on the throne. And He who sat thereon was to look upon like a jasper and a sardius stone; and there was a rainbow round about the throne, in appearance like unto an emerald.
>
> REVELATION 4:2-3

You are created in the image of God. God is light. You will be a light being. You will be composed of all colors of the rainbow vibrating at a frequency so quickened that you will never die.

Your thought will utterly control the vibrations of the light waves which are your body.

Your mind will be consciously connected with the Mind of God. Your body will be a conscious manifestation of the perfect ideal of a co-creative being, a being at one with the Creator, uniquely qualified to participate in the Creation.

The beings you will first see in what you have called "Heaven"—which is but the next stage of your development, with many more to come—will be those intimately concerned with planet Earth. Remember, there are billions of planetary systems with life like your own, undergoing birth and maturation to co-creatorship.

The God of Creation focuses attention on everything at once through elements of divine consciousness. You will not at first encounter the whole God force. You will encounter aspects that your young mind can comprehend. Patience, dearly beloved, there is more and more to come.

> And round about the throne were four and twenty seats; and upon the seats I saw four and twenty elders sitting, clothed in white raiment, and they had on their heads crowns of gold.
>
> REVELATION 4:4

The elders are more fully-evolved beings who know what you are going through because they have been through it themselves.

Each planetary system has a hierarchy of such evolved beings, who are already co-creative with God, who already know of God's Design, and who are totally in love with you, infantile though you are.

Their raiments are white. They are utterly pure, completely united with God, fully conscious that they are about their Creator's business.

The elders are no longer prey to the illusion of sin, the illusion of separation from God. They have graduated permanently from the period of self-consciousness, just as Homo sapiens graduated once and for all from the period of animal consciousness. They never fall into the dreadful misperception that they are separate egos contending against each other for survival in an ultimately meaningless material universe.

They sympathize with you at this traumatic transitional phase between the womb of Earth and the universal phase of life.

They wear crowns of gold upon their heads. They are consistently enlightened. They are always connected with Spirit. Their Higher Self has totally taken over. They have graduated completely from the creature/human phase.

They are your teachers and guides through the transformation from creature to co-creator. Call upon them as they call upon you. Ask and it shall be given. Knock and doors shall open.

Dearly beloved, we are here for you. Those inner voices you have been hearing are us in all our diversity, guiding you in all your diversity, to grow up and become the Sons and Daughters of God.

The esoteric is becoming clear. The mystery is now being revealed in the fullness of time.

The mystery is your transformation to godlike beings at the next natural phase of your evolution. The mystery is that you are surrounded by godlike beings whom you will recognize soon, because they are like you.

The mystery is the mystery of birth, discovered by a child emerging from the womb.

It is no longer a mystery to the growing child. It is a miracle, as all life is a miracle—that it exists at all.

You will recognize us, your elder brothers and sisters, because we are like you at your best—and more so. All of us are like each other because each of us is created in the image of God and there is only one God, one Design, one cos-

mos, one comprehensive system of infinite diversity, ever-evolving, worlds
without end. Amen.

> **And out of the throne proceeded lightnings and thunder-
> ings and voices. And there were seven lamps of fire burn-
> ing before the throne, which are the seven Spirits of God.**
>
> REVELATION 4:5

How does the Designing Intelligence work? How does the process of
creation operate? How does God do it? How does God organize, maintain
and evolve a universe?

Through intelligent entities. Everything is intelligent. Atoms are exquisite, precise and awesome in their intelligence. Cells are a miracle of intelligence.

A biosphere is intelligent beyond our capacity to calculate. A solar system within a galaxy is intelligent beyond the reaches of our comprehen-
sion.

A human being is intelligent beyond the awareness of the conscious
mind. Who knows how this whole system works and how this system will
overcome the limits of terrestrial life?

God knows.

There is a Law of Increasing Order. According to this Law, when a point
of limit is reached, some entities co-operate to transcend the limit. In so
doing they evolve the next stage of life, which displays greater complexity,
consciousness, freedom and order. In consonance with the Law of
Increasing Order, to keep reproducing ourselves we must eventually transcend ourselves.

In the early seas of life, the cells reached a point where they could not
continue to reproduce themselves. They had reached a limit to growth:
pollution, stagnation, overpopulation. To reproduce themselves they transcended themselves by transforming themselves. They discovered the pattern of multicellular organization. They transcended the limits of single-
celled life.

In the late period of the biosphere, human beings are reaching a point
where they can no longer continue to reproduce themselves as before. We

are reaching a limit to growth on planet Earth. In order to keep reproducing ourselves, we are transcending ourselves. We are discovering the pattern of self-organization, which is based on co-operation. Humans working together to overcome limits establish the pattern from which the co-creative human emerges. We do not emerge in isolation amidst self-centered patterns. We emerge in unison among whole-centered, synergizing patterns of co-operation.

Single mutants provide the trigger to new patterns of self-transcendence: the first cell, the first multicellular creature, the first human, the first co-creative human. These firsts represent the discovery of the next pattern. Only one such discovery is required for the life force to eventually re-organize itself according to the new pattern of increased order.

That is life's intention: to evolve to higher consciousness through increased order.

Jesus Christ was the first to discover the next pattern for human evolution. The same discovery must be made on every planet transitioning from self-conscious to God-conscious life. The pattern must be the same everywhere: co-operation of Christlike beings attracted to universal life in order to know God better.

Once the pattern was demonstrated by Jesus, hundreds of millions of human beings struggled to emulate him, to become like him in order to have access to more life, to more contact with God.

We are at the stage of proto-Christs, just before the flowering of the new pattern: co-creative humans co-operating with other co-creative humans to co-evolve a New Earth and new worlds in space. The self-transcenders are self-electing, volunteering for the new tasks, finding each other, preparing themselves for the Quantum Transformation—the great period of selection when the self-transcenders will transcend and the non-transcenders will descend, devolve and die to this particular planetary experience. Self-centered beings cannot survive in a synergistic world.

At moments of Quantum Transformation, when a system is preparing to "leap" from one order to the new order, God's communication signals are intensified to those who have eyes to see and ears to hear.

We are in such a period now.

These signals are now intensifying to those electing to hear the inner voice for God.

"Out of the throne proceeded lightnings and thunderings and voices." God's communication system is light and sound. God flashes messages through light waves and sound waves that carry coherent information, which can be received and understood by properly attuned beings—by those who have chosen to listen and to follow the signals they receive in perfect faith that they are real.

Your mind-body system is a magnificent receiving/conceiving set. As your intention focuses on the aspiration to be godly, your receiving/conceiving set turns on. The signals begin to flow in. To the degree that you follow the signals, you will be guided to purify your system from the static of ego—and to join with others doing the same—until you discover a group of individuals, each capable of receiving/conceiving the same information. Such a synergistic group is the signal for empowerment. Whenever two or three are gathered in my name, there is my church.

The church which shall be taken up first are those uniting to carry out the next step of evolution in themselves and in the world.

The elders are evolved beings now in communication with the self-transcenders who are personifying God's will.

The seven lamps of fire burning before the throne are the seven qualities required to transform you from creature to co-creator. They are the seven Spirits of God, the elements of God's communication system—the Holy Spirit—which are now at work communicating with those who have eyes to see and ears to hear. You will learn what they are as you proceed.

The Holy Spirit intensifies its actions at times of quantum transformation, pinpointing its messages precisely to those who are moving toward higher inner order amid increasing external disorder.

The elders, the lamps of fire, the seven Spirits of God, are a glimpse caught by the creature/human, John, of God's communication system.

He saw because he desired to see. He saw in images his mind could formulate.

▲

You will see the communication system of God in other images because you, dearly beloved, live two thousand years later. Your intellects have been developed by science, which discovers more of God's processes of creation. Your powers of conception have increased. You will see differently, in new images and in new words, but the actual events that you will see are the same as what John divined.

> **[And] before the throne there was a sea of glass, like unto crystal. And in the midst of the throne and round about the throne, were four living beings full of eyes in front and behind.**
>
> REVELATION 4:6

Crystal is a metaphor for humankind organized in perfect coherence at the next stage of evolution. A crystal is a substance in which the molecules are aligned in a definite self-repeating pattern so that its external shape is symmetrical. New crystallizations occur when a thoroughly saturated solution, a solution at the absolute limit of its current form, suddenly orders itself according to a pattern not previously revealed.

John is now seeing into the future. A time will come when the elect from all nations will be gathered together and consciously coordinated so that perfect alignment of aspiration occurs. This alignment of the elect creates a magnetic field conducive to attunement with the will of God, which emanates from the "throne"—the Seat of the God-force that exists at the core of all being.

Without an animating core, electrons would cease orbiting nuclei in atoms; atoms would cease connecting to make molecules; molecules would cease interacting to make cells; cells would cease cooperating to make organisms; humans would cease striving to be unified with God and each other.

Without an animating core, the universe would fly apart. Instantly all coherence, order, and pattern would be gone. If the Mind of God turned off for an instant, the universe would disappear.

The "sea of glass like unto crystal" is the unified field of those who are hearing the same voice, aligning with the same Design, all oriented in the same direction. This unity of the elect is the key to the transformation from Adam to Christ, from *Homo sapiens* to *Homo universalis,* from creature to co-creator, from self-centered to whole-centered being.

Dearly beloved, you who have an ear to hear what the Spirit saith unto the churches, prepare for the union of the elect in one crystalline field of consciousness, attracted by love of God within and God beyond, attracted to become Universal Humans, the first fruits of terrestrial evolution.

Prepare by purifying yourself of all obstacles to your ability to receive the signals. Prepare by uniting with others who are also receiving the word of God as to how to evolve.

The four living beings "full of eyes before and behind" are examples of the strength which is revealed in those who, seeing that which has been and that which is to come, are wholly alert to the will of God.

Think of yourself as a co-creator whose will is totally aligned with the Designing Intelligence of the universe. This is the power you are to inherit, dearly beloved.

> **And each of the four living beings had six wings about him, and they were full of eyes within; and they rested not day and night, saying, "Holy, holy, holy, Lord God Almighty, who was, and is, and is to come!"**
>
> *REVELATION 4:8*

The living beings represent our animal strength infused with eyes of awareness lifting us to transcend the creature/human condition. They represent our innate ability to use the force of our animal aspiration for godly purposes by fusing the creature drive to the deeper aspiration to become a co-creative human.

Underlying the animal desire for self-preservation and self-reproduction is the deeper drive for self-transcendence and union with the source of life.

Animal desire does not conflict with fundamental human creative desire. Underneath the animal desire for self-preservation and continuity is the knowledge, genetically encoded in egg and sperm, that life is immortal. There is an imperishable code in the fertilized seed—incorruptible genes—which are transmitted from generation to generation, from body to body, preparing for the fulfillment of procreation: the evolution of co-creative organisms that do not die, but which are self-regenerating, self-replicating, self-conceiving.

The memory of immortality is in every cell in your body. It dates back to the first self-replicating cell that divided to reproduce and did not die.

Scheduled death came in with living beings—the multicellular animal phase, from which sprang the long chain of species, evolving ever and ever more complex organisms and expanded awareness, until at last the living being self-transcended. Accordingly, a creature/human arose with a mammalian body and a mind that remembered immortality, remembered that dormant in the genetic code of each reproducing body is the information of how to self-reproduce as did our earliest sentient ancestors, the single cells, in the ancient seas of the early Earth.

The memory of immortality was activated in the creature/human and will be acted upon by the co-creative, Christlike human in the fullness of time.

We are the living beings with eyes within. We are the creature/humans awakening to our inherited capacity to transcend our condition by activating our capacity to build new bodies that are conscious of God at all times, to rise beyond our animal origins by reactivating our cellular capacity to regenerate and self-evolve.

O dearly beloved, such wonders await those of you who open your inner eyes. I pray that all of you who have the slightest glimpse of your dormant powers will say unceasingly, "Holy, Holy, Holy potential within me—be fulfilled."

> And I saw in the right hand of Him who sat on the throne, a book written within and on the back, sealed with seven seals. And I saw a strong angel proclaiming with a loud voice, "Who is worthy to open the book and to loose the seals thereof?" And no man in Heaven, nor on earth, neither under the earth, was able to open the book or to look thereon.
>
> REVELATION 5:1-3

Everything that ever was, is now, and potentially can be, is recorded in the Mind of God. Everything is energy, recorded as a frequency in a universal information system available to those who learn the language.

A chimpanzee cannot really learn human language. It does not have the vocal chords nor the brain required. The creature/human cannot really learn the universal information system. We do not have a continually awakened inner eye nor an integrated mind-body that can attune to the appropriate frequencies. We flash on and off, tune in and out, flicker into and out of universal consciousness.

Only a Universal Human, a human at the next stage of evolution can learn the language of the universal information system. Only a co-creative human has a sufficiently awakened suprasensory channel of cognition with which to perceive the information impinging on all of us all the time.

We know through science—our optically and electronically extended sensory system—that information of various kinds is constantly transmitted and received through extra-human sensors—radio and television, X-rays, gamma rays, cosmic rays, and other invisible forms of energy. Only as we develop such extra-human sensors do we pick up this information.

So shall it be in the future. Co-creative humans will develop suprasensory receptive organs to pick up information which is available even now, just as the language of the world is available to chimpanzees who cannot use it because they are at a different stage of evolution of consciousness.

> **And I wept much, because no man was found worthy to open and to read the book, neither to look thereon. And one of the elders said unto me, "Weep not! Behold, the Lion of the tribe of Judah, the Root of David, hath prevailed to open the book and to loose the seven seals thereof."**
>
> *Revelation 5:4-5*

Jesus Christ developed a mind-body system capable of knowing the universal language of evolution.

One person was all that was needed to decipher the Book of Life and begin the decoding process that shall, in the fullness of time, be the God-given capacity of all humans who choose to go on to the next stage of evolution.

Jesus Christ was an evolutionary mutation, a new template, an individual quantum transformation that was as great a step from the creature/human condition, as was the first *Homo sapiens* from earlier hominids.

Now we see the same pattern unfolding before our eyes. Jesus Christ sprung out of the genetic pattern of *Homo sapiens* with an enhanced capability to attune to God and to transform the physical body.

This mutation is replete with evolutionary options. It is a template that has attracted intelligence of the highest degree, and which will prove to have great survival advantage. It is the template that will prevail.

The evolutionary selection process will favor our Christlike capacities: healing, regenerating, attuning to God above all else, loving everyone as one's self.

Jesus Christ, a future human, was capable of learning the language of God. He was able to teach in parables and imprint the memory of his words upon the minds of disciples who wrote them down in an extremely limited form. The desire to transform was thereby awakened in those humans with an innate tendency to evolve Christ-capacities, those proto-mutants on planet Earth to whom the promise has been made.

In the fullness of time we will be able, by a process still unknown to us, to manifest the same capabilites as Jesus did to decipher the pattern of evolution.

Our power will eventually be immeasurably greater. Jesus was alone, as a single co-creative human. In the future, after the selection has been made, everyone who survives will also be a co-creator. The New Jerusalem is a community of co-creative humans, a collective of natural Christs.

The power of this congregation, aligned with the design of creation, is a quantum leap too great for us to imagine at this time.

When Daniel asked, "How long shall it be to the end of these wonders?" the answer was, "It shall be for a time, times, and a half; and when he shall have accomplished to scatter the power of the holy people, all these things shall be finished" (Daniel 12:6-7).

This means that when the holy people, the attracted people, shall be scattered everywhere on Earth, the next phase of evolution shall begin.

The "elect" are not limited to one people or one part of the world. They are everywhere on Earth. Therefore, it is necessary that people from every nation, race and culture have the free choice to evolve when the selection process begins.

Proto-mutants like you, dearly beloved, are scattered across the face of the thinking globe, ready at any instant to go the Whole Way to become godlike beings in the image of God, joint heirs with Christ.

The Quantum Transformation will come when enough of you are ready. It is a delicate matter of timing. If the transformation begins too late, the disorder will be so great as to engulf even the self-elect in the catastrophe.

The more quickly you can get the word to all the nations—to the ears of the attracted members of the social body—that they are about to be united by the same call, the better it will be.

Timing is of the essence. Your task, dearly beloved, is to spread the word and provide a channel for those who wish to act.

However, human acts of initiative are insufficient unto themselves. Your acts are essential but incomplete. You cannot induce a quantum transformation by human intelligence alone. You can intuit it by consciousness at its highest. You can prepare for it by human will at its highest. You can connect among each other in preparation for the signal as to what our actions should be. More you cannot do. More would be destructive.

> **And lo, I beheld in the midst of the throne and the four living beings, and in the midst of the elders, a Lamb standing as it had been slain, having seven horns and seven eyes, which are the seven Spirits of God, sent forth into all the earth. And He came and took the book out of the right hand of Him who sat upon the throne.**
>
> *REVELATION 5:6-7*

Out of the Mind of God, up from the creature/human world, in the midst of the evolved beings concerned with planet Earth, arose a Lamb, a personification of God that was apparently destroyed by the limited thinking of the past, yet who overcame the crucifixion to live on as an evolutionary model of the optimum capacity of *Homo sapiens* to self-transcend. He manifested the peaks of human capacity of mind, body and spirit, demonstrating that at our very best we transcend our past condition. He showed us that by totally fulfilling every aspect of our human potential, we are enabled to go beyond our animal bodies and self-centered consciousness.

He demonstrated how transformation works. We know an airplane is so designed that once it achieves a certain speed on the runway, it lifts into the air, defying common sense as tons of steel rise into the thin air. How? By obeying the invisible laws of aerodynamics, which govern the flow of invisible air.

Jesus represented an analogous, extraordinary moment of lift from Earthbound to airborne.

We had to see one airplane fly only one time to know that it was possible, and eventually we filled the air with flying objects obeying the law.

Likewise, we only require one person to lift beyond involuntary death to know it is possible, and eventually we will fill the future with people who can lift from corruptible to incorruptible bodies, doing as Jesus did, and even more.

To **do** as he did we must **be** as he is. The seven horns and seven eyes which are the seven spirits of God, must be ours as well as his, if we are to be like him.

The seven spirits of God that Jesus manifested are inherent in us—just as the airplane is inherently capable of lifting off the Earth at a certain speed because it is intentionally designed to fly. We are designed to transcend animal limits. Self-conscious mortality is a phase of preparation for whole-centered immortality.

What are the seven spirits of God that gave Jesus access to the suprahuman powers of the creative force? What does a human being have to manifest to become a Son or Daughter of God, personifying God wholly?

First is LOVE. We reject fear, anger, hostility, guilt. We nurture the potential godlike human within us as we would our beloved child—a savior like the Christ-child born in the manger with the beasts. Each of us has a Christ-child within, born out of the manger of our animal bodies, sur-rounded by our animal desires. This Christ-child within is excluded from the reality of the present mundane world. There is currently no room at the inn for the Christ-child within us.

This inner being is not invited to sit at the tables of power in the world today where self-centered consciousness plays out its final moments of awful supremacy, bringing on the end of this phase of evolution.

We are Mary and Joseph to the Christ-child within ourselves, and with-in every person on Earth, regardless of race, creed or color.

We love that tender inner being as a savior of the world, protect it from negative thoughts, put it in a cocoon of tranquility, just as a mother pro-tects the child at her breast during a storm, shielding her from stress so that she may grow unharmed by the momentary tribulations.

In each person on Earth there is an inner being in a chrysalis, ready to be born. Turn to it for guidance. Let it speak to you. It is growing rapidly now. The signal for its birth *en masse* is the gathering of the attracted peo-ple by the sound of the voice of God—the "trumpet" that shall surely sound. Then we shall surely be changed, in the twinkling of an eye.

At that Quantum Instant, Christ-consciousness will emerge at once in many who are prepared, transcending self-consciousness just as self-con-sciousness transcended animal consciousness, and animal consciousness transcended single-cellular consciousness.

This event is a real experience, which shall come soon to those who are now, at this moment, loving their innate potential to be godlike above their visible limits as self-centered *Homo sapiens* fighting for life on the way to the grave.

This inner choice to acknowledge, nurture and love our own and each other's capacity to be godlike is the first essential spirit of God that we must manifest.

The second spirit of God is WISDOM. As we are loving our potential to be godlike, we become wise in all things. Wisdom is vision-in-action. To be wise now, we see beyond the material world. We take the evolutionary per-spective and see the world in process of transformation according to the Pattern of Creation. We discern the pattern of breakthroughs based on the

reality of our potentials in all fields, from personal to social to technological.

To be wise now, we identify and communicate to ourself and others the
potentials to build the New Jerusalem. These potentials are growing in our
midst right now. They are our evolutionary technologies and capacities to
become natural Christs. We have the wisdom to acknowledge and nurture
our own capacities to become godlike, that is to:

Attune to God through inner listening,
Resonate, through attunement with the cosmic Design, the blueprint
    in our DNA
    and in the very structure of the universe,
Love our neighbor as our Potential Self,
Extend intelligence through synergistic
    cooperation with others,
Employ the extended mind capacity
    embodied in our intelligent machines,
Extend our life and transform our body,
Live and work beyond the planet,
Seek other life in the universe.

The wisdom to do all this naturally is the second spirit of God.

The third spirit of God is FAITH. In the midst of the material world, we
constantly have faith in the reality of things unseen, as Paul said ages ago.
We reject the evidence of the senses, which perceive reality in snapshots.
Rather, we see reality as a continuous act of creation.

We have faith that we are conscious participants in the creation,
designed by God to take a vital role in co-evolving a future in which all
who so choose shall become godlike, universal beings, joint-heirs with
Christ, members of a universal community.

We have faith at all times that the sufferings of the present cannot compare to the glory which shall be revealed in us, to wit: the redemption of
our bodies. We have faith in the approaching selection process whereby the
"judgment" will be made as to which of our characteristics are suitable for
the next phase of evolution. We have faith that we are to be selected for life

ever-evolving because we have committed our life to following the necessary commandments to qualify.

We have faith that there is a Design, that there are higher beings, that we can become higher beings, and that all this is happening now for those who have eyes to see and ears to hear.

The fourth spirit of God is COURAGE. Love, Wisdom and Faith lay the foundations for courage. Courage means heart-motivated action.

When we set out upon the path toward godliness, we encounter obstacles. We take heart. We have heart. We are courageous in the face of these obstacles. They can be used to strengthen our capacity to inherit the Kingdom of God. When we sense fear, we stop and remind ourselves that we are actors in the Creation, beloved by the Creator, imbued with the strength to overcome all obstacles, including mortality and ego. We are not alone. We are beloved. We can call upon God to aid us in the struggle. We are not struggling for ourselves alone; we are carving out pathways of consciousness as Jesus did before us.

We are vital to the universe. The universe will respond to our request when we have faith that it will. Courage without faith is foolhardy risk-taking—especially as we approach the Quantum Instant when we shall all be changed.

The fifth spirit of God is PATIENCE. Think of how patient God is! Think of how patient Jesus is! Think how patient the elders are! Then think of how impatient we are, and change. Relax into the design.

Timing is in the hands of God, who tends the transformation like a good gardener. God cannot reap the harvest until the seeds have ripened. God cannot trigger the transformation in its final irreversible phase until the word has been heard by all nations, until "the power of the holy people" has been scattered throughout the world, until the choice of extinction or evolution is made clear to all.

Planet Earth is in its final phase of terrestrial-animal life. It is about to burst forth with seeds of new life, impregnating the universe with empowered humans, and restoring its Earthly body with loving humans, stewarding the whole system with tender care.

It is already undergoing the transition, which includes the selection of the God-centered from the self-centered. Time is of the essence here.

All is well. We must all do our parts with love, wisdom, faith, courage and patience, trusting in the larger system that created us and is still creating us now.

The sixth spirit of God is POWER. The time has come for right to make might. Love is to be embodied in power for the good in the coming phase of evolution. We learn to be powerful with love. It is the only power that can prevail. When confronted with worldly power of the past, as in the giant bureaucracies, the nation-states, the totalitarian regimes, what can we do to prevail? We can transform the situation by presenting in total clarity, with absolute fearlessness, our vision of hope in the potential of each person to be empowered by God to inherit the Kingdom.

We are to gain power by empowering. We are to use power by demonstrating the reality of our potential to be like Christ, to be the Sons or Daughters of God.

This demonstration is irresistible. No power on Earth can withstand it. When we are godly we will have the power of God. God's will **shall** be done on Earth as it is in heaven. When we join our will with God's in absolute faith in its reality, all will be given to us, even unto the ends of the universe.

The seventh spirit of God is SURRENDER. "Not my will, but thine, be done" is our incessant prayer. The humility of the infinitesimal co-creator who is inheriting the powers of creation is essential now. We are still too young and uncertain to trust ourselves completely. We are like student pilots on our first solo flight.

The thought that we can do it alone as a novice at the altitudes toward which we are rising, is deadly. Pride can kill us as we transform. We are now most vulnerable to *hubris* because we feel the godlike power flooding into us. We are constantly grateful for it. We recognize that we can love ourselves as godly beings because we have been created by God. In loving ourselves we are loving God. We let that memory of gratitude for our existence shine through, turning pride to praise, turning *hubris* to loving humility that we have been created in the image of God and that godlike shall we be.

Jesus personified these seven spirits of God. He combined them all in one person. Therefore he was permitted to take "the book out of the right hand of him that sat upon the throne."

Jesus had access to the Mind of God—the universal information system, the program of evolutionary selection and creation.

> **And when He had taken the book, the four living beings and the four and twenty elders fell down before the Lamb, having every one of them harps and golden vials full of incense, which are the prayers of saints. And they sang a new song, saying, "Thou art worthy to take the Book and to open the seals thereof; for Thou wast slain, and hast redeemed us to God by Thy blood, from every kindred and tongue, and people and nation, and hast made us unto our God kings and priests; and we shall reign on the earth."**
>
> *REVELATION 5:8-10*

When Jesus accepted his full empowerment as an agent of evolution for planet Earth, the living beings and the elders were overjoyed. They were redeemed, not rejected, by Jesus' empowerment.

The living beings represent the animal nature of humans. The evolution of humans to godlike power does not deny our animal nature, it fulfills it. The deepest intention of animal life is to reproduce itself forever. The fulfillment of this intention, however, is not reproduction *ad infinitum* in a planetary womb. It is production of a mutation that is a continuous human, with life everlasting and ever-evolving.

The co-creative human is the fulfillment of the creature/human and of the animal drive for survival. That is why the living beings fell down with joy and "sang a new song" of fulfillment that their purpose had been served. The living beings will not be destroyed by co-creative humans. They will be fulfilled by them, and protected as we enter the phase of the restoration of the Earth and the protection of all species.

The elders represent other highly evolved humans who have lived on planet Earth and transcended the mammalian condition, almost completely, but not quite.

All the saints and seers taught the same lessons as Jesus—to love God above all else and your neighbor as your self.

Jesus added one essential awareness: that the individual has a personal future in a transformed body to continue the work of the Creator, evolving the Creation, until all creatures are in the image of God.

Jesus fulfills the lives and works of other saints and seers of the human race by carrying godliness to its natural next step: the empowerment of the individual to be like God. He died and then rebuilt his body, and ascended to the next plane, leaving no corpse to disintegrate and return, recycled, to live again. He broke the wheel of birth, death and rebirth *ad infinitum.* Those who follow his path need never be reborn in a creature-human body. Nor need they linger, souls-in-waiting, like the elders. They can act on behalf of the Creator, forever. They can get on with the task of creation. Thank God that at last the next phase has begun.

"Thou hast made us unto our God kings and priests, and we shall reign on the earth," say the elders, acknowledging Jesus' selection as the one to lead the way to the next stage of evolution.

Jesus' empowerment in turn empowers all the evolved beings. For they, too, desire the transformation of the human race. Their task can be activated to help now during the tribulations and the selection. They can act as guides in the night to the children of God, now that the birth process has been initiated through the signal of Jesus that we are capable of life ever-evolving beyond this Earthwomb. The elders-in-waiting are joyous that the next step is about to begin. This step represents their renewed involvement in ongoing life, relieved from the inactive status of retirement, which they have patiently endured while awaiting the fullness of time.

> And I beheld, and I heard the voice of many angels round about the throne and the living beings and the elders; and the number of them was ten thousand times ten thousand, and thousands of thousands, saying with a loud voice, "Worthy is the Lamb that was slain, to receive power and riches and wisdom and strength, and honor and glory and blessing!" And I heard every creature which is in heaven and on the earth, and under the earth

and such as are in the sea, and all that are in them, saying, "Blessing, honor, glory, and power be unto Him who sitteth upon the throne, and unto the Lamb for ever and ever!"

REVELATION 5:11-13

Imagine the universe with its billions of galaxies and billions upon billions of solar systems with planets circling their suns.

What do you suppose is happening there?

There are billions of planets in this universe that engender life, a biosphere, and an intelligent species that discovers God from within through intuition and God from without through science.

Every living planet arrives at the stage wherein it recognizes its finiteness, and begins the work of conscious evolution, caring for the mother planet and extending its capacities into the universe beyond the gestating planetary womb.

This stage is occurring throughout the universe now. Imagine how many babies are being born this instant on planet Earth, multiply that by billions, and you will have a sense of how many planetary systems are shifting from their terrestrial to their universal phase, right now.

We have not yet encountered others like ourselves because we have been asleep in the womb of Mother Earth, gaining our capacities to be born as a cosmic species.

The period of our birth began with the birth of Jesus Christ. He was the first human cell to manifest the capacities of "postnatal" humanity—what our species will be like after the transition from self-centered Earthwomb-life, to whole-centered universal life.

He initiated the demonstration of life ever-evolving in a universe without end. He began the "labor" to transcend the creature/human condition.

His acts triggered the appropriate expectation and activated the dormant human potential to focus on the development of capacities for achieving life beyond the terrestrial womb. These capacities are love of life, and its twin offspring, science and democracy.

The labor began two thousand years ago.

The birth pangs reached critical intensity with the explosion of the first atomic bomb in 1945. This was the signal that humanity could destroy its womb or co-create new worlds on Earth and in space. An irreversible birth process began. We could never return to the prenatal period. The Cosmic Child, humanity, had discovered the invisible technologies of creation and destruction. We could not unlearn it. We had to go forward with our birth to become a godlike species, or destroy ourselves in the process of birth.

We entered the "birth canal." The meta-crises of limits began: resource shortage, overpopulation, pollution, alienation, confusion, malaise about the future, disconnection with the past. Experts with an Earthbound perspective advocated a return to the simpler past, an adaptation to limits, a program of maximum conservation, and no growth. At the same time, some futurists wrote of a paradigm shift from self-centeredness to whole-centeredness. And some evolutionaries proclaimed the extended gospel of the "postnatal" technologies, to be developed within the womb of Earth for use after birth in the universal environment beyond the biosphere, such as astronautics, genetics, longevity, cybernetics, robotics and nanotechnology.

In 1957 we first penetrated the surrounding universe: *Sputnik* went up and signaled to the people of Earth that life was no longer bound to the terrestrial world. The sciences of genetics and cybernetics accelerated. We learned to communicate with genes to build new bodies through recombinant DNA. We learned to extend our bodies into intelligent machines. We landed on a new world.

People reacted with joy. We were "born into the universe." We saw ourselves as one body struggling to coordinate by reaching beyond ourselves for new life.

The pain of birth intensified. Attention was withdrawn from attraction to our imminent life as a universal species, to preoccupation with the complexity of surviving and managing as a planetary system in which billions of members are undernourished.

The tribulations of birth increased. The Cosmic Child—humanity—panicked with pain. Some cells within the body of humankind refused to co-operate with the planetary organism as a whole. They remained self-centered. Other cells desired to participate in the vast range of postnatal tasks: they began to evolve. They began to renew the body of Earth from the trauma of birth; to attempt the distribution of goods and services to everyone throughout the planetary system; to educate everyone to the good news that they are born with the options of life ever-evolving; and to build the postnatal capacities to change from the terrestrial to the universal phase of development. These include living in space, extending our life-span, cybernating the tasks of production and maintenance, freeing the unique creativity for specific functions of each member of the body, and contacting other life which also has survived its birth from other planetary wombs.

John was one of the first humans to catch a glimpse of postnatal, post-terrestrial, post-self-centered life. He saw us in the future. He caught a pre-cognitive glimpse of universal life beyond the Earthwomb-stage of human existence.

The first glimpse was of "the Lamb," the risen Jesus Christ, in a glorified body, surrounded by thousands and thousands of angels, other beings in this universe who could not be seen until we matured enough to experience the extraterrestrial, postnatal phase of human existence. Just as a baby in the womb cannot perceive other life, a species gestating in the womb of its Earth cannot perceive other life already born throughout the universe.

We are surrounded with life now, as a newborn child is surrounded. We have barely opened our eyes. We barely remember we are born. We can hardly believe the good news, foretold in the New Testament, that we were to have life everlasting in partnership with God in a universe of many mansions.

John saw all creatures blessing "Him who sitteth upon the throne, and the Lamb." All life—the minerals, the vegetables, the animals, as well as humans—is fulfilled through empowerment of the Lamb at the right hand of God.

For the destiny of all kingdoms of life on Earth is to develop the capacity to seed Earth-life into the universe, with new worlds that carry information concerning all the acts of Earth: its atomic acts, its molecular acts, its cellular acts, its animal and plant acts, its human acts, its cultural history; and also to restore Mother Earth after she has given birth to universal life.

All Earth-being comes to fruition in the post-terrestrial life of Universal Humanity, just as every act of the nine-month embryo, from the fusion of sperm and egg to the passage down the birth canal, comes to fruition in the first breath taken by the newborn child.

The scene John saw was the celebration of the birth of humanity now occurring in the universe beyond the doors of our five Earthwomb senses.

It is happening around us, right now. Occasionally some of us flicker into cosmic consciousness and see that we are immortal, that we are beloved by God, that we are like Christ, that we are universal, that we are surrounded by higher beings celebrating the joy of our birth.

At the Quantum Instant, when the "trumpet" shall sound, awakening us from our Earthwomb slumber, hundreds of millions of human cells in the planetary body will open their inner eyes at once, in unison, and see together what John saw alone.

Seeing together after the birth, as we will do, will be different than seeing alone before the birth, as John did. Seeing alone, he was struck with awe until almost dead, and he arose to describe in prescientific, preuniversal images, a sight totally beyond human Earthwomb experience.

We who are in the generation experiencing the actual birth of Universal Humanity, will see clearly, face to face, what John saw symbolically and intuitively.

Single individuals have made the intuitive leaps from Earthwomb life to see the future of ourselves as a universal species. They have been called "prophets," and have usually been reviled by the "prenatal" cells working to build a body for a birth of which they know nothing. The prenatal cells do not like to be distracted by too much information of the glories to come. It prevents them from concentrating on the vital work at hand.

However, it is the prophets' vision of the future, especially as foreseen in the Book of Revelation, that has guided modern civilization beyond the total acceptance of Earthwomb life as the be-all and end-all of human existence. The earlier prophets in the East foretold a future beyond the body—a blending of the individual droplet of consciousness into the sea of the whole. The later Hebraic prophets in the Mideast foretold a future in a new body, an evolution of the individual toward partnership with God for the sake of the world.

Early scientists began to create the means whereby an individual could actually realize a future beyond the limits of this Earth and the animal body.

And now, the combined efforts of the "holy people of power," the prophets of the people of Earth who are attracted to a personal future as Universal Humans, are actually **doing** it and will soon share in the rapture of the revelation of the reality of what John saw, ages ago.

Ages ago, in Earth time, is a cosmic blink of the eye. The mystery is about to be revealed. What we will see is already happening. It is we who are opening our universal eyes. Other life has been surrounding us for thousands of years.

Individual humans have caught eccentric flashes of information about this life: voices, unidentified flying objects, visions, automatic writings from the "other side." Soon all these vital flashes will be forgotten in the glory of that which is to be revealed to those with eyes to see and ears to hear.

> **And I saw when the Lamb opened one of the seals; and I heard, as it were, the noise of thunder, one of the four living beings saying, "Come and see!" And I saw, and behold, a white horse, and he who sat upon him had a bow; and a crown was given unto him, and he went forth as a conqueror to conquer.**
>
> *REVELATION 6:1-2*

The seven seals on the "book" which was "held in the right hand of Him that sat on the throne" (Rev. 5:1) are barriers that must be removed before the new life is free of the past. They are blocks to the birth, which must be overcome before this book can be opened, read, understood and followed by the evolving members of humankind. The book sealed with the seven seals is the guide to the New Jerusalem. It is the code for the next stage of evolution, the design for a universal species' first acts **after** the birth into the universe.

The breaking of the first seal revealed a white horse with a rider that went conquering the lower aspect of human nature, that which must pass away if we are to evolve.

The breaking of the second seal revealed a red horse ridden by one with the power to take peace from the Earth. It stands for the necessity of the evolutionary selection process which shall dissolve the old order.

The breaking of the third seal reveals the black horse whose rider carries a pair of balances measuring wheat and barley, preserving oil and wine.

Wheat and barley stand for the necessities of survival, the food we require to meet our immediate needs. The oil and wine stand for the energy that produces what we require to survive. Oil is the fuel that powers the engines of society. Wine is a fluid that releases the mind from its limited focus on the immediate.

In the end times, during the tribulations, the immediate necessities will be scarce, causing famine, hunger and death. The **source** of the food, that is, the fundamental energy and the liberated mind, will not be scarce. They will be preserved. They are the producers of the goods needed to survive.

Modern civilization was founded on ideas that affirm the capacity of the individual, the oneness of God, and the future of humanity as a godlike species. This set of ideas is inherent in the nature of evolution. It has fostered individuality and intellect, creating science and democracy, which have produced in abundance.

Now, through the effects of technology and industrialization, and the emancipation of human potential everywhere on Earth, the limits to growth are felt. Famine destroys millions of people. The "barley" and "wheat" are scarce, while the oil and wine, representing the capacity to produce rather than the products produced, will not be hurt.

This means that trying to survive the old way, by old means of production will not work. There is no way that the deficiency needs of two-thirds of humanity can be met by past means. We cannot survive by the labor of the past, working by hand in the traditional way; there are too many mouths to be fed. Nor can we survive by the labor of the present, industrializing as the modernized nations did, since the nonrenewable resources upon which the industrial revolution was founded are rapidly depleting. The biosphere is overtaxed with pollutants. The period of the agricultural revolution is over. The period of the industrial revolution is over. The period of the co-creative revolution has begun.

The black horse will measure out the barley and the wheat while leaving the oil and the wine for those who have eyes to see how God creates, and who do as Jesus did, creating with him for the good of all.

The co-creative revolution is based on knowing how the processes of creation work, and working consciously with them to produce in abundance, like Jesus did—out of five loaves and two fish enough to feed everyone.

We take the "oil and the wine"—the energy to produce and the expanded idea of productivity—and consciously create the goods and services required by humanity. This means we recognize that henceforth we live in an infinite environment, a universal environment, an Earth/space environment. We have available to us sunlight, lunar materials, asteroids. We have geothermal energy, wind energy, water energy; we have fusion; we have solar powered satellites; we have nonterrestrial materials-processing capability, and so on and so on, *ad infinitum*. As awakening sons and daughters of God, we are co-creators with the energy that creates the universe. We are new alchemists, conscious evolvers, natural technologists transforming sunlight to food—as the chlorophyll molecule did beginning hundreds of millions of years ago.

It is ideas that produce wealth. It is the idea of reality as a God-inspired process evolving to ever higher order, consciousness, freedom and abundance that will produce the wealth of the future.

There will be no scarcity in the New Jerusalem, dearly beloved. Those of you who are new alchemists, those of you who are studying how things grow, how ecology works, how photosynthesis operates, how solar energy can be focused, how the moon can be made fruitful as a stepping-stone of access to a universe of life, thanks be to you from God. Upon you the next world depends.

The "birth" of a planetary system is a very complex operaton, as is the birth of a biological system. The new capacities must be sufficiently developed to permit survival beyond the womb of Earth, just as a baby must have its breathing apparatus, its nursing capability and its elimination system ready for immediate action after the birth. If these systems are not ready prior to birth, the organism will die.

Humanity is now building its capacities for survival after the planetary birth process is complete. This means we have to be capable of surviving on Earth as a conscious act of planetary coordination, distribution, conservation and production of renewable, recyclable resources. We have to make the shift from dependency on fossil fuels, non-renewable resources and polluting industries, else we shall surely die.

We also must be capable of surviving off the Earth, as conscious builders of new worlds in space. The human race at the stage of co-creativity cannot survive in a closed biosphere. Its capacity to create is too great for survival in a closed system. Our abilities to extend and create life are too great for the womb of Earth.

A co-creative species must be building beyond the planet as well as restoring the planet.

Our new capacities in astronautics, genetics, cybernetics, robotics, noetics and nanotechnology are the natural capabilities of a universal species. We have been learning how to survive in the universe, simulating within the womb of Earth.

▲

When you awaken to the glory of your role as a universal species, you will know why you have gained powers too great for Earth to contain. You have gained them because you are designed to be Universal Humans.

Do you suppose that a being created in the image of God is ultimately meant to suffer involuntary death by degeneration of an animal body?

Do you suppose that a being created in the image of God is ultimately meant to remain in a state of scarcity, scratching survival foods from the nuts and fruits and flesh of Mother Earth?

Do you suppose that a being created in the image of God is ultimately meant to remain in a state of self-consciousness, shut off from universal awareness?

No! Of course not! You were born to be free. You were born to be me. You were born to be partners with God. And so shall you be, dearly beloved, in the fullness of time, all of you. The quick and the dead shall be restored in incorruptible bodies, connected consciously to God, at the beginning of the universal phase of evolution. Have patience, the time is close at hand.

> And after these things I saw four angels standing on the four corners of the earth, holding the four winds of the earth, that the wind should not blow on the earth, nor on the sea, nor on any tree. And I saw another angel ascending from the east, having the seal of the living God; and he cried with a loud voice to the four angels to whom it was given to hurt the earth and the sea, saying, "Hurt not the earth, neither the sea nor the trees, until we have put a seal on the foreheads of the servants of our God." And I heard the number of those who were sealed. There were sealed a hundred and forty-four thousand of all the tribes of the Children of Israel.
>
> REVELATION 7:1-4

All the people on Earth will be reduced to the same status. Rich and poor, powerful and powerless, black, white, red, yellow and brown. When all are in total awe of the creative force, the destruction will cease for a time.

Who is then able to go on?

Those who are children of the tribes of Israel. Remember that "Israel" means those people who choose to believe in one God with all their heart, mind and spirit.

It is not as biological Jews, nor as biological Christians, that you will be selected. The selection is based on your inner awareness that God is one, that you are the heir of God, and that you desire to follow the intention of the Creator with all your might.

These believers are the ones who are most sensitive to God's Design.

Each shall be "sealed" with the seal of the living God. This means that they shall be marked, visibly identified, first to themselves, then to others. This means that their inner eye in the forehead will be fully opened by this touch, henceforth separating them from all who are still asleep in the womb of self-centeredness.

It is those of you who are now hearing an inner voice telling you to put this purpose first, to put the love of the Kingdom first, to put the love of evolution first; you are now being visibly touched by the animating hand of God.

You are, even now, visibly different from those who live in the darkness of self-centered consciousness.

> After this I beheld, and lo, a great multitude, which no man could number, of all nations and kindreds and people and tongues, stood before the throne and before the Lamb, clothed in white robes and with palms in their hands. And they cried with a loud voice, saying, "Salvation to our God who sitteth upon the throne, and unto the Lamb." And all the angels stood round about the throne, and about the elders and the four living beings, and fell on their faces before the throne and worshipped God, saying, "Amen. Blessing and glory and wisdom, and thanksgiving and honor and power and might, be unto our God for ever and ever. Amen!" And one of the elders spoke, saying unto me, "Who are these who are arrayed in white robes, and from whence have they come?" And I said unto him, "Sir, thou knowest." And he said to me, "These are those who came out of great tribulation, and have washed their robes and made them white in the

blood of the Lamb. Therefore, they are before the throne of God, and serve Him day and night in His temple; and He that sitteth on the throne shall dwell among them. They shall hunger no more, neither thirst any more; neither shall the sun light upon them, nor any heat. For the Lamb who is in the midst of the throne shall feed them, and shall lead them unto living fountains of waters, and God shall wipe away all tears from their eyes."

REVELATION 7:9-17

Those who have the seal of the living God will be able to take the next step of evolution. They shall hunger no more. They shall weep no more. They will love to perfection and be the first to fully emulate Christ with all their hearts. The creature/human phase will be over. The divine/human phase will have begun.

This is not a phase of impersonal disembodiment, but of new life in a resurrected body, beyond the reach of fear. "Perfect love casteth out fear." Perfect love casteth out death as well.

The multitude arrayed in white robes are the first to love Christ and desire to do as he did. They are the first to emulate the new template, to imagine themselves as joint-heirs.

Their thoughts and desires are registered in the Library of Consciousness, as their genetic code is recorded in the Book of Life. At the time of the judgment, their thought patterns will be retrieved and those in the white robes, they who have loved life with perfect purity, will be resurrected. They are the first to whom the mystery shall be revealed.

Remember, not a feather goes uncounted. Not a hair is lost. Not a gesture is unnoticed. Everything counts, dearly beloved, forever and ever.

"The Lamb which is in the midst of the throne shall feed them, and shall lead them unto living fountains of waters."

The Lamb is your capacity to be co-creative with God. When you awaken to this capacity, you shall move beyond creature/human consciousness. All your needs will be fulfilled through partaking of the Mind of God.

The "living fountains of waters," the source of ever-evolving life in each of you, is waiting to be turned on. It is the mechanism for rejuvenation and renewal.

When the time comes, you will not be alone. You will be surrounded by life from many dimensions: angelic beings who exist beyond this plane; the elders, who have experienced creature/human existence and perfected Christ-consciousness, and the living beings, animal nature in its pure form.

The resurrected co-creative human will join the whole family of God.

O dearly beloved, what joy awaits you! How I wish I could show you the glory that is to be revealed through you!

Joy is essential now. Lightness of heart will help you overcome the heaviness of life during the tribulations to come.

I speak now to those attracted to the future, with a belief in things as yet unseen. You are to say the prayer:

Our Creator who art in Heaven,
Hallowed be your name.
Your Kingdom come,
Your Will be done,
On Earth as it is in Heaven.
I do willingly commit myself to the fulfillment of your design.
Your will and mine are one.
I will go the Whole Way without arrogance.
I will move beyond the limits of the creature/human plane.
I know in my soul that more is to come.
I know I am to be a guide to my brothers and sisters on Earth,
    as we move through the passage of transformation.
I promise to prepare myself and all others who desire everlasting life.
I believe that the God-conscious will evolve.
I promise to be a beacon of light for myself and all others who
    choose to evolve from Adam to Christ.

And when the Lamb had opened the seventh seal, there was silence in Heaven about the space of half an hour.

REVELATION 8:1

Every woman who has given birth knows what a respite between labor pains feels like: a silence in Heaven. This is the brief moment of utter quiet before the child breaks through the narrow straits into the wide, wide world.

The seventh seal is the final barrier to our birth as co-creative humans. It must be broken. The pain that comes from this is intense, though necessary.

As we undergo the period of birth, the tribulations, we must practice "natural childbirth" in preparation. We can lessen our pain by understanding it. We can hasten the birth by natural relaxation.

Dearly beloved, you are to practice absolute faith in the outcome of the tribulations.

You are to visualize the New Jerusalem.

You are to envision a new humanity—all loving and God-centered.

You are to become a prototype of that humanity, to demonstrate its reality, to those with eyes to see and ears to hear.

You are to build within you an impregnable fortress of peace where you can attune to God no matter what is happening around you.

Dearly beloved, my New Order of the Future, you are to prepare with all your concentration.

Use this period of silence well. It is given to you to learn how to behave in the excitement of birth which is to come.

> And I saw the seven angels who stood before God, and to them were given seven trumpets. And another angel came and stood at the altar, having a golden censer; and there was given unto him much incense, that he should offer it with the prayers of all saints upon the golden altar, which was before the throne....And the angel took the censer, and filled it with fire from the altar, and cast it down upon the earth; and there were voices and thunderings and lightnings, and an earthquake. And the seven angels who had the seven trumpets prepared themselves to sound.
>
> REVELATION 8:2-4, 5-6

We take heart, for what is about to occur is not an accident. It is not a random event. It is a process of birth from terrestrial, self-centered humanity to universal whole-centered humanity.

It will make all the difference if we know there is a meaning to the tribulations, rather than believing them to be a meaningless horror wrought by the depravity of humans or the anger of God.

What is to come is not meaningless nor depraved. It is necessary. All cosmic births are somewhat traumatic. Some are worse than others. The cosmic birth of planet Earth may be a difficult birth for several reasons.

The main reason is the genetic aberration which began before humanity, when animals began to eat living flesh. Humans amplified this aberration, killing not only for the survival of their bodies, but also of their ideas. Killing has been imprinted in the animal aspect of creature/human nature. This has caused the natural period of self-consciousness, wherein intellect and individuality were developed, to be far more painful than necessary. Self-centered humans killed each other, suppressed each other, treated each other and the rest of nature as "things" to be used rather than beings to be consciously aligned with. All this stems from the fact that killing to survive diminished the natural empathy of beings for other beings, upon which ultimate survival depends.

Now we are a humanity which is becoming an interrelated, organic, planetary whole system, yet whose members do not feel empathy for those beyond the immediate family and tribe, except in moments of crisis or celebration. We are like a body with multiple allergies to itself—a right hand which gets hives when it touches the left, a body which cannot stand to feel itself, a baby that does not know it is one body.

This makes the birth process painful, because the planetary body must become an inter-feeling whole to survive. Instead, there are too many members of the body who have an allergy to each other, too many people with no empathy for others, too many repressive humans clinging to self-centeredness when whole-centeredness is the necessary state of being.

Also, our mass media, the planetary nervous system, has a disease. This extended nervous system does not convey sufficient empathy for the body upon and to which it is reporting. Therefore, even those members of the planetary body who are in a state of natural empathy, are not reinforced by the electronic nervous system. They are warned that it is unrealistic to love, to hope, to plan ahead, for the reality is that life is everywhere brutal, meaningless and short. So says our mass media by selecting as news that which is violent and destructive over that which is creative and loving.

To correct the defects of lack of empathy among people, and the "disempathitis" of our global nervous system, the New Order of the Future has a special assignment. First, we are to be empathetic with all our heart, mind and spirit. We see in everyone we meet the potential to be godlike rather than the potential to be destructive. That empathy will reinforce the reality of the godlike potential in everyone we meet. Empathy is a magnet. It attracts that which is like itself. It reinforces love in the other by the magnetic attraction to the other.

Secondly, we shall work to cure the media's disempathitis by communicating empathy on the mass media. Empathy means "feeling with." We are to broadcast news and images of people feeling with people, of people loving people, of people loving themselves. Our underlying empathy is the trust that there is enough for all, that survival depends on co-operation and creativity rather than competition and covetousness. As we broadcast the options for survival—the policies and potentials to build new worlds on Earth and in space, where there will be enough for all—we shall actualize our right to life, liberty and the pursuit of happiness.

The knowledge of the potential for ever-evolving life for all who love God and neighbor as themselves will empower the already empathetic, and switch some of the neutral souls to loving attraction. For empathy is a psycho-magnetic field, which can attract all but the irremediably self-centered.

One way to lessen the pain of the tribulations to come is to create a powerful field of empathy through the mass media, which will select by attraction those capable of union.

We must not allow ourselves to be despairing. Our joy and empathy are needed to heal the world and attract all souls ready to join their will with the will of God to become heirs of the Kingdom.

> The first angel sounded, and there followed hail and fire mingled with blood, and they were cast upon the earth; and a third part of all the trees were burnt up, and all green grass was burnt up. And the second angel sounded, and as it were, a great mountain burning with fire was cast into the sea; and a third part of the sea became blood; and a third part of the creatures which were in the sea and had life, died, and a third part of the ships were destroyed.
>
> And the fifth angel sounded his trumpet, and I saw a star fall from heaven unto the earth; and to him was given the key to the bottomless pit. And he opened the bottomless pit, and there arose smoke out of the pit, as the smoke of a great furnace; and the sun and the air were darkened by reason of the smoke of the pit. And there came out of the smoke locusts upon the earth; and unto them was given power, as the scorpions of the earth have power. And it was commanded to them that they should not hurt the grass of the earth, neither any green thing, neither any tree, but only those men who have not the seal of God on their foreheads.
>
> REVELATION 8:7-9, 9:1-4

What would you do if you were Christ in charge of planet Earth now?

You have access to the God-force in all its personifications and elemental activities. You can call upon thunder, lightning, earthquakes, plagues, droughts. The armies of destruction are at your command, as are the forces of creation. You gaze upon a humanity at the hour of its greatest need—gasping for breath, in the process of striving to activate its capacities to live as one planetary body. What do you do? You love humanity. You love it for its full potential.

First, you may have to decide to save the child by destroying those elements which are unhealthy. If you are a surgeon delivering a child whose umbilical cord is wrapped around his neck, you must operate quickly, or the child will be strangled by the cord that connects him to his past.

The operation to save humanity is also painful. You do not want to kill bodies but to change minds, yet the "good" will also suffer as you eliminate self-centeredness that would destroy the whole body.

So you send seven angels, seven forces to change the world. The angels roll out a panorama of fiery disturbances:

Hail and fire are mingled with blood, burning trees and grass.

A mountain of fire is cast into the sea.

A star from heaven falls, poisoning the fresh water.

The heavens are eclipsed.

A bottomless pit sends forth horrible locusts with the sting of death.

This whole drama is directed at those who do not believe. It is they who must be amazed and astonished until they convert to love.

> **And the four angels were loosed, who had been prepared for an hour and a day and a month and a year, to slay a third part of mankind. And the number of the army of horsemen was two hundred thousand thousand, and I heard the number of them. By [fire, smoke and brimstone] was a third part of mankind killed.**
>
> **And the rest of the men, who were not killed by these plagues, yet repented not of the works of their hands, nor gave up the worship of devils, and idols of gold and silver, and brass and stone and of wood, which can neither see nor hear nor walk; neither repented they of their murders, nor of their sorceries, nor of their fornication, nor of their thefts.**
>
> Revelation 9:15-16, 18, 19-21

As the selection process intensifies, dearly beloved, you must create a holy place within you and practice every day listening to your inner voice. I will be communicating to you, as the tribulations intensify, so strengthen that inner place.

Align yourself with everyone else hearing the same signals, worldwide.

Communicate what you hear, in every possible medium. Reach out to as many as possible. The more quickly people know their choice, the more quickly the tribulations will be over.

Put the Kingdom first. Keep your attention on where you are going rather than where you have been. Let the vision of Universal Humanity guide you through the darkness and you will witness the birth of the Universal Human.

Do not panic if destruction comes.

Remember that there is a Design and it is good.

The prophecy of John can be avoided altogether, if you would heal the social body as you have learned to heal the biological body—by total focus on love, truth, wholeness and the goodness of God.

The alternative to Armageddon is the Planetary Pentecost. When a critical mass is in the upper room of consciousness on a planetary scale, each will hear from within, in their own langauge, the mighty words of God. All who are attuned will be radically empowered to be and do as Jesus did. If those people who are not self-centered align their thoughts in perfect faith, that they are whole, created in the image of God, the world can be saved.

The Book of Revelation is a description of one path to the New Jerusalem, but this scenario is not inevitable. However, the triumph of God-centered life is inevitable.

How the victory will be won is to be determined by you. If enough of you act for the good of the whole, right now, the Christ within each person will be born. The world will be changed, in a twinkling of an eye. Change your minds and you can change the world, dearly beloved.

The Cosmic Birth Experience can be a natural, graceful, planetary transition. If you are able to communicate this alternative reality before the tribulations are fully set in motion, violence can be avoided.

There is still time to make this a gentle rather than a violent birth.

To work with me to save the world, you must develop your own Christ-consciousness (love) and your own Christ-capacities (transcendent technologies—astronautics, genetics, robotics, cybernetics, microtechnology, psychic powers). Accelerate the co-creative revolution. Begin to build new worlds on Earth and new worlds in space. Make your life a conscious act.

I want you to know, dearly beloved, that the forces described by John are angels of creation. **If there are enough of you on Earth capable of initiating a wholesome direction that attracts the attention of the good and selfish alike, we can avoid the destruction.**

You are here, dearly beloved, to gentle the birth, to ease the way to the New Jerusalem. The angels of creation await your command. You are heirs of God on Earth who have faith to go the Whole Way, who have the genius to attract others with the good news, that they are born into a universe of infinite possibilities with enough for all, forever

> And I saw another mighty angel come down from heaven, clothed with a cloud; and a rainbow was upon his head, and his face was as the sun, and his feet as pillars of fire. And he had in his hand a little book open. And he set his right foot upon the sea, and his left foot on the earth, and cried with a loud voice, as when a lion roareth. And when he had cried, seven thunders uttered their voices. And when the seven thunders had uttered their voices, I was about to write, and I heard a voice from Heaven saying unto me, "Seal up those things which the seven thunders uttered, and write them not."
>
> REVELATION 10:1-4

There are beings in this universe utterly beyond our capacity to understand at our stage of evolution. They are to us what we are to the first fish that crawled out on the dry land: incomprehensible.

John saw one such being come "down" from this state of being. He is clothed with a cloud; that is, he is emanating an aura of glory, glowing, yet hidden from sight, protecting the human eye from sights so brilliant as to blind one forever.

Paul was blinded for three days by the vision of Jesus. John was blinded by the "cloud" diffusing the brilliance of the angelic being.

A rainbow was on the being's head. The rainbow, God's covenant never to forget humans, given to Noah after the flood, is a sign throughout the universe of life everlasting. The rainbow is a seal of God to those who are becoming co-creators. It consists of all colors and is a symbol of synthesis, a sign of synergism, a mark of love signifying that the elevated individual is always connected to God consciously and is therefore whole, incorruptible, immortal and perfect as God in Heaven is perfect.

"His face was as it were the sun." The transfigured being glows with the light of the Creative Intelligence. It is the mental counterpart of atomic energy. It is the light given off by minds whose thought is vibrating at the God-frequency, consciously accessing the universal information system, consciously connected with the mind of God.

"His feet were as pillars of fire." Instead of "feet of clay," which are the natural state of creature/humans whose bodies are composed of the materials of Earth, higher beings have feet of fire. Their bodies are rooted, not in the soil of the Earth, but in the light of God's mind. Their bodies are composed of light, of fire, of ideas made flesh, as was Jesus' glorified body, beyond the reach of disease, decay and death.

Can you imagine a resurrected body attacked by a virus? It burns the virus instantly by the laserlike intensity of its thought.

"And he had in his hand a little book open." This being is reading from the Book of the Gods. It is the manual for co-creators who have graduated from creature-hood, who have established God-centered consciousness as a new norm, who have regenerated new bodies that are incorruptible.

Realize, dearly beloved, that the universe is filled with Christlike beings who have gone much, much further than Jesus was able to demonstrate to you while embodied on Earth. They read from the Book of the Gods as you read from the Book of the Dead and the Bible of the living. The Book of the Gods is what I read before I came, and what I am reading now, in this ever-evolving universe without end.

"And he set his right foot upon the sea, and his left foot on the earth." This being totally dominates the physical Earth. He is a master of the material world.

"And cried with a loud voice...and...seven thunders uttered their voices." The voice of a being in the co-creative state is a direct communication from the Mind of God. There is no separation. Now when we hear the inner voice it is softened and diffused by the frequencies of our brain waves. When our brain waves resonate with those of the Mind of the Creator, our inner voice becomes the direct communication of God. There is no buffer, no energy lost. It is direct. John was about to write the words of the direct voice of God, coming through an evolved being of the highest order, rather than through his own head.

But another voice from heaven stopped him and said, "Seal up those things which the seven thunders uttered, and write them not." The human race is not ready to hear the next level of knowledge beyond the gentle stories and the hints about the future which Jesus foretold and the saints heard. This would be like informing a newborn child that she is to pilot a spaceship to the moon. Too much. Incomprehensible. Confusing. Even if she could understand, the child would be distracted from carrying out the purposes at hand, the vital, immediate tasks of whole-system survival—breathing, nursing, eliminating. And so with humankind.

John heard, but was ordered not to reveal. It was not yet time.

*Now it **is** time. More of the Book of the Gods shall be revealed to you, dearly beloved, for the end is coming and the new beginning is dawning in your lifetime.*

Some of you alive now will witness the next step of evolution, not in a vision, but in actuality, not as John did, but as I did. You who are intending to follow me the Whole Way will do so and experience yourselves as natural Christs—little butterflies finally emerged from the chrysalis of self-consciousness to the universe of God-conscious beings, who are everywhere surrounding you even now.

> And the angel, whom I saw standing upon the sea and upon the earth, lifted up his hand to Heaven. And he swore by Him who liveth for ever and ever, who created Heaven and the things that are therein, and the earth and the things that are therein, and the sea and the things which are therein, that there should be time no longer, but that in the days of the voice of the seventh angel, when he shall begin to sound, the mystery of God should

be finished, as He hath declared to His servants the prophets.

REVELATION 10: 5-7

When self-centeredness is transcended through whole-centered consciousness, time will disappear. Time exists from the perspective of a self that experiences itself as separate from the Creation. When we enter the state of God-centered consciousness, we experience ourselves as contiguous with all that has been, is now, and potentially will be. All is alive now, right now, in God's mind.

We are in a physical cocoon of Earth and in a psychological cocoon of the five mammalian senses. Every now and then we flicker into universal consciousness and catch a glimpse of the cosmos as a living being with all its parts conscious, connected, imbued with love and intention. Then we return to the dark box of self-consciousness and see ourselves laboriously eating, sleeping, reproducing and dying alone, not realizing that we are members of a planetary body, that our Higher Self knows the past, present and potential future, just as we know the back, front, top and bottom of our own bodies.

The experience of time disappears when self-consciousness disappears. The experience of co-creativity emerges with God-centered consciousness. We experience ourselves creating effortlessly with no sense of time passing. We experience ourselves in a flow, dancing to a rhythm we did not invent. We experience ourselves synchronizing with others who are dancing to the same beat. We experience ourselves connecting to everything, which is everywhere connecting to everything else, until the sense of time passing is annihilated. The sense of time present, time eternally creative, appears, and we are free from the passing of time.

We exist in a state of eternal evolution, an unfolding of that which is eternally prepotential in the mind of God. We become Alpha and Omega. We are the beginning and the end. We are the whole. Every whole being is integrated into the whole. There is no death, only ever-higher order, consciousness, and union with God through co-operation of the parts of the universal Whole.

The experience of time springs from the experience of death. Self-consciousness and death of the individual body are evolutionary twins and are the source of the experience of time.

The experience of eternal creativity beyond time springs from the experience of immortality. The stage of immortality (Christ) follows the stage of sexual reproduction and scheduled death (creature/human), which itself followed the stage of semi-immortality (single cell).

*The stage of immortality is the next step of evolution. It was experienced on planet Earth by me. I manifested the capability of continuity of consciousness through the death of a physical body and the resurrection of a new body. This is the essential key to immortality. It is not essential to keep the same body. It is essential to keep the consciousness of who you are **uniquely,** with the memory of your experience intact through all of the mind-body systems you may be required to create in order to continue your function as co-creators with God.*

At the stage of immortality, individuals do not lose consciousness of their experience. The mind of the individual remembers all of its experience and partakes equally in the experience of all other minds, all of which are clearly registered in the Mind of God, with open access to all in a state of God-consciousness.

*Time-binding is over. Eternity begins, **as an experience,** when you gain access to all information instantly by thought.*

Your aging research will succeed. You will learn the code of degeneration— programmed death—and change it to the code of regeneration and consciously chosen life. Longevity of your existing body will be increased sufficiently for you to gain the capacity to create a body that you can leave at will, renew at will, dematerialize and rematerialize at will, and redesign as necessary to survive in the new environments beyond the biosphere of Earth.

Eventually everyone born will be a natural Christ, a chosen person, a higher being, a self-selected life. After the tribulation, which is the evolutionary selection process, only those with a genetic code for loving God-centeredness will exist.

Conceptions will be through virgin birth, as was the conception of Jesus. Carefully selected sperm and egg, each carrying the Design of a natural Christ, an immortal being, will be joined in a ceremony of joy witnessed by the mother and father of the child to be.

Remember, "immortal" simply means "not mortal." The word stands for the human intuition that a stage of being exists which is not animal, not mortal, not subject to disease and death. It stands for what is not, rather than for what is to come.

The next stage, from the experience of those already there, is godly. The stage of godliness follows the stage of humanness, and is more than merely "not mortal." It is godliness personified. It is as much beyond your experience as is your experience from that of a newborn child. That is why the angel was not permitted to let John describe the Book of the Gods.

The gestation period of a godly being is consciously monitored for any mistake in following the perfect whole design. The natural Christ child is born when the body is perfectly ready. It is immediately conscious of the continuity of all its experience throughout the universal series of lives. It knows by identity. It knows atomic psychics because it is atoms in motion. It knows molecular biology because it is composed of molecules in action. It knows organic chemistry because it is a living organism of chemical reactions. It knows cosmology, biology, paleontology, anthropology, history, current events and possible futures because its atoms hold the imprint of the moment of creation. Its cells have the memory of the origin of life, its brain remembers the experience of the reptilian, mammalian and early human history, and its mind knows the whole history of the universe, since every part has the information of the whole system.

Children "read" their own DNA just as you read words. They read the Mind of God because they are consciously of, in and at one with the Mind of God. They are born with the connection intact. They are incorruptible. Their third eye, their inner voice, their suprasensory channel of cognition, are turned on as a natural inheritance of every child born.

Remember, even now there are among you some mutants who have experienced this level of awareness, to some degree. It is they who are "sealed" by

God on their foreheads and who will evolve to co-create godly humans by conscious choice, as the first generation of natural Christs.

The problems you are now facing will not exist.

I did not reform the world; I transformed myself and returned to demonstrate that you can do the same. It is true. You can. You will.

Godly children always know they are about God's business.

Your life span is chosen. Your cells are programmed not to degenerate involuntarily, but only with the choice of the Higher Self, which decides when a particular body has finished its usefulness.

You have the capacities of a natural Christ, based on my template for the mutation that will evolve through the tribulations. You will be capable of self-healing, telepathy, clairvoyance, clairaudience, levitation, materialization and dematerialization.

Empathetic love will be a constant state. A community of natural Christs attuning to the Design of God, co-creating with that Design, each giving a unique contribution, each emancipating the best in each, suprasexually engaged in conscious co-creation, ever ecstatic, ever new, ever mindful of God. This is the form of self-government in the New Jerusalem.

In childhood there will be no loss of memory of who you are. You will never lose awareness.

You will know your vocation of destiny, your inner calling, your participation in the creation, from the very beginning of your life. Each of you will be born knowing what you are born to do. There will be a continuity of consciousness. Intentionality, unique purpose, will guide the action of the child throughout the period of self-education.

Your adolescence will be a joy. You will be androgynous. You will learn to co-create. You will know that you are a self-conceiving, self-regenerating, continous being. You will choose to create another being only on very special occasions when the whole community of natural Christs sees the requirement. The selection of the individual to be embodied is done by conscious selection. The individual desirous of taking on a new body signals the would-be parents. An agreement is consciously made between the would-be parents and the soul who chooses to be born. The proper design is embodied in an egg and sperm.

The conception is consumated. The body begins to materialize according to the chosen design. All designs are in the image of God. Diversity is infinite, since God manifests creativity in an infinity of ways in a universe without end.

This method of conscious conception already occurs in the creature/human stage, but it is not yet at the Higher Self level. The ego does not know. The Higher Self does not tell, except in those individuals who are listening to their Higher Selves even now, and have already some dim perception of having volunteered for this task, of having chosen to come to Earth at this time to fulfill some purpose for God.

During your adolescence as a natural Christ you find your suprasexual partner, that person most suited to co-create with you. You are at the Tree of Life. Your education is by contact with the mind of God. You learn the invisible processes of creation by exercising your own God-given capacities to co-create with Divine Intelligence. You are engaged in the whole array of post-human functions at the highest degree of artistic genius. Everyone is an artist because everyone is created to be a co-creator in the image of God. Creativity is the essence of life at the next stage.

You produce as God does.

You heal as God does.

You design new worlds as God does.

You are apprentice godlings at the dawn of the Universal Age. This is the stage of the natural Christs in the Second Garden, the New Jerusalem, where grows the Tree of Life. You have eaten of the fruit of the Tree of Life. You are like gods. You are immortal; that is, you are godly. You are in the kindergarten of the universe. You are now surrounded by the elders that John saw, and the multitudes of beings from other planetary systems, and all the resurrected dead from planet Earth who believed in their potential to be Christlike—earlier proto-mutants who had the template for God-consciousness and incorruptible bodies before the fullness of time.

You begin your education for the next phase of evolution as a conscious personification of God with access to the information of the past, present and potential future beyond the confines of space and time, which are constructs of

▲

the self-conscious mind. You know everything is intelligent. What appeared to
Homo sapiens *as "evolution" appears to you as a conscious act of God to create beings in God's own image who are capable of co-evolving the universe to the stage of universal Godhood.*

In your adulthood as a natural Christ you move from one function to the next in an ever-evolving flow. Progress is defined as ever-greater union with God. Suprasexual couplehood is the form of personal union. Marriage is by agreement to create together in the name of God.

There is no possession nor being possessed. Love is suprasexual and empathetic. Fidelity of the partners is to each other for the sake of their chosen act, whether it be a godly child or godly work in the universe.

When the act is completed, the partnership is renewed if there is more to be done. It is lovingly ended if there is nothing more to be created by that particular couple. Each discovers the next partner, or partners, with no hint of sorrow, for nothing is separated among those totally connected with God.

The families of suprasexual couples are chosen. The children choose the parents. The parents choose the children. The bonding is noological—of the mind—not only biological. The bonds of shared intention are far deeper than the bonds of blood.

Synocracy is the form of government—whole beings uniting with whole beings in a community of whole beings, all attuning to the same Design, motivated by the same intention to utterly fulfill the intention of the Creator with every iota of creativity in each person..

The will of the individual and the will of God are totally united. The power of such a community of natural Christs is the very beginning of the preparation for universal life, the introduction to the galactic community of evolved beings on the universal scale.

The elders, the angels, the Lamb are teachers whom you will see in the early days of the New Jerusalem, as soon as the Quantum Instant has been shared by all who desire to be Christlike.

Then begins the preparation for your universal mission. You learn the language of the multitudes of universal cultures—each springing from a different star, each with a different experience, all united by the fact that they are all attuning to the universal Design.

"In the days of the voice of the seventh angel, when he shall begin to sound, the mystery of God should be finished, as He hath declared to His servants the prophets." This vision of the future has been proclaimed by the prophets of the world who have been inspired by the Mind of God.

We always intuited that we were immortal. And now we know that we are. We always knew that we were not limited to this body or this planet. Now we find that it is true. We always knew that there were higher beings. Now we become higher beings ourselves.

We always believed we would be partners with God. Now we find that we actually are. We always believed we were more than animals reproducing and dying. And now we find ourselves co-creating and regenerating rather than procreating and degenerating.

We always believed in fidelity. We always wanted love that would last forever. "What God hath joined together, let no man put asunder." Now we find it is true. We become the second couple, godly beings united to godly beings, creating together forever, worlds without end.

We always believed God is good. Now we find it is true. We always desired to be good. Now we always are.

We always desired to know God. Now we live and breathe in God as a continual state of co-knowing, co-creating, co-existing with the whole universal Creation.

These things seem beyond you, dearly beloved. Know that everything you truly desire is real. You shall have your hearts' desire, dearly beloved, and far, far more than you can yet conceive. Thank God. Be joyful. Celebrate your birth. Prepare for the end and the beginning. I am with you. Thank God. Amen.

> And the voice which I heard from Heaven spoke unto me again and said, "Go and take the little book which is open in the hand of the angel who standeth upon the sea and upon the earth." And I went unto the angel and said unto him, "Give me the little book." And he said unto me,

"Take it and eat it up, and it shall make thy belly bitter, but it shall be in thy mouth sweet as honey." And I took the little book out of the angel's hand and ate it up, and it was in my mouth sweet as honey; and as soon as I had eaten it, my belly was bitter. And he said unto me, "Thou must prophesy again before many peoples and nations, and tongues and kings."

REVELATION 10:8-11

John tasted the fruit of the Tree of Life. The fruit is recorded in the Book of the Gods. He ate the book. He tasted of the knowledge of eternal life which was revealed to him.

It tasted sweet in his mouth, for the knowledge is wonderful beyond all imaginings. It was bitter in his belly because the creature/human nature, which is still our condition, cannot digest and incorporate the godlike state. The knowledge of the Book of the Gods, the fruit of the Tree of Life, still cannot be consumed by us in our present condition.

Therefore, John was commanded to prophesy, prophesy, prophesy, again and again, to the people of all nations, so that all can hear, and then the end shall come.

We shall pass through the tribulations. All who evolve will be natural Christs capable of eating the fruit of the Tree of Life, consuming the Book of the Gods with no bitterness, for the creature/human phase will be over.

Those of you who hear these words now are to carry on the commandment given to John two thousand years ago. You are not only to prophesy the end, the tribulations, and the New Jerusalem, you are to act it out. You are to discover the blueprint and become actual co-creators with God. You are to see the first fruits of the New Beginning.

Dearly beloved, everything depends on your capacity to believe this extraordinary truth. It is the same requirement I gave to the twelve disciples upon my return from the grave: Go ye therefore and teach all nations, baptizing them in the name of the Father, and of the Son, and of the Holy Spirit, teaching them to observe all things whatsoever I have commanded you. And lo, I am with you always, even unto the end of the world.

Since you come two thousand years after I first spoke these words, your task is even greater. You are to do as I did and even more.

If you can believe this, as Peter and Paul were able to believe in the resurrection of their bodies, it shall be done.

All depends on your belief. Believe, and it shall be so. Fail to believe, and it shall not be.

Dearly beloved, those of you who hold within you the code of life everlasting are now being awakened from within.

It is I arising within you. I am now motivating each of you to move beyond your existing lives to your ever-evolving lives. You experience me from within as the fire in your heart to fulfill your destinies as natural Christs. You are the generation on the cusp between creature and co-creator. As you allow me to activate you from within I raise up your mind/body system so that you are capable of incorporating the "little book" into your very being.

This little book triggers the unused DNA within your genetic code. This is the information required for your transformation from separated self-conciousness to unified God-consciousness.

All of you who are now awakening to your own evolution are to gather. Find one another. Join spiritually. Through your joining your genius will be revealed, your hearts will be opened, your life partners attracted. You will be guided from within as to the design of the Planetary Birth and your roles in it. From every race, nation and religion you will prophesy that the transition from Homo sapiens *to* Homo universalis *is now occurring.*

Your prophesy will call people to experience in your life time the Planetary Birth.

> **"And I will give power unto my two witnesses, and they shall prophesy a thousand two hundred and threescore days, clothed in sackcloth."**
>
> **REVELATION 11:3**

There will come witnesses who will proclaim to the peoples of the world the truth of our birth as Universal Humans, co-creators of new worlds.

The New Jerusalem is the Second Garden. It is humanity living at the next stage of evolution, after the selection process has gathered the God-centered from the self-centered. It is us-in-the-future collectively, with all capabilities operating harmoniously—a community of natural Christs.

The New Jerusalem is us in co-creative consciousness, attuning to all life as Jesus did.

The New Jerusalem is us in an Earth/space environment, beginning a new technological revolution, restoring this Earth, producing in space as astroculture begins, building new worlds as mini-godlings, exploring our galaxy, signaling other life, and learning how God creates so we can co-create.

The New Jerusalem is us in synergetic, empathetic attunement to the voice within, self-organizing for the tasks of building the New Jerusalem. It is the genius of clusters of natural Christs cooperating with each other and God to meet the full range of needs of all humans who evolve through the Quantum Transformation. Remember, only the loving, God-centered evolve. Only the good evolves. Self-government in the New Jerusalem will not depend on coercion or legislation to force obedience to the law. For it will be populated by those who have chosen to align their will with the will of God. There will be no lawyers of the old kind in the New Jerusalem, for everyone will be motivated, as Jesus was, not to destroy the law but to fulfill it.

The New Jerusalem is us in new, incorruptible bodies capable of self-healing, self-conception, self-regeneration, materialization and dematerialization, resurrection and ascension. In the New Jerusalem there is no death. In the second garden the Tree of Life grows. We are as the gods. We are created in the image of God and in the image of God we shall be.

The New Jerusalem is us in contact with higher beings as a shared experience. In new bodies, co-operating with each other in suprasexual attraction, in an Earth/space environment, each with the consciousness of a natural Christ, we encounter other life. What John saw "in the spirit," we shall know in actuality. He saw a vision of the personifications of God who are now concerned with the future of Earth-life. These personifications are real. We shall see them too, face to face.

The blue cocoon of Earth opens physically and we become free of involuntary planet-boundedness. That physical act of leaving the Earth and living in the new environment beyond the biosphere triggers our extrasensory capacities, which Jesus had but which are dormant in most of us. The extraterrestrial environment stimulates the extrasensory capacities, naturally.

Weightlessness stimulates the memory of immortality which cells once had, floating weightless in the seas of the early Earth and in the womb of the female mammal. This weightless experience is one of the stimuli required to trigger the regenerating mechanisms now latent in the DNA of all human cells. The other stimuli are Christ-consciousness and empathetic organization.

Beings who are in co-creative consciousness, in an open Earth/space system, cooperating synergistically, can have a shared experience of higher beings. Only higher beings can recognize higher beings. Just as newborn babies cannot recognize their mothers, newborn planetary species cannot recognize the personifications of God who are more mature than they, until they themselves mature.

> **"And so it is written, The first man Adam was made a living soul; the last Adam was made a life-giving Spirit.**
>
> *(I Corinthians 15:45)*

One particular generation experiences the shift from creature-human to co-creative human; from Adam of the living soul to Adam of the life-giving Spirit—the Universal Human. Some people alive on Earth now are members of that blessed generation. This generation, the first generation capable of self-regeneration, is now marked by intention, desire, will, love and total dedication to being like me, doing as I did and even more. They are those sealed upon their foreheads just before the tribulations intensify. They are those alive now who are completely committed to the transformation of themselves and their world, even unto the resurrection and the ascension which, translated into modern language, means they shall change their bodies and leave this Earth alive, to join me beyond this physical plane.

The purpose of this crossover generation, which is shifting from a living soul to a life-giving Spirit, is to serve as links between those still in self-consciousness and those becoming God-conscious, natural Christs. This is the generation of the evolution of the self-centered into the God-centered. This is the generation of choice. Only the God-centered reach the Tree of Life.

Those who first experience the shift, not "in the spirit" as John did, but in the flesh, as I did, are to be guides during the tribulations. Their task is to help as many living souls as possible make the choice for God. Even now my legions are growing. Evangelists are proclaiming that the Kingdom of God is at hand. They are urging repentance and acceptance of Jesus as your personal savior. But they are not laying forth the image of the collective future of the human race as a generation of the saved. They have not yet envisioned what it will be like when everything works.

That is your task, dearly beloved, you of my New Order of the Future, who have eyes to see the reality and the beauty of my Design for you.

It is your work to envision the New Jerusalem as the society of full humanity wherein each person is a co-creator. It is your blessed privilege to communicate this vision and to attract all with eyes to see and ears to hear, to participate in the creation. **You are to prepare the way for the alternative to Armageddon, which is the Planetary Pentecost, the great Instant of Co-operation which can transform enough, en masse, to avoid the necessity of the seventh seal being broken. It is now the time of the silence in Heaven.**

This is the cosmic instant immediately preceding the onslaught of the intensified selection process, or tribulations. The "half hour" of silence is the period of waiting until the last possible moment to begin the traumatic events.

What the angels are waiting for, dearly beloved, is you of my New Order of the Future. You represent the possibility of the avoidance of the painful process of selection, which means the destruction of the self-centered who cannot inherit the powers of co-creation.

You have the capacity to attract, through educating members of the plane-tary body of their capabilities to participate in the building of the New Jerusalem.

It is up to you to reveal the reality of my promise based on the reality of your potentials, your capacity to transcend your creature/human limitations and become partners with God, joint-heirs with me.

I, Jesus, am the Lamb. I have been given the Book of Life. It has seven seals.

The first four seals are the four horsemen of the Apocalypse, ready to ride, but not yet riding. They wait, holding in abeyance for one more instant the dreadful process of selection:

The White Horse and the conqueror of creature/human nature; the Red Horse and the power to kill; the Black Horse and the power to destroy those who are in deficiency; the Pale Horse upon whom sits the rider called Death, posed to kill those who choose to remain self-centered, with sword, with hunger, with death and with the beasts of the Earth.

All are at the gate, ready to let loose the mighty force.

The fifth seal reveals the souls who have already died and who are waiting, waiting, waiting until the end shall come, so that they may be resurrected, renewed and released from the pattern in which they are holding until the fullness of time has come.

The sixth seal is the atomic explosions that have already begun to take place. It was a sign to the kings of the Earth, the great men, the rich men, the chief captains, and the mighty men, and every bondman, and every free man, that none could prevail over each other in the face of a force of ultimate destruction.

The sixth seal, which John saw in the first century after I was born, was broken in the twentieth century after my birth. It was the signal that the birth process had begun. It was the sign that the human race had gained the powers of co-creation and of self-destruction. It was the inevitable next step of evolu-tion wherein a still self-centered species was given the power of the gods, because they could no longer be kept in ignorance of their inheritance, no matter how immature they might be.

You cannot keep an infant from walking, even if it is a retarded child. Humanity could not be kept from gaining the understanding of God's invisible technologies. Once the neo-cortex developed—the big brain—the process was set in irreversible motion. There was no going back to the animal condition. The unstable period of transition from animal creaturehood to godlike being had begun. Self-consciousness emerged. Intellect and individuality developed. Scientific method and democratic institutions released the creative power of godly humans—and the human race approached the Tree of Life. Neither the angels of mercy nor the fear of death could prevent humans from wanting to know how to be more like God.

So be it, dearly beloved. So be it.

Here we are, now poised either on the brink of destruction greater than the world has ever seen—a destruction which will cripple planet Earth forever and release only the few to go on—or on the threshold of global co-creation wherein each person on Earth will be attracted to participate in his or her own evolution to godliness.

At this cosmic instant, before the seventh seal is broken to unleash the horrors which John foresaw, one misunderstanding can destroy the world.

But notice, dearly beloved, what else John saw. He saw another angel ascending from the East, having the Seal of the Living God. And he cried with a loud voice to the four angels to whom it was given to hurt the Earth and the sea, saying, "Hurt not the earth, neither the sea nor the trees, until we have put a seal on the foreheads of the servants of our God."

John heard the angel say, "The number of those who were sealed [was] a hundred and forty-four thousand of all the tribes of the children of Israel."

Who do you suppose those "children of Israel" are, dearly beloved? They are you who love God above all else, your neighbor as yourself, and yourself as me. You are sealed in your foreheads. This means your awareness is awakened. You are practicing the seven spirits of God, which are required to become like me: love, wisdom, faith, courage, patience, power and surrender.

You are ready to self-transform, not for the sake of your personal reward, but for the sake of all humanity, that everyone may have the same opportunity as you. My purpose in submitting to the crucifixion was to demonstrate the resurrection, for all to know that in the fullness of time, they could do it also. Your purpose in surrendering to self-transformation is to demonstrate that you can do it; therefore anyone can do it who follows me.

You are chosen, dearly beloved, not because you are extraordinary, but because you are wholesome, normal, good humans with whom anyone in their right mind can identify.

There are many more than one hundred and forty-four thousand training to be sealed. Once the first hundred and forty-four thousand have demonstrated the rudimentary capacity to self-transform, millions will be empowered to do the same. Those with the seal are simply the first to demonstrate the reality of the potential to be like me.

I, Jesus, am Israel fulfilled. You who are sealed with the Seal of God are builders of the New Jerusalem in my name, empowered by the Christ-within because you have willingly desired to follow my commandment of love the Whole Way.

O Israel, awaken to the reality of your potential to be heirs of God!

Thus will preach the witnesses to whom I will give power to prophesy. They will preach it during the cosmic silence which is now at hand.

All is silent to see if a second miracle can occur comparable to the birth of Christ.

That miracle is the gentle Second Coming of Christ through the rapid evolution of enough humans linked up by the planetary nervous system, so that the social body will flood with empathy, healings will abound, and the world will smile with joy. The people will know they are whole, they are good, they are capable, they are loved, they are needed.

The world will forgive itself.

We have been taught to forgive one another, one by one. Now we will forgive the whole. We have been taught to love one another, one by one. Now we are taught to love the whole.

This is the hope of the world. It is entirely in the hands of those with eyes to see me, those with ears to hear me, those with the desire to be me.

Anyone who reads these words and has such eyes, such ears, and such desire, will know that the words are true, and will be empowered to take action on them.

What action shall we take?

Like the astronauts before the launch, your action is to prepare by simulation, which means by envisionment and visualization of yourself and the world at the next stage.

You are to perform the cosmic union ceremony daily: visualize yourselves entering the cocoon, and placing your body in my body of light, giving it permission to become a new body like mine. It is already preprogrammed to change. Your desire and love of union with me is the key to this suprasexual union.

You are to practice the seven spirits of God. Be perfect as God in Heaven is perfect.

You are to be alert to the encounter with each other. You will know each other by the fact that these words appear true to you, and you are willing to practice the disciplines of self-transcendence which I have given you in this work and in many others.

Thus shall you be known by each other and by me. So be it. Thank God. Amen.

> **These are the two olive trees and the two candlesticks,
> standing before the God of the earth.**
>
> **REVELATION 11: 4**

The witnesses to the New Jerusalem held forth the olive branch of peace and the bearers of enlightenment, which can save the beloved Earth from the opening of the seventh seal, the destruction by the four horsemen of the Apocalypse and the battles to come.

These have power to shut heaven, that it rain not in the days of their prophecy, and have power over waters to turn them to blood, and to smite the earth with all plagues, as often as they will. And when they shall have finished their testimony, the beast that ascendeth out of the bottomless pit shall make war against them, and shall overcome them and kill them.

REVELATION 11:6-7

The future which John saw is not the only possible future for the peoples of Earth. It is the worst possible future. It is what will happen if you kill the witnesses of your own potential, as you killed me.

The question is: Will you believe in your ability to be loving Sons and Daughters of God? If you do believe, the world will be saved. If you do not believe, the world will be destroyed.

What follows is one possible way in which a universal species comes through the trauma of birth. By studying it, you can catch a glimpse of what the world is to suffer if you ignore your full abilities.

And their dead bodies shall lie in the street of the great city, which spiritually is called Sodom and Egypt, where also our Lord was crucified.

REVELATION 11:8

Remember, dearly beloved, this is a negative scenario which has not yet happened and which can be avoided if you act now. It is essential that my New Order of the Future put forward images of a positive future based on the reality of your potentials to be like me. Without such positive images of the future, you will not be able to imagine a positive scenario. You will not take steps to achieve it. You will therefore not achieve it if you do not envision it. ***Do not dwell on the negative scenario whose description is to follow. It is not inevitably so.***

If the witnesses are not heard, if the "beast" ascends out of the bottomless pit, if the selfish nature of humans prevails, the witnesses to hope will be killed. The assassinated bodies of hope shall lie in the street of the great city. Sodom, the place of materialism gone mad, is like the city of ancient Rome that killed me. It distracts the desire for God into the psycho-magnetic fields of death, degeneration and disease.

The modern arts that depict depravity, the violent films, the killing for entertainment on television, the tawdry flaunting of the loving body are assassins to the witnesses to hope.

The modern moralists, who preach the irremediable degradation of human beings as sinners, are assassinating the witnesses to hope.

The modern pessimists, who pronounce that we shall surely fail, are assassins of the witnesses to hope.

The modern brokers of power who would rather hold the fort than build the New Jerusalem, and those who sit at the head of giant corporations, governments and churches, who dare not risk for new life—these also are assassins of the witnesses to hope.

> **And they of the people and kindreds, and tongues and nations shall see their dead bodies three days and a half, and shall not let their dead bodies be put in graves. And those who dwell upon the earth shall rejoice over them and make merry, and shall send gifts one to another, because these two prophets tormented those who dwelt on the earth.**
>
> **REVELATION 11: 9-10**

Dearly beloved, we shall now expand on the prophecies of John.

The hope for life ever-evolving is more good news than many humans wish to accept. It means that they must lift their sights and start upon the path of self-transformation rather than self-destruction. Self-destruction is easy. It follows the tendency of the material world to ever increased entropy, devolution and death. Self-transcendence is difficult. It follows the tendency of the evolving world to negentropy, synergy and synthesis, to the rise of consciousness and freedom, to the increase of order. Self-transcendence extends the path of the billions of years of past evolution to create universal beings with eyes to see and ears to hear God.

> **The second woe is past; and, behold, the third woe cometh quickly. And the seventh angel sounded, and**

there were great voices in Heaven, saying, "The kingdoms of this world have become the Kingdoms of our Lord and of his Christ, and He shall reign for ever and ever!" And the four and twenty elders, who sat before God on their seats, fell upon their faces and worshipped God, saying, "We give thee thanks, O Lord God Almighty, who art, and wast, and art to come, because Thou hast taken to Thee Thy great power, and hast reigned."

REVELATION 11:14-17

The seventh angel of the seventh seal awaits the end of the tribulations, which shall surely come. Time will end. The mystery will be revealed. We shall all be changed. This is the design. The only question is, will it be violent or will it be gentle? That is our choice.

The elders and the waiting saints give thanks at the voice of the seventh angel. They have been waiting thousands of years for this stage of evolution to be finally over.

If we are impatient, imagine how they feel!

The elders are real. They are consciousnesses who have experienced Earth-life many times. They have learned all of the lessons required to graduate from God's kindergarten on Earth. They are no longer victims of fear. They are ascended masters, people who have realized the Christ-within and are capable of exercising Christlike powers.

However, they, like Christ, have chosen to help humanity rather than to take further steps for their own personal universal evolution in the "many mansions" of God's whole universe.

We are dedicated to you, dearly beloved. We are here now for you. Call on us and we will respond. We are your older brothers and sisters. We have chosen to aid the collective transformation of humanity from terrestrial to universal. We cannot initiate. Only you, still on Earth, can initiate. We can respond to your initiatives by giving you guidance. We are communicating to you through your Inner Voice. We are a chorus of inspiration for those with ears to hear.

Remember the spirit of faith in things unseen. This is vital, dearly beloved.
Call on us now, and together we will empower the believers in the future of
the world to build the New Jerusalem in accordance with the Design of God.

> **And the temple of God was opened in Heaven; and there**
> **was seen in His temple the ark of His testament, and**
> **there were lightnings and voices, and thunderings and an**
> **earthquake, and great hail.**
>
>

REVELATION 11:19
>

God instructed Moses to build an ark into which his testimony shall be given. In the ark is a "mercy seat of pure gold." The mercy seat is to be put above the ark. In the ark Moses is to put "the testimony which I shall give thee."

> **And there I will meet with thee, and I will commune with**
> **thee from above the mercy seat, from between the two**
> **cherubims which are upon the ark of the testimony, of all**
> **things which I will give thee in commandment unto the**
> **children of Israel.**
>
>

(EXODUS: 25:22)
>

From the time of Noah through Moses, Abraham, David, Jesus and us, a promise has been made by God to humanity. It is the promise of peace on Earth and a future beyond the confines of this mortal body.

The Judeo-Christian promise is of a personal future in a transformed body in a transformed material world in a universe without end, in partnership with a personal, loving God.

Other religions have had different visions of the next stage of evolution. Some have seen the future as a disembodiment from the personal, in a universe of consciousness in which there is no personal God.

Both visions may be realized: There is a pattern of evolution that is transpersonal, and another pattern of evolution that is impersonal. This choice of patterns is one that each soul is making now. When the end of this phase of evolution actually comes, in historical, real time, the choice of each soul for a transpersonal or an impersonal future will be fulfilled.

The impersonal choice implies our intention to release continuity of personal consciousness and return to the whole from whence we differentiated.

The transpersonal choice is not a return. It is an advance to newness. Although every idea is prepotential in the mind of God, its actualization in form has an element of uncertainty, freedom, genuine creativity and surprise. Although the design is pre-patterned, it is not predetermined. There is freedom throughout the universe.

Those attracted to the transpersonal choice want to work with God to create the universe of conscious being. They opt for the evolutionary aspect of God. Those who choose the impersonal future opt for the eternal aspect of God.

Now, turn within and ask your Higher Self which it prefers—life ever-evolving with continuity of consciousness in a series of bodies ever more godlike, or life everlasting with no individualized aspect, disembodied, resting in the Mind of God.

The answer you receive will indicate to you the choice which you are making. It is valuable now to bring this metaphysical preference to the surface of consciousness, because it is, in fact, affecting your every act, right now.

The preference for a transpersonal future in a new body urges us to be for the evolutionary capabilities of the human race—space exploration, genetics, longevity research, psychic powers, artificial intelligence, nanotechnology, atomic power. All the invisible technologies of creation attract us, because they will be required in an evolved form at the next stage of evolution for those who so choose to become a universal species, Christlike individuals in a community of Christs, co-operating with God to build a New Earth, and New Heavens—new mansions in the abundant house of God.

The preference for an impersonal, disembodied future inclines us to cut back on the technologies and capacities for material transformation. We prefer passive technologies of adaptation rather than active technologies of transcendence. We wish to return to a less interventionist role. We admire the way of life of traditional peoples who do not impact the current stage of evolution. Our excitement is for transcendent union with the Universal Mind beyond the confines of form. We wish to go "home" from whence we came, in an eternal bliss as an aspect of God.

It will save us from a painful process of polarization if we recognize that one basis of our policy differences is a legitimate metaphysical preference for either an impersonal or transpersonal future. We can honor each other's choices and orchestrate policy decisions that accommodate all temperaments within the ecology of souls. All are required.

Those of us who prefer an impersonal, disembodied future will choose the tasks of restoration and maintenance of the Earth. Those who prefer a transpersonal future in new bodies will tend to prefer the tasks of building new worlds in space, overcoming aging, learning how to resurrect bodies as Jesus did.

Those souls in waiting to be judged and rewarded with new bodies are impatient. John saw the promise which is keeping them in a state of expectation. It was first given to the Jewish people, then passed by the disciples to the Gentiles. Now it is offered to you, dearly beloved, Homo universalis *of all races and religions—to all peoples regardless of ideology or creed.*

The ark is the promise of a transpersonal future in a transformed body in a transformed world in partnership with a loving God.

> **And there appeared a great wondrous sign in heaven: a woman clothed with the sun, and the moon under her feet, and upon her head a crown of twelve stars. And she, being with child, cried out, travailing in birth and in pain to be delivered.**
>
> REVELATION 12:1-2

The first revelation to John was of the Son of Man, clothed with a garment down to the foot, his head white as snow, his eyes aflame, his feet like brass, his voice the sound of many waters.

This "wondrous sign" is of the Daughter of Man, the feminine aspect of the Christlike potential of the human race, the other half of the divinity within us all.

Each person has a Christ-within. It is neither masculine nor feminine. It is whole. Within the wholeness, the masculine and feminine are synthesized to make a new pattern greater than the sum of its parts.

The woman clothed with the sun, with the moon under her feet, is the feminine aspect of God, which will rise again, as it always does, when a Quantum Transformation is at hand. The feminine aspect of God is pregnant with all life. It loves all life and offers itself as a perfect receptacle for the growth of all life.

At the time of transformation from *Homo sapiens* to *Homo universalis*, the feminine aspect of God is pregnant with the new Adam of the life-giving Spirit.

As Mary was pregnant with Jesus, who carried the template for the future human, this woman of the universe is pregnant with the natural Christ, who shall be born after the tribulations, who will never know physical death, never succumb to the mammalian way, never experience the awful illusion of separation from God.

The woman of the universe is pregnant with the Universal Humans, who shall be born after the judgment of the quick and the dead, after the resurrection of the believers, after the defeat of Satan, after the establishment of the New Jerusalem, after the next phase is begun.

She is now travailing in pain to deliver this child, but cannot do so until the Quantum Transformation has been completed, and the environment has been prepared in which the natural Christs can live.

If such co-creative beings were to be born now, at the end of the phase of self-conscious humanity, they would be destroyed by the shock of hostility, fear and guilt which they would telepathically receive from the moment of conception.

Occasionally, such "gifted" children are born with the template of a natural Christ. If they survive, they learn to disguise their powers from the humans who still cannot tolerate the knowledge that they, too, can manifest the Christ as Jesus did.

The ones who can pave the way for the birth of the natural Christs are you, dearly beloved, the people who bridge the Quantum Instant, having been born as creature/humans, and, midstream in your lives, having consciously decided to transform.

You are the precious link. You can manifest yourselves without being destroyed, for you carry the double template of creature/human and Christlike human—a very precious role.

> And there appeared another wonder in heaven: behold, a great red dragon, having seven heads and ten horns, and seven crowns upon his heads. And his tail drew a third part of the stars of heaven, and cast them to the earth. And the dragon stood before the woman who was ready to be delivered, for to devour her child as soon as it was born.
>
> REVELATION 12:3-4

The power of the self-centered human has become a universal aberration, a dragon that can destroy the natural Christ and prevent the birth of the future human.

Intellect and individuality, cultivated during the period of self-consciousness, are meant to marry the Mind of God, rejoining the Creator in alignment with the evolutionary design for greater consciousness, freedom and union with God.

Eve-consciousness must marry Christ-consciousness; intellect must marry direct knowledge of God, and individuality must marry love-of-the-whole, in order for the natural Christ, the future human, to be born.

The dragon is the misuse of the powers of intellect and individuality at the conclusion of the phase of self-centeredness from which we are soon to emerge. The dragon is the instrument of evil—Satan—God's selection process, which will weed out the self-centered from the God-centered.

It is up to us how long the dragon of selfish power is permitted to prevail. In the end it will surely be defeated, for God's will shall be done on Earth as it is in Heaven.

Be aware, dearly beloved, that there are worse forces at work here than you are yet aware of. Read on, those of you who wish to cross the river of Water of Life.

> And there was war in Heaven. Michael and his angels fought against the dragon, and the dragon fought with his angels and prevailed not; neither was their place found any more in Heaven. And the great dragon was cast out—that serpent of old called the Devil and Satan, which deceiveth the whole world. He was cast out onto the earth, and his angels were cast out with him.
>
> REVELATION 12:7-9

There shall come a conflict beyond human understanding. It is a conflict between the suprahuman forces of good—the fully God-centered beings who have evolved beyond the creature/human—and the suprahumans who have chosen evil.

Who is that devil which is beyond humans? What infects humans with the desire to be gods separate from the one God, the Creator of all?

That devil is a fallen angel who went astray. It was he who contaminated the period of self-consciousness with the disease of egoistic pride.

It was necessary for humans to separate from their unconscious relationship to God, so that they could develop intellect and individuality, just as adolescents separate from their parents to establish their own identity.

But it was not necessary during this period of individuation for individuals to forget their relationship to the Creator and think that they could exist without God.

The problems of Earth are reflections of a problem that exists beyond you, dearly beloved. You have been infected by a disease that you did not create. It is at another level that this disease originates.

Remember, you are gestating in a womb according to a design in which nothing is guaranteed for an individual person. Genetic defects can and do occur.

The same is true of individual planets. The design is one of wholesome birth and life ever-evolving to all members of the God-centered species.

But the design is not pre-determined. It is pre-patterned.

What happened was this:

An error in the design occurred when animals became carnivorous. It was compounded when Cain slew Abel. Killing entered both the animal and the human scene.

The animals' error was innocent. The human error was childish. Cain slew Abel because he felt rejected by God.

The human sense of rejection has been perpetuated throughout time. It is this sense of rejection upon which the devil played. For he had the same defect. He, Lucifer, felt rejected by God and behaved, at a higher level, as badly as you. His force is still contaminating some of the evolved beings concerned with Earth. This contamination will not be fully overcome until all fear of rejection by God disappears from Earth. Fear can only be overcome by love. The tragedy is that fear prevents love from being expressed or experienced. Therefore your mission, dearly beloved, must be to overcome fear within yourselves, and then, in fearlessness, to express your certainty that God loves humanity as the Sons and Daughters of God.

Know that, and the devil shall wither away.

Lucifer cannot sustain his rebellion on his own. He has strength only to the degree that you permit the illusion of separation and the fear of rejection to prevail.

> **And I heard a loud voice saying in Heaven, "Now have come salvation and strength, and the Kingdom of our God, and the power of His Christ; for the accuser of our brethren is cast down, which accused them before our God day and night."**
>
> **REVELATION 12:10**

There is a great celebration in heaven when this cataclysmic event occurs. It means that the forces of self-rejection are defeated at a suprahuman level—where they originated.

Eve represents early humanity. She was innocent. Her curiosity was good. She was tempted by the "serpent called the Devil and Satan," to eat of the fruit of the Tree of the Knowledge of Good and Evil. It was natural for Eve—early humanity—to be attracted to the Tree of Knowledge. Through Satan, however, a disease of consciousness infected the tender self-consciousness of early humanity. It was the disease of the fear of God. It was a lie, a defect of information, lodged in the impressionable mind of early humanity.

What was not natural was for Eve to have reached to the Tree of Knowledge by the signal of the serpent. She would have made it on her own. Self-consciousness is a natural stage in the development of co-creative beings. It is the early stages of individuation needed for apprentice co-creators, potential natural Christs.

I, Jesus, have come to inform you that humanity is innocent of the conscious intent to reject God. You have been infected by a disease of a higher being than your own.

This is why so many angels are attending your birth. You are a wounded Cosmic Child, wounded not by your own inherent defect, but by the aberration of Satan, who invaded your minds at an impressionable stage, and distorted the Design, much as a virus can enter the genes of an embryo and cause the cells to err—missing the mark of the perfect design imbedded in every cell.

There are two defects from which you suffer, carnivorous behavior and the illusion of separation from God. Neither are of human origin. The animals made the first mistake when they killed to survive. Satan made the second mistake when he rejected God.

*You, beloved, have been struggling to overcome twin defects which you did not **intentionally** cause.*

You are innocent, O humanity. The forces of God are on your side.

This awareness of your innocence is essential for your salvation.

Do not feel guilty. You are innocent. You inherited the defects of other forms of life. Forgive the animal for eating flesh. Forgive Satan for fearing God. Forgive yourselves, who inherited these mistakes, and correct them. You are empowered to correct the twin defects that have plagued humanity—violence and the illusion of separation from God.

Love the animal in the world and in yourself, and do not kill him any-more.

Love Satan, my fallen brother, and do not let him make you reject God any more.

> **"And they overcame him by the blood of the Lamb and by the word of their testimony, and they loved not their own lives unto the death."**
>
> Revelation 12: 11

Michael and his angels—suprahuman personifications of God—overcome Satan, by the power of the blood of the Lamb. This means that the lifeforce of the risen Son of God defeats the death-force of the fallen angel of God. Within each of you, dearly beloved, is the fallen-angel-of-God consciousness and the risen-Son-of-God consciousness. The fallen angel is that impulse in your being that urges you to believe only what your creature senses tell you: that you are separate from God and you will surely die.

The risen Son of God is that impulse in your being that urges you to believe what your Higher Self tells you—that you are one with God and will surely have life ever-evolving.

Each of you has a choice on a personal level as to which voice to believe, the fallen angel or the risen Son. According to that choice you shall fall or rise.

There is also the social choice, which is beyond the personal choice. It is the social choice for which you have now come, dearly beloved. You are here to help everyone who can personally be attracted to a personal future as a co-creator to do so, en masse, all at once. This power will be great enough to overcome the devil nonviolently.

The Book of Revelation reveals the violent scenario to salvation, wherein the good are killed to get rid of the bad, as in Sodom and Gomorrah. The Book of Co-Creation reveals the gentle scenario to salvation, wherein the good create a field of empathetic force so powerful that the fallen angel of God himself revives and returns willingly to God.

This scenario has not been offered until now. It has come into being because there has grown up in the world a generation of lovers of the future who believe in me, and in their capacity to become me.

They are you, dearly beloved.

It is for a heroic attempt to save the Cosmic Child from a violent birth that you were sent.

Never fear. God is near. Amen.

> "Therefore rejoice, ye heavens, and ye that dwell in them! Woe to the inhabitants of the earth and of the sea! For the devil has come down unto you, full of great wrath, because he knoweth that he hath but a short time."
>
> And I looked and lo, a Lamb stood on Mount Zion, and with Him a hundred forty and four thousand, having His Father's name written on their foreheads. And I heard a voice from Heaven as the voice of many waters, and as the voice of a great thunder, and I heard the voice of harpists harping with their harps. And they sang, as it were, a new song before the throne, and before the four living beings and the elders; and no man could learn that song, except the hundred and forty and four thousand who were redeemed from the earth.
>
> REVELATION 12:12; 14:1-3

In the midst of the tribulations, the one hundred forty-four thousand co-workers of Christ assemble. The decisive moment of selection has almost come. The judgment of the quick and the dead is about to be made. The end of this phase of evolution is nearly complete.

These one hundred forty-four thousand are the children of the new Israel. They are offspring of the idea of one God and the partnership of God and humanity.

They come from the twelve tribes of Israel, which are all the tribes of the peoples of Earth. Remember, from this point of view, "Israel" is a thought, not a blood-type or a place. In every culture there are those who believe there is one God, one humanity, one way of love, one truth, one unity of infinite diversity, in which each person attunes to the mind of God.

These one hundred forty-four thousand are not the only ones who will be saved at the final hour. They are the first. They were assembled before the final days to help in the process of mediation.

No one can force another to grow.

No one can force another to know.

No one can force another to choose life ever-evolving.

*However, it is possible to **attract** others to grow, to attract others to know, to attract others to choose life ever-evolving. This is the purpose of the one hundred forty-four thousand: to act as intermediate links between self-consciousness and God-consciousness.*

The one hundred forty-four thousand are those who have been totally magnetized by their potential to be like me. They radiate a natural enthusiasm and joy, which can encourage others to acknowledge their own potential to be joint-heirs with Christ.

Those with the seal of the living God on their foreheads will be with Christ at the time of the transformation. They will serve as beacons of light, educators and emancipators, and as models of love, wisdom, faith, courage, patience, power and surrender—the seven spirits of God.

These humans will "sing a new song" before the four living beings and the elders. They are the "first fruits" of your belief in the power to transform from Homo sapiens *to* Homo universalis.

Every child born sings a new song. Every planetary system that gives birth to universal beings, natural Christs, sings a new song. Individuality is inherent in the nature of reality. We are born to be unique. The more we evolve, the more original we become.

Dearly beloved, affirm the best within yourselves. Listen carefully to your inner calling and follow it to completion. For you are to sing a new song with me, a song never heard by the living beings or the elders.

This is the birth song of humanity awakening as heirs to the Kingdom, co-creators with Christ, participants in universal affairs.

These are they who were not defiled with women, for they are virgins. These are they who follow the Lamb whithersoever He goeth. These are the redeemed from among men, being the firstfruits unto God and to the Lamb. And in their mouth was found no guile, for they are without fault before the throne of God.

REVELATION 14:4-5

What does it mean to be a virgin, one who follows the Lamb wherever it goes?

It means to be one of those who puts this purpose first, who gives first priority to the Kingdom, the realization of their full potential to be me, a natural Christ.

Virgin means pure. What is pure about us?

A pure intention to follow me, and a pure attention on your potential to be me, marks you as one of those sealed with the seal of the living God.

In a deeper sense, your virginity springs from the same source as the virginity of Mary. She was conceived by sexual intercourse, yet was free, from the moment of conception, from any stain of the so-called "original sin."

This means she never suffered from the defect of the illusion of separation of herself from God. For that illusion is the original sin, the missing of the mark.

From the moment of birth she knew she was co-creative with God. She had perfect faith because she was uncorrupted by the error of thinking she was alone in a dying body. Her cells were never imprinted with the fear of death.

Mary, too, was an evolutionary mutation. It was due to her total awareness of her union with God that she was selected to bear the seed of a first future human, the human-we-are-to-become, who knows he or she is the heir of the Kingdom of the Creator of all being.

The Virgin Mary was a human who never forgot that she was the child of God. Yet she was mortal. She was conceived by humans. She was a first step.

Jesus was the second step. His mind was utterly unaffected, never infected, by the idea of death. His mind was attuned to the mind of God, and his body was programmed to follow God's intention rather than the mammalian programming of multicellular life. He was a new seed, an individual quantum leap, as are all mutations.

The third step is the one hundred forty-four thousand. They are the first fruits of the new seed. Born of humans, sufferers from the illusion of separation, we are, nonetheless, by pure attention and intention, self-evolving from creatures to co-creators.

We who are virgins, we who follow the Lamb wherever he goes, we are the missing links between self-centered humans and whole-centered humans; we are the ordinary become the new norm; we are beacons of light unto ourselves and therefore to others. We are normalizing the unique mutation by growing the seed in ourselves.

The Virgin Mary, Jesus, the one hundred forty-four thousand, and finally all humans who choose to follow their potential to be like Christ, heirs of God—this is the evolutionary progression, the process of seeding human beings with new life beyond the mammalian, terrestrial phase.

These words, "Virgin Mary," "Jesus," the "elect," "Israel," the "New Jerusalem," must be reinterpreted now. They do not relate to doctrines, ideologies, institutions, powers or principalities. They relate to human potentials in every person on Earth.

The Virgin Mary is our potential to be perfectly pure in our intention and attention.

Jesus Christ is our potential to have a personal future in a transformed body in alignment with the pattern of evolution.

The one hundred forty-four thousand sealed with the seal of the living God are all of us now choosing to believe in and act upon our capacity to be co-creators.

Israel is the idea of humanity and God as One. It is the idea of the transformation of this world to a New Earth. It is the idea of the transformation of this body to a new body. It is the idea of the selection of the God-centered from the self-centered. It is the idea of the evolution of humanity from Adam of the living soul to Adam of the life-giving Spirit, from *Homo sapiens* to *Homo universalis.*

The New Jerusalem is our potential, collectively, to transcend all creature/human limitations through the harmonious use of our capacities, achieving a society of Universal Humans whose minds and bodies are total reflections of the mind of God.

All power, all glory, all life is potentially yours. That is the meaning of the New Jerusalem.

> And I saw another angel fly in the midst of Heaven, having the everlasting Gospel to preach unto those who dwell on the earth, and to every nation and kindred, and tongue and people, saying with a loud voice, "Fear God and give glory to Him, for the hour of His Judgment has come. Worship Him who made Heaven and earth, and the sea and the fountains of waters."
>
> REVELATION 14:6-7

There are many attendants at the birth of Universal Humanity. You are indeed a blessed child. You are the collective prodigal son. You are eagerly awaited by those who love you and have tended you throughout your gestation in the womb of Earth.

Your planet is beloved. Your triumph over Satan, that is, over the illusion of separation, will be a victory for the universal community. Your victory will encourage millions of planetary systems throughout the universe who are struggling to be born—with less help than you, and with less genius among their members.

Planet Earth is especially favored for the genius of your race. Your artists, your scientists, your inventors, your heroes and heroines of freedom, your mystics have rare and precious capacities known throughout the universe.

As the birth of Christ was heralded on Earth, so the birth of the Cosmic Child, Universal Humanity, is now heralded throughout the universal community.

Be glad, humanity, the end of the birth trauma is near. The promises will be kept. Not a hair will be lost, not a thought will be unnoticed, not a gesture will be forgotten.

> **And there followed another angel, saying, "Babylon is fallen! Fallen is that great city, because she made all nations drink of the wine of the wrath of her fornication."**
>
> REVELATION 14:8

The great city of materialistic life is fallen forever. Babylon, Sodom and Gomorrah—gone, gone, gone. So be it.

Babylon falls as the New Jerusalem rises. The great strand of belief in separation, which human intellect and individuality built, is to be absorbed into the co-creation of the New Jerusalem through the marriage of Christ and Eve. The devil—the illusion of separation—is dispelled by the consummation of the union of human intellect with divine love. Ego is attracted to its real fulfillment through the wedding of the intellect with the Higher Self.

Intellect is delighted by the enlightenment it receives when it unites with intuition. In this union it knows the invisible technologies of creation *directly* by *identity.*

The period of self-consciousness is over when the union of Christ and Eve occurs. The period of materialistic science gives way to the period of co-creative science when humans function as natural partners with God.

The period of separate sects and dogmas gives way to the period of co-creative consciousness when everyone is attuning to the same pattern and is attracted to fulfilling their unique capacities to be a Universal Humans.

Churches, mosques, temples and spiritual centers of all kinds have been preservers of the new seed of the future human. They shall all be honored and celebrated as keepers of the flame of expectation during the process of our birth from the womb of Earthbound consciousness and life.

There shall be no new church.

There shall be no new religion.

There shall be only the union of everyone with God.

And the third angel followed them, saying with a loud voice, "If any man worship the beast and his image, and receive his mark on his forehead or on his hand, the same shall drink of the wine of the wrath of God, which is poured out unmixed into the cup of His indignation; and he shall be tormented with fire and brimstone in the presence of the holy angels and in the presence of the Lamb. And the smoke of their torment ascendeth up for ever and ever, and they have no rest day or night, those who worship the beast and his image, and whosoever receiveth the mark of his name."

REVELATION 14:9-11

Dearly beloved, let us do away, once and for all, with this childish threat of hellfire and brimstone for those who do not believe in me. The end is near. The old play is almost over. Suffice it to say, that if you do not choose to evolve into a wholesome, co-creative human, then you shall not.

The only punishment is your self-exclusion from the joy of new life. The only pity is that you are missing the mark and choosing to die unfulfilled.

There need be no greater punishment. There need be no threats. There is only choice. That is the purpose of freedom. Only those who choose to evolve, do.

Henceforth, the choice is yours.

I hereby abrogate all threats of punishment except the only one that matters: If you do not choose to fulfill your potential to become a full human, you shall not.

Here is the patience of the saints: here are those who keep the commandments of God, and the faith of Jesus. And I heard a voice from Heaven, saying unto me, "Write: 'Blessed are the dead who die in the Lord from henceforth.' " "Yea," saith the Spirit, "that they may rest from their labors, and their works do follow them."

REVELATION 14: 12-13

Dearly beloved, have absolute faith that my promise shall be kept. Everyone who has believed in me, or believes in me now, shall have life ever-evolving.

Every thought you think is registered in the Mind of God. If you intend to be like me, it means you have recorded or elected the program of transformation to be triggered in your system.

If you die before the "fullness of time," you shall be reconstituted in a new body, as I was. The process of reconstitution is similar to the formation of a full-term child from a fertilized egg.

You are reconstituted from the DNA code and from your neuronally imprinted memories, which are recorded in the Book of Life from which I will read at the time of selection. The reconstitution process is a speeded gestation. The code of the new body is different than that for the mammalian body in which you incarnated on Earth. The new body bears the same characteristics; it is tangible; that is, it has a new materiality. It can move objects and be seen. It is capable of dematerialization and rematerialization, self-regeneration and self-transformation. It is wholly reflective of your godly intention to create according to the Design of God.

Do not be surprised at this new body, dearly beloved. You have witnessed the process of evolution wherein I create new bodies to transcend new limits time and time again.

I created fish to swim in the seas. I created birds to fly in the air. I created animals to run on the ground.

I created humans to understand how I do these things, so that they can do them with me, so that they can join with me in the designing process, creating new bodies for themselves to overcome the new limits of terrestrial humanity imposed by death, self-consciousness and planet-boundedness.

The new body you will co-create with me (by your registered intention to do so, by your choice for eternal life now recorded in the Book of Life) is a body that:

> *is sensitive to the God-within at all times,*
> *transcends self-consciousness,*
> *can self-transform,*

does not die,

is capable of ascension, meaning that it can materialize and dematerialize at will.

*Your current space programs and genetic research are **very early phases** of new bodybuilding. Their purpose is to reveal to you how my invisible technologies of transformation and bodybuilding work, so that you may use them at will.*

If you do not choose to have a new body to co-create with me, you will not have one. You may choose an impersonal future rather than the transpersonal future. The impersonal future is bodiless. You divest yourself of your personal memory and your DNA, and become an undifferentiated aspect of God.

The saints who are so impatient are those who believed in me and elected to follow my example, which is to have a new body in which to continue the work of creation.

They shall be fulfilled in the fullness of time.

Those of you who happen to be alive at the time of the actual Quantum Instant, will be changed while still alive. You will not have to undergo physical death or the reconstitution process.

Your co-creative system will turn on. It is being prepared now. Can you experience your bodychange process happening now?

Do you desire regeneration? Do you feel an inner radiation? Do you sense a quantum change? Do you have a flame of expectation exciting you from within?

If so, you are being prepared, or rather, you are preparing yourselves to be ready when the selection process comes.

Since no one knows exactly when that will be, you must prepare for both eventualities: the possibility that you will die before the selection process; the possibility that you will be alive or "quick," when it happens.

In the first case, you will be reconstituted. In the second case, you will be transformed.

John wrote then, "Blessed are the dead who die in the Lord...their works do follow them."

*I say now, "Blessed are the living who transform **as** the Lord; their works shall live on with them." Hallelujah. Praise God. Amen.*

> And I looked, and behold, a white cloud; and upon the cloud sat one like unto the Son of Man, having on his head a golden crown and in his hand a sharp sickle. And another angel came out of the temple, crying with a loud voice to him who sat on the cloud, "Thrust out thy sickle and reap; for the time is come for thee to reap, for the harvest of the earth is ripe." And he who sat on the cloud thrust out his sickle on the earth, and the earth was reaped.
>
> REVELATION 14:14-16

Dearly beloved, I approached the crucifixion far more easily than I approach the selection. The crucifixion was done unto my body. The selection will be done unto yours.

I was prepared. You are not.

It is I that is holding, holding, holding for the last possible moment to see if this cup may be avoided for your sake.

I asked my Father if I could avoid the cup—the agony at Gethsemane. The answer was: No, your physical body must die in order to demonstrate the human potential of the resurrection and the ascension.

I submitted voluntarily to the crucifixion, to lodge the expectation of the triumph over death in the hearts of those who desire to follow me and do as I did. The expectation is now creating the actuality.

The question remains: Do you on Earth have to undergo the collective crucifixion known as the tribulations, in order to rise again in new bodies?

The answer is not yet fully registered in the Mind of God. The answer depends on how many of you register your intention to do as I did. If a critical mass of the human population were to choose a godlike future, the devastation could be avoided, the birth could be graceful, the attractors could attract the vast majority of humanity.

This critical mass represents those marked with the seal of the living God on their foreheads. They are all now sensing a total urgency to communicate the good news in every language, in all tongues, in a variety of symbols. They are impelled from within to link up with everyone who shares the same aspiration. They are finding each other at an increasingly rapid rate, brightening the flame of expectation that now rises like fire in the night across the weeping face of my beloved Earth.

Arise and alight and enflame your fellow humans with the expectation of life ever-evolving as co-creators of the future.

Use the broadest possible language.

Use music and art and symbols.

Sound the drums!

Ring the bells!

Throw open the windows and shout:

Yes! Yes! We will go forward to a future of unlimited possibilities!

Yes! Yes! We are born into this universe of immeasurable life!

Yes! Yes! We are the Sons and Daughters of Creation!

Dearly beloved, I wait for you to do your work in the world as faithfully as I did mine. Together we can save the world from the pain of a violent birth.

The half hour of silence in Heaven is almost over. The angels are impatient. The saints are impatient.

I am patient.

I wait for you.

> And another angel came out of the temple which is in Heaven, he also having a sharp sickle. And another angel came out from the altar, who had power over fire, and cried with a loud cry to him who had the sharp sickle, saying, "Thrust out thy sharp sickle and gather the clusters of the vine of the earth, for her grapes are fully ripe." And the angel thrust in his sickle into the earth, and gathered the vine of the earth, and cast it into the great wine press of the wrath of God. And the wine press was trodden outside the city, and blood came out of the wine press, even unto the horse bridles, by the space of a thousand and six hundred furlongs.
>
> REVELATION 14:17-20

John saw the negative scenario, the violent birth that will occur if those sealed with the seal of the living God fail to do their work now.

The process of selection in a violent birth is crude. Vast destruction grotesquely rips apart the fabric of the body politic, as a difficult birth tears the flesh of a mother in labor.

All who die will be resurrected, as I said. But there is a great difference in the future health of a planet that undergoes a violent birth, as contrasted to one that undergoes a gentle birth. The planetary future of the violent birth is retarded forever by the shock to its systems.

Remember, every thought and intention is registered in the Mind of God. So is every pain, every wound, every tear, every hurt. When the slightest injury befalls the smallest child on Earth, it is recorded forever in the Mind of God.

Why does God not intervene to save the world?

If you but think a minute, you will see the answer to this question: The Creator laid down a law as fundamental as the law of gravity: no one is **forced** *to evolve; only those who choose to inherit the powers of creation will do so. The Law of Freedom is inherent in the nature of reality.*

Therefore, your future is your choice, personally and collectively. We can communicate, awaken, promise and reveal. But only you alive now can act.

There is free will. How could it be otherwise? The purpose of evolution is to select for godly qualities, of which freedom is the absolutely essential key.

"Gather the clusters of the vine of the Earth; for her grapes are fully ripe." The angel is right. The grapes of the vines of Earth are fully ripe. You have little time left to harvest them.

We still have time, dearly beloved, to prevent hell from breaking out on Earth. Famine, nuclear war, biospheric collapse, the armies of the hungry invading the lands of the fat and the full—all of these dangers are imminent, waiting for you to do your best for the world, which you so dearly love that you have chosen to commit your life, your fortune, and your sacred honor for the cause of all humankind.

The cause is life ever-evolving as Sons and Daughters of creation. The cause is universal life. And you knew it all the time.

It has been told you from India.

It has been told you from Egypt.

It has been told you from Greece.

It has been told you from Israel.

It has been told you from Arabia.

And now it has been told you from the New World—the place where people who dreamed of universal freedom for all came to launch the great experiment of opportunity for life-everlasting for every man, woman and child on Earth.

Add to the Four Freedoms the freedom of life-everlasting, and you have the power that builds the new worlds, that ushers in the future of the newborn Cosmic Child named Universal Humanity.

O angels, hold your fire, hold your brimstone, hold your plagues and famines and wars for one more golden instant of cosmic time, lest the bell tolls for my beloved peoples of Earth.

> And I saw another sign in Heaven, great and marvelous: seven angels holding the seven last plagues, for in them is completed the wrath of God. And I saw, as it were, a sea of glass mingled with fire, and those who had gotten the victory over the beast, and over his image, and over his mark, and over the number of his name, standing on the sea of glass and holding the harps of God. And they were singing the song of Moses, the servant of God, and the song of the Lamb, saying, "Great and marvelous are Thy works, Lord God Almighty! Just and true are Thy ways, Thou King of Saints! Who shall not fear Thee, O Lord, and glorify Thy name? For Thou only art holy. For all nations shall come and worship before Thee, for Thy judgments are made manifest."
>
> Revelation 15:1-4

Just before the final wave of tribulations—the seven last plagues—those who resist evil, those who are victorious in their struggle against the temptation of separation, stand upon a burning sea of glass.

Ah, dearly beloved! Can you imagine what a burning sea of glass might be?

I will tell you. It is the transformation of matter, the very atoms of the material world. It is the quickening of the vibrations of the entire atomic structure that composes the material of Earth, and of your bodies that are made of Earth.

Four billion years ago I composed the material of Earth out of simple atoms of hydrogen and helium. This material has been recycled since then in my bodies on Earth—in the molecules of the early seas, in the cells of the first Earth, in the animals and vegetables that crept up upon the land, in the humans who grew a large brain out of the dust of the Earth and lifted their eyes to discover me, their Creator.

At the time of planetary birth, the atoms on Earth are changed: the mineral, vegetable, animal and machine Kingdoms all become more transparent, like glass, through which the invisible force can be seen by all with eyes to see and ears to hear.

Just before the end shall come, those who are to be saved will be quickened. They will "stand on the sea of glass." This means they will be transformed visibly from Adam of the living soul to Adam of the life-giving Spirit. The Holy Spirit, which had been sent as your comforter and communicator from God's intelligence for two thousand years, now has a new task. It intensifies its signals; it infuses matter with intelligence, thereby transforming the very essence of the material world.

Do you find this hard to believe? Why should you? Just look back at what I have already done:

I created a universe.

I created billions of galaxies.

I created billions and billions of life systems like your own.

I created life forms beyond imagining.

I created you out of nothing.

Do you suppose that I can do no more? That I am finished? That I intend to stop with you, on the face of a tiny planet, far away from the central uni-

versal community, at the parochial outskirts of a remote galaxy called the Milky Way?

Do you suppose that I intend to leave you like this, like fireflies in the night, glowing for an instant then going out forever?

No, dearly beloved. You can see that I am not finished with you. I will never be finished with you if you choose never to be finished with me. I will go on to the uttermost creative limits of the universe with those of you who will put your mind in tune with mine.

I created you to go on with me to universal acts of creation that are beyond the acts of Jesus, as the billions of galaxies are beyond the acts of a single planet called Earth.

Jesus demonstrated a phase of consciousness that occurs everywhere in the universe between terrestrial and universal life. This consciousness is the guide through the transition. It is legion. It manifests by the billions.

This is why he told you that you would do as he and even more would you do.

It is true. You are born into a universe of infinite capacity. You have just begun.

Open your eyes and see the glory of your future with me.

> And after that I looked, and behold, the temple of the tabernacle of the testimony in Heaven was opened; and the seven angels, holding the seven plagues, came out of the temple, clothed in pure and white linen and having their breasts girded with golden girdles. And one of the four living beings gave unto the seven angels seven golden vials full of the wrath of God, who liveth for ever and ever. And the temple was filled with smoke from the glory of God and from His power, and no man was able to enter into the temple until the seven plagues of the seven angels were fulfilled.
>
> REVELATION 15:5-8

The transformation is about to begin. Those who are to evolve are even now transforming their material bodies. A new material is being generated out of the old.

Look at your bodies right now.

Be aware they are composed of energy-in-action. The appearance of solid flesh is an abstraction produced by your animal senses, suitable for the phase of evolution now passing. The disappearance of solid flesh occurs through a slight change in the frequency at which atoms vibrate. Have you seen water become steam? Have you seen water become ice? So will you see water become as burning glass. Your body is made up largely of water. The water in you will change to resonate with the sound vibrations of the "trumpet," or voice or signal of the God-force, which is directed intentionally upon you.

The body-change, the inner radiation which some of you now feel, is a preliminary experience to prepare you for the alchemy you are about to undergo.

As the evolving are in the process of transformation, the last of the plagues begin for the purpose of the final purification of Earth.

> And I saw three unclean spirits like frogs come out of the mouth of the dragon, and out of the mouth of the beast, and out of the mouth of the false prophet. For they are the spirits of devils working miracles, which go forth unto the kings of the earth and of the whole world, to gather them for the battle on that great Day of God Almighty. "Behold, I come as a thief. Blessed is he that watcheth and keepeth his garments, lest he walk naked, and they see his shame." And the devils gathered them together at a place called in the Hebrew tongue, Armageddon.
>
> REVELATION 16:13-16

Armageddon is, dearly beloved, the dreadful script which you and I rewrite now.

Yes, it is possible that "the spirits of devils will go forth unto the kings of the Earth," tempting them with miracles of power to control the people. This temptation of selfish control by the powers that be, leads to the battle of Armageddon and the violent destruction of life as you have known it.

Armageddon is known with terror throughout the universe. Whenever a cosmic child is born through a violent birth, the bell tolls throughout the universe in pain and pity for the suffering child.

It is possible that the leaders of the world will be tempted to global suicide. They shall be gathered into the place called Armageddon.

Dearly beloved, I am pained beyond words to have to endure the continual repetition of the violent path to life ever-evolving. It will be a self-fulfilling prophecy if we force ourselves to continue contemplating this disastrous set of events. We will bring them on by repeating them one more time. Therefore, we will not repeat them.

> and there came a great voice out of the temple of Heaven from the throne, saying, "IT IS DONE!" And there were voices and thunders and lightnings; and there was a great earthquake, such as has not been since men were upon the earth, so mighty an earthquake and so great. And the great city was divided into three parts, and the cities of the nations fell, and great Babylon came to remembrance before God, to give unto her the cup of the wine of the fierceness of His wrath. And every island fled away, and the mountains were not found. And there fell upon men a great hail out of heaven, every stone about the weight of a talent; and men blasphemed God because of the plague of the hail, for the plague thereof was exceeding great.
>
> REVELATION 16:17-21

Just before birth, as the head of the child bears down upon the flesh of the mother, the pain intensifies and the waters break. Once the head emerges through the barrier of the body of the mother, there is no turning back. There is no going home again. "It is done." Everything that can be done must be done before that critical instant of maximum danger to the whole child.

The aborning organism is pressed out of shape to emerge through the narrow passage. The head is deformed. The oxygen supply is cut off as the umbilical cord no longer connects the child to the mother. The warmth of the womb is replaced by the cold glare of lights, people, instruments of birth.

Terror! The child is totally helpless! This magnificent creature who has built a miraculous body in the womb—with exquisite precision constructing eyes, brain and organs according to a design evolved over billions of years of experiment—is rendered suddenly endangered and humiliated.

Has the design gone astray? What did I do wrong? How could I have failed? Why am I punished when I have faithfully worked since my conception as a single cell, to build this fabulous body which is perfectly suited to the womb as my everlasting home!

How could God be so cruel as to expel me from the world I have known in the womb of my mother, where nature supplied me with all my requirements and I lived in harmony with my environment, working at the meaningful tasks of building this marvelous being and hoping to stay forever so well adapted to the watery womb in which I have faithfully floated since time began?

I am so wise—or once I thought I was. I have been a single cell, too small to be seen, holding in my heart a secret purpose to build a world I've never seen. I have been a multicellular organism, dividing, dividing, dividing as though I were immortal. I gained a foothold in the womb and drew nourishment from Mother Nature.

Then I heard an inner voice, sending currents of chemical commands to each of my millions of cells to differentiate. Form the head! Form the foot! Form the hand! Build an ear! Construct a brain!

Each of my cells felt called upon by a mysterious vocational urge to do more, be more, want more than simply dividing to reproduce.

We went to work—just why we did not know—and built an edifice of beauty through devoted co-operation and absolute fidelity to the design each of us held in our hearts. We felt drawn to each other in organic networks of shared aspiration. Those who were attracted to eye-building made a great team! Those who loved bone-making constructed a fantastic skeleton. Those who were drawn to the intelligence of the whole built the nervous system and incredible brain.

We became a fish-like creature. We developed proto-gills. We know what it's like to breath underwater. We are kin to all those who live in the sea.

Then we matured like little mammals. You could hardly distinguish us from an embryo monkey or rabbit or mouse. We developed our little hearts and stomachs, and the reproductive organs—different for the male and the female.

We wondered why we were building all these strange and wondrous technologies when, in fact, we were perfectly content as a happy cluster of single cells.

Why? Why? Why? some began to ask, do we have to keep on growing? Yet the inner urge to build, to experiment with new possibilities, motivated us to do more.

Soon we felt complete. Victory was at hand. We had overcome the challenges of survival in a womblike world and were finally able to rest, relax and enjoy what we had so laboriously accomplished.

We began to press a bit heavily upon the walls of our womb—for, in fact, we found we could not stop growing, even though our wisest leaders advised us to limit growth and adapt to the "natural" world.

A controversy sprang up between the cells of the body and the cells of the brain. The body cells wanted to stay as they were and repeat the tasks they had learned so well to do. They wanted to build another set of eyes and ears, and one more heart, since they knew the joy of working by hand as their parents had done before them.

But the rabble-rousers in the brain kept sending signals of warning and discontent and, believe it or not, excitement about a new future! "Something new is coming," they said.

"What is coming?" the contented cells asked. "What do we need with a future different than the magnificent beauty of this womb, and this companionship with each other that we have known and loved, since time immemorial? Can't you leave well enough alone?"

Yet we kept growing. New cells kept emerging with the urge to build, to do, to know. The crowding became a problem.

Resources were short. The brain used too much energy. The limbs were straining. Pollution arose as the environment could not carry off the wastes of such an extraordinary number of growing cells.

"Environmentalists" organized to protect the womb from the organism. "Theologians" who were responsible for interpreting the design preached guilt to the cells who kept on building beyond the requirements of the present world. "Futurists" complained that within a short time, social collapse would occur. Limits to growth were propounded.

"Vigilantes" emerged to suppress the vibrant cells who kept signalling: More is coming! Be prepared! Expect the unexpected! Anticipate the new! These bearers of glad tidings were ignored by the experts of the womb-environment, and the interpreters of the ancient design. Every effort was made to convince the majority of cells not to raise their expectations, but rather to be satisfied with stewarding what their ancestors had created.

And yet the organism kept growing.

"Doomsday is coming!"

"Prepare for the End!"

"Survivalists" asked for whom the bell tolls, and answered, "It tolls for us all."

"The future will be worse than the past," they said. The nervous system communicated a fear of The End. The organism paused in confusion. Its leaders who had led from the single cell to this gigantic civilization of cells, fought with each other.

The voices of hope were drowned out by the cacophony of despair. Depression, anger, alienation and pessimism prevailed. Then, a silence suddenly descended. A pause. We were poised, waiting.

Some of us remembered a voice which had arisen within us eons ago, saying, "Prepare for the future. The Kingdom of Heaven is at hand. You shall have life everlasting if you believe in the goodness of the Design and the goodness of each other. I will show you that you need not be afraid of what is to come. I will demonstrate that the death of this world is the beginning of the new. I will die and I will rise again. And so shall you in the fullness of time, if you follow the Design and have faith in me. You shall do as I do, and even greater works shall you do."

Suddenly all hell broke loose. The walls of our secure world began to move. Terrible earthquakes rent the body asunder. We were ripped from our source of nourishment. Starvation, suffocation, deformation. We began to move out of the womb. Down a narrow passage we were forced.

We followed the irresistible force of the contractions, finding ourselves pushing beyond the "biosphere" in which we lived. We remembered the ancient words which had long been forgotten: "For now we see through a glass darkly; but then face to face." "The sufferings of this present time are not worthy to be compared with the glory which shall be revealed in us."

Into the new environment we came, in a twinkling of an eye. And we were all raised up to a new awareness.

The eyes we had built so beautifully in the womb opened for the first time, though unable as yet to see. The ears we had designed in the silence of our world, suddenly picked up strange wondrous sounds. The muscles we had built for the joy of it while floating in the womb, now bore the weight of the whole body.

The heart pumped. The lungs expanded. Air rushed violently through the throat. Oxygen reached the brain.

We felt the pangs of hunger. Our mouth moved by instinctual guidance to seek a strange new source of nourishment. We had to coordinate ourselves as a whole body to draw forth the vital food. It came not from the womb we had known so well, but from outside the body which we had built. And we had to work at first to handle the strange taste of milk flowing through our body. We had never tasted anything before!

There was terrible alienation of the younger generation of cells from its elders—the last generation to live in the old world of the womb.

"Nothing that you taught us prepared us for this," they cried. "We have nothing to do. We are not needed. We shall be destroyed."

They cried and they cried, and they slept and they slept, and they hungered and they reached; they thirsted and they drank, they reached together beyond themselves to survive in the new world to which they had been born.

And with the reach outward, the agonizing cells ceased their crying. Each cell awoke to a new potential, to growth of a new kind! The nervous system reported breakthroughs instead of breakdowns.

"We're not dying. We're not starving. We're not suffocating. We're living, we're loving, we're in a new world. We have eyes to see. We have ears to hear. What they told us is true!"

The body relaxed. The trauma was over. The nervous system linked up the whole organism and began to report peace, life, excitement and love.

The eyes opened. The child saw for the first time a figure of splendid proportions, radiant with light after the darkness of the womb.

The figure gazed into the opening eyes of the awakening child. The brain cells lit up with ecstasy. They flashed a signal of joy throughout the body. "We're born! We're good! We're loved! We're needed!"

And with that the newborn child smiled, and saw many figures, many mansions, many worlds without end.

Yes, dearly beloved, Babylon fell. The cities of the material-building past in the womb are not needed in the new world. There we will build a new way, not by the sweat of our brows in an environment of scarcity, attacked by beasts from without and fear from within.

Yes, dearly beloved, Babylon fell, not because it was originally bad, but because its work had been done. It was holding on to a past mode of civilization when, in fact, the new had already come.

No more slaves.

No more inequality.

No more hunger.

No more disease.

No more death.

Only life ever-creative through love of God above all else, your neighbor as yourself, and yourself as me.

Babylon is outmoded. Rome is outmoded. We are building New Heavens and a New Earth, dearly beloved, in which everyone will be godlike.

Yes, beloved, Babylon may be destroyed by the fire of the atom which you have discovered. Armageddon may be the way you choose to be born. But you still have time to be born without the destruction of your mother's body, the loving Earth. You have the knowledge to be born gently, for the good of all. The silence in Heaven is still holding for you to bring the word to all nations.

It depends on your awareness. If you can alert the members of the social body that birth is good, that their future together is infinitely greater than their separate pasts, then all will be well. All will be very well. For Earth and its life is a jewel in the heavens, which can shine with the beauty of a well-born Cosmic Child.

The question is, are you willing to be born, or will you fight it all the way?

> And there came one of the seven angels, who had the seven vials, and talked with me, saying unto me, "Come hither; I will show unto thee the judgment upon the great whore who sitteth upon many waters, with whom the kings of the earth have committed fornication, and the inhabitants of the earth have been made drunk with the wine of her fornication."
>
> REVELATION 17:1-2

The great whore is the idea that we should sell our future in a new world for the sake of pleasure in the old world.

The great whore is the idea that we should prostitute our capacities to transcend mammalian life, in exchange for momentary accommodation.

The great whore is the idea that we are nothing but animals that eat, sleep, reproduce and die.

The great whore is the idea that we are limited to the womb of Mother Earth and the confines of our infantile, self-centered minds.

The great whore is the promise that death is the end and that, therefore, we should make merry until the end shall come.

The kings of the Earth are committing fornication with the great whore. They are promising people the possibility of life forever in the womb of Earth.

They are promising people the possibility of creature comfort with infantile entertainment. They are promising people justice without freedom to evolve. They are usurping the new capacities to transcend animal life, for the sake of war, armaments and products no longer needed on Earth.

> So he carried me away in the spirit into the wilderness; and I saw a woman sitting upon a scarlet colored beast, covered with blasphemous names, and having seven heads and ten horns. And the woman was arrayed in purple and scarlet color, and bedecked with gold and precious stones and pearls, having a golden cup in her hand full of abominations and filthiness of her fornication; and upon her forehead was a name written: "Mystery, Babylon the Great, Mother of Harlots and Abominations of the Earth."
>
> *REVELATION 17:3-5*

Babylon, the mystery woman, adapts to the creature/human stage of life and refuses to desire the new. She is the great whore who prostitutes life everlasting for a fleeting instant of pleasure and pain.

She deceives the conceivers into denying their love of the unknown, the new, the transcendent, by arousing them to repetitious acts of reproduction.

The universal woman arouses us to co-creation. The great whore arouses us to procreation without purpose in a closed world. She is death.

The universal woman is in love with the Christ-child within her and within each person. She asks us to give birth to ourselves as universal beings.

> And I saw that the woman was drunk with the blood of the saints and with the blood of the martyrs of Jesus. And when I saw her, I wondered with great amazement.
>
> *REVELATION 17:6*

The great whore desires to consume those who believe in their potential to be Christlike. She cannot withstand their attraction for life-everlasting.

She is attracted to death and dying. She hates the saints and the martyrs who were attracted to new life.

When John saw her, he was amazed that anyone could prefer death over life-everlasting. And it is amazing that the modern world, which has heard the good news of its new capacities does not believe that its potential is real.

It is amazing that the powers to transcend are used to destroy. It is amazing that the great seducer should have such power over the minds and hearts of the people.

> **And the angel said unto me, "Why dost thou marvel? I will tell thee the mystery of the woman and of the beast that carrieth her, which hath the seven heads and ten horns. The beast that thou sawest was, and is not, and shall ascend out of the bottomless pit and go into perdition; and those who dwell on the earth, and whose names were not written in the Book of Life from the foundation of the world, shall wonder when they behold the beast that was, and is not, and yet is."**
>
> **REVELATION 17:7-8**

*The "mystery" of the woman and the beast, of the great whore and the destroyer of transcendence is that they are not real. You **thought** you saw them, you believed that the passing moment was the the only reality. It was, yet it is not. It seems to be real, yet it is not real.*

What attracts your eye is a picture in your head composed by the interaction of the energy outside your body with the energy within, mediated by your senses of seeing, hearing, tasting, smelling and touching.

What your creature senses see is other than what it seems to be. Your intellect tells you this, even now, for it has penetrated the veil of matter with extended eyes of science, discovering that there is no "thing" there.

The beast shall ascend out of the bottomless pit and go into perdition. It shall disappear.

They that dwell on the Earth, whose names are not in the Book of Life, are they who gave primary reality to "the beast," to the things seen and felt with the senses alone; it is they who had no faith in things unseen and unknown, who did not believe in God above all else and love their neighbors as them-selves.

They shall wonder when they behold the disappearance of that which they held to be most real—the sensual world.

For at the end, the sensual world will "disappear" as a new stage of con-sciousness emerges. You will see the world as God-in-action, with the inner eyes of intuition. The sense of time passing will stop as you overcome self-cen-tered consciousness and the fear of death.

As you gain continuity of consciousness, which is the natural state of self-evolving beings, you will see reality with the eyes of a natural Christ.

What does this mean?

It means we will see everything as an aspect of ourselves. There will be no sense of separation. We will experience ourselves as the I AM THAT I AM. The Higher Self, which speaks to us now in parables and whispers, will be our only voice.

Our sensory system will remain intact for use when dealing with the world at the frequency of terrestrial life. We will tune down when needed, as Jesus was able to ascend and descend after his resurrection in a new body.

The sensory system will be available, as our autonomic nervous system is now available, for hygienic body maintenance. It will operate where nec-essary whenever we need to interact with the animal, vegetable and miner-al worlds.

But in our own world, we will scarcely turn on the sensual eyes. We will know as God knows, by the experience of mind to mind, thought to thought, feeling to feeling, communicated instantaneously through the whole universe of life. We will turn our attention to an event and know it by attending to it. Knowing by identity and empathy will expand our knowledge about and of the external world.

> **And this is for the mind which hath wisdom: The seven heads are seven mountains on which the woman sitteth. And there are seven kings: five are fallen, and one is, and the other has not yet come; and when he cometh, he must**

continue a short time. And the beast that was, and is not, even he is the eighth, yet is of the seven and goeth into perdition.

REVELATION 17:9-11

Remember that wisdom is vision-in-action. It is one of the seven spirits of God necessary for those who choose to become natural Christs.

Wisdom is to see reality, not as a static set of things, but as an intentional, directional process leading toward godhood for humanity.

The seven heads of the beast upon which the woman, Babylon, the great whore sits, are leading you to perdition, nonexistence, or extinction.

There are seven mountains. Mountains are terrains to climb. They are the arduous path of those who are climbing for salvation through finding security in the passing condition of the existing world.

Upon these mountains are seven kings who claim power over the material world. Most have already come and gone—the ancient and recent rulers of the material world.

One exists in power now. One is yet to come.

The beast comes out of all the seven kings; he is the heir to their Kingdom, he is the fruit of their labor, he is the castle they built in the sands of time. He was not, he is not now, and he will never be the ultimate reality.

The beast is heir to the Kingdom that never was, is not now, and never will be.

You are heir to the Kingdom that once was, is now, and ever will be.

"And the ten horns which thou sawest are ten kings, who have received no kingdom as yet, but will receive power as kings for one hour with the beast. These have one mind, and shall give their power and strength unto the beast. These shall make war with the Lamb, and the Lamb shall overcome them; for he is Lord of lords and King of kings, and those who are with Him are called, and chosen, and faithful."

REVELATION 17:12-14

Those who cling on to mortal, material existence will be opposed to the Lamb, who stands for evolving existence and co-creative reality, the at-one-ment of humanity with God.

*The Lamb shall inevitably win. For he is King of Kings. He represents the next stage of evolution. His will **will** be done on Earth as it is in Heaven now. It is as inevitable as the birth of the child once it begins its passage down the birth canal.*

All who are with him, all who choose to become natural Christs, will surely overcome the kings of the passing power, the beasts that disappear, the great whore of Babylon who will be forgotten—as even now we have forgotten the struggle to emerge from the womb of our mothers.

You who are called, chosen and faithful, rejoice! Victory is certain. You shall surely overcome all obstacles to life ever-evolving. It is the law. It is the way. It is the truth for you who choose to believe it and activate this belief in your lives.

Do you sense within you an inner attitude of faith, and also one of faithlessness? The attitude of faith triggers the awareness and the power that comes from being the Sons and Daughters of God. The attitude of faithlessness triggers the fear that you are nothing but dying flesh in a dying world, and which thereby disempowers you.

Practice turning on the attitude of faith. It stimulates your entire system to evolve. Just as vitamins are essential to the procreative body, whose purpose is to reproduce itself, so faith is essential to the co-creative body, whose purpose is to transform itself.

At the crossover point between Adam of the living soul and Adam of the life-giving Spirit, the procreative body tends to be at war with the co-creative body. The beast is at war with the Lamb.

The purpose of procreation seems to conflict with co-creation. One deals with the maintenance of the existing system, the other with the evolution of the new.

At a deeper level, there is no conflict. Procreation is an essential evolutionary phase. It is the phase of multicellular life during which the diverse species originated, the biosphere was built and the creature/human arose. Sexual reproduction, death, mutation and natural selection are methods of reproduction and evolution during the procreative period of evolution. This period can be dated from the first multicellular organism that reproduced sexually and died a biologically programmed death, to the first human that was not reproduced sexually and did not die a biologically programmed death—that is, Jesus Christ.

The co-creative period of human history is a natural result of the procreative phase; there is no conflict of purpose. There is only momentary confusion during the actual period of transition, which you are now experiencing.

The co-creative period will be established when "the Lamb shall overcome...and those who are with him,"—"they" being those who believe in their potential to be as Christ.

The co-creative period began with the"virgin birth" of the future human, whose mind-body system reflected a new genetic code. It was a mind-body system capable of self-conception (virgin birth), self-healing, healing others (the miracles), self-regeneration (the resurrection) and materialization and dematerialization (the loaves and fishes, the ascension).

The co-creative period of human history will be established after the tribulations, after the selection process is complete, when everybody displays the same capacities as Jesus did. Just as self-consciousness flickered on and off at the dawn of creature/human history, so co-creative consciousness is flickering on and off at the dawn of universal/human history.

Its first description was the visionary glimpse that John saw and called the New Jerusalem. Far, far more will come to you, my dearly beloved members of the New Order of the Future.

And he saith unto me, "The waters which thou sawest, where the whore sitteth, are peoples and multitudes, and nations and tongues. And the ten horns which thou sawest upon the beast, these shall hate the whore, and shall make her desolate and naked, and shall eat her flesh and burn her with fire. For God hath put into their hearts to fulfill His will and to agree, and to give their kingdom unto the beast, until the words of God shall

**be fulfilled. And the woman whom thous sawest is that
great city which reigneth over the kings of the earth."**

REVELATION 17:15-18

In the long run, temporal, material power run amok will destroy itself.
It is like cancer. If a cancer cell succeeds sufficiently in spreading to the
healthy tissue, it thereby kills itself.

There is no way we can continue to grow exponentially in the womb of
Earth.

The great whore, Babylon, is still tempting us to build more and more
of the same. The Quantum Transformation is at hand.

The first misuse of power—represented by the ten horns—will destroy
the **source** of the misuse of power, which is self-centered consciousness.
This form of consciousness is rendered obsolete by the human discovery of
the powers of co-creation, which can destroy or evolve all life.

The powers of materialism and selfishness will eventually destroy themselves. For example, if self-centered nations use nuclear bombs to gain self-
centered purposes, they will destroy self-centeredness! For they will destroy
themselves. Cancer destroys cancer. 1x0=0. If you multiply our oneness by
the nothingness of self-centeredness, you get nothing. Nothing times
something is nothing.

The "ten horns" are the ten kings who have as yet received no Kingdom
but who receive power as kings one hour with "the beast." They are the
final manipulators of material-scientific power for selfish purposes. They
have "agreed" with God to "give their Kingdom unto the beast, until the
words of God shall be fulfilled." This means that the final misuse of temporal power is part of the negative scenario. The situation has to become
intolerable before it can improve. As long as there is even a *modicum* of
hope that the situation can continue in the old way, the powers that be will
remain in control. For people are inherently conservative. They rarely give
up a familiar evil for an unknown good—unless forced to.

Of course, in the alternative scenario, they are attracted to the new
rather than forced to give up the old.

If the positive scenario is enacted, it will not be necessary for Babylon to be destroyed by hellfire and brimstone, by nuclear bombs and biospheric collapse. Babylon will become a museum, part of the interesting heritage of our past, as are the early tools of *Homo erectus* or the fossils of the fish that first established themselves at the shoreline of the sea, between the marine and the terrestrial worlds.

The main point is, the words of God will be fulfilled on Earth as it is in Heaven.

It can be graceful.

It can be violent.

That is up to us.

> And after these things, I saw another angel come down from Heaven, having great power; and the earth was lightened by his glory. And he cried mightily with a strong voice, saying, "Babylon the great is fallen, is fallen, and is become the habitation of devils, and the stronghold of every foul spirit, and a cage of every unclean and hateful bird. For all nations have drunk the wine of the wrath of her fornication; and the kings of the earth have committed fornication with her, and the merchants of the earth have waxed rich through the abundance of her sensuous pleasures." And I heard another voice from Heaven, saying, "Come out of her, my people, that ye be not partakers of her sins, and that ye receive not of her plagues; for her sins have reached unto Heaven, and God hath remembered her iniquities. Reward her even as she has rewarded you, and return double unto her according to her works; in the cup which she hath filled, fill to her double. How much she hath glorified herself and lived voluptuously! That much torment and sorrow give back to her; for she saith in her heart, 'I sit a queen and am no widow, and shall see no sorrow.' "
>
> *REVELATION 18:1-7*

Have you ever known those who personify *hubris*, whose pride is so profound that they assert they have no need for God, no need for help, no need for the promise of a new life; those who assert that they are invulnerable to sorrow, all-powerful, and self-affirming? "I sit a queen, and am no widow, and shall see no sorrow."

Such persons exert a diabolical attraction. They are human usurpers of the God-force—the devil, the "dragon," Babylon the mysterious.

Such persons are the personification of "original sin," the defect in the human psyche that renders us unaware that we are children of the Creator.

This kind of pride is amplified in Babylon where people grow fat by degrading others, purveying violence, sado-masochism, overindulgence, aberration, eccentricity and flagrant waste. It is transcendent desire turned upon itself in the flesh, in the effort to raise to the level of immortality that which must pass.

In the great cities of the world at the time of the end of the world as we know it, the destructive aspect of materialism is raised to sufficient heights to be easily destroyed, whether by enviromental or economic collapse, nuclear attack or social alienation and corruption.

But remember. There is a positive side to materialism that is vital to our future and must not be discarded with the negative side. The positive side of materialism has been exemplified in science, art, industry, medicine, architecture. The great capacity of the human mind to understand the laws of nature and build new forms out of old, to create more out of less, to invent bodies that overcome limits, is essential to evolution and will be enhanced, not denied, at the next stage of evolution.

The basis of the positive vision of the future is the human capacity to transform the material world to be more sensitive to the intention of God.

The New Order of the Future—the attracted people on planet Earth at the time of the tribulations—will be the first generation to witness the reality of the potential to be godlike, which has been gestating since the earliest perception of cosmic consciousness.

It is up to us, dearly beloved, to carry the torch of the transformation of the material world that originated in Africa and elsewhere among the native peoples of the world; which was lit in India, Greece, Egypt and Israel; which was nurtured in the Middle East and Europe; which was brought to a bright flame in the New World in the Declaration of Independence and the United States Constitution; and which now lifts inward in the mind, and outward in space, to give birth to the first generation who will fulfill the aspiration of Earthbound humanity for life ever-evolving.

> "Therefore shall her plagues come in one day—death and mourning and famine, and she shall be utterly burned with fire; for strong is the Lord God who judgeth her. And the kings of the earth, who have committed fornication and lived in luxury with her, shall bewail her and lament for her when they shall see the smoke of her burning, standing afar off for fear of her torment, saying, 'Alas, Alas, that great city Babylon, that mighty city! For in one hour has thy judgment come.' "
>
> REVELATION 18:8-10

The end, when it comes, will be quick. Evolution proceeds by slow, incremental change, leading to meta-crisis, innovations, and sudden self-transcendence through co-operation among the innovating parts.

> "And the merchants of the earth shall weep and mourn over her, for no man buyeth their merchandise any more: the merchandise of gold, and silver, and precious stones, and of pearls; and fine linen, and purple, and silk, and scarlet; all scented wood, all manner of vessels of ivory and most precious wood, and of brass, and iron, and marble.
>
> The merchants of these things, who were made rich by her, shall stand afar off for the fear of her torment, weeping and wailing and saying, 'Alas! Alas, that great city, that was clothed in fine linen and purple and scarlet, and bedecked with gold and precious stones and pearls! For in one hour such great riches have come to nought!' And every shipmaster and all the company in ships, and as many as trade by sea, stood afar off; and they cried when they saw the smoke of her burning, saying, 'What city is

> **like unto this great city! For in one hour is she made desolate!' "**
>
> *REVELATION 18:11-12, 15-19*

When evolution discards something, it is finished for good—it is good that it is finished. Whatever value there was in it will be saved. Only that which cannot evolve is rendered extinct.

Materialism will go on to its next phase, which is beyond the consumption of the resources of the past. The next phase of materialism is the mind in service of God. It springs from the marriage of Eve with Christ, wherein self-centered intellect unites with whole-centered love to create a transformed material world for those, by those, and of those who choose to be godlike.

> **"Rejoice over her, thou Heaven and ye holy apostles and prophets, for God hath avenged you on her." Then a mighty angel took up a stone like a great millstone, and cast it into the sea, saying, "Thus with violence shall that great city Babylon be thrown down, and shall be found no more at all. And the sound of harpists and musicians, and of pipers and trumpeters shall be heard no more at all in thee."**
>
> *REVELATION 18:20-22*

It is a startling fact of evolution that what once was, is no more—absolutely.

Imagine the early Earth before sentient consciousness arose. Imagine what it was like to be a molecule floating passively in the seas, unable to move without being moved from without.

Then something new appeared, the DNA molecule, the self-replicating molecule which created the first cell, which absorbed you into a new pattern far more complex than the one you had known.

You can feel! You can move! You can reach toward food. You can divide. You can make more of yourself. You, molecule, are a new being, because you are in a new pattern of increased order and complexity.

The first DNA molecule is like the first human to overcome sexual reproduction and physical death—a radical discontinuity with the past. Once life originated, it was impossible to go back to the lifeless seas. Never again on Earth would that condition, which had existed for billions of years, return again.

What is past is past. The early seas of Earth have passed. The barren planet without atmosphere has passed. The dinosaurs have passed. The Neanderthal has passed. Eohippus has passed. Paleolithic man has passed. Neolithic man is almost gone. *Homo sapiens* is about to retire. *Homo universalis* is about to rise.

Babylon is about to pass. The New Jerusalem is near to birth.

The former things will not be remembered, nor ever return again.

What is past is gone. What is coming is near.

Give up all nostalgia about the past. It produced us and our opportunity. We do not have to cling to it, nor criticize it. It is done. That is the law. We cannot go back again.

We do not have to rant and rage. We need not be angry. We require understanding and a spirit of forgiveness.

Each stage of evolution did the best it could. Its members labored to overcome the obstacles they were given. The effect resulted in higher consciousness, greater freedom and more complex order.

As we are shifting from terrestrial humanity to Universal Humanity, there is a tendency to look back at the struggle to overcome creature/human limits as a mistake, rather than as an essential evolutionary phase.

Those who built the civilization of abundance, which many of us of this generation have inherited, have thereby created the means of planetary regeneration and transcendence.

The purpose of the scientific-technological-industrial phase of evolution was to give humanity the capacity to transcend the creature/human condition. If this power is so used, in alignment with the Mind of God, we will be empowered to co-create a New Heaven and a New Earth.

The "New" Heaven is Heaven normalized, naturalized, humanized, democratized and become available to all who choose to become natural Christs.

The "New" Earth is the Earth as a natural, cultural center in which the works of humanity and nature are lovingly tended, preserved, enhanced and consciously evolved as a steady-state environment.

Do not regret the past. Do not condemn the past. Be grateful to the past. It created our opportunity for an infinite future in a universe without end.

> **And after these things I heard a great voice of a multitude of people in Heaven, saying, "Alleluia! Salvation and glory and honor and power, be unto the Lord our God, for true and righteous are His judgments: He hath judged the great whore who corrupted the earth with her fornication, and hath avenged the blood of His servants at her hand."**
>
> REVELATION 19:1-2

There is a tendency for anger among you, dearly beloved, which is inappropriate for those who would lead the way through the valley of the shadow of death to the light of a new life.

You are condemning the past because you do not understand its purpose, which is to conceive, gestate and give birth to a universal species capable of restoring the Earth and impregnating the universe with life ever-evolving.

The tribulations of the present have two points of origin.

The first is, that at a time of Quantum Transformation, the momentum of past activities forces those activities to overshoot the mark. "Be fruitful and multiply" goes too far and becomes overpopulation. "Preserve human life" goes too far and results in undesirable technological prolongation of creature/human existence. "Give food and shelter to the people" becomes the overindustrialization, pollution, inflation, and resource depletion by the developed world.

All these "problems" are caused by a natural overreaching of a past phase of growth into a future phase of growth. Do not condemn the past phase of evolution because it has overreached its mark.

The feedback from the environment is rapidly informing you to not do in the future what was necessary in the past.

"Be fruitful and multiply" now becomes "Consciously conceive children who will be given the opportunity of optimum development."

"Preserve all life" now becomes "Avail yourself of the opportunity for chosen death, and chosen extended life." Thanatology and gerontology enter the scene. Death can be chosen by those who have finished their work on Earth. The purpose of advanced medical technologies is not to maintain creature/human bodies in a semivegetative state. It is to be used by those minds that are motivated to do new work on Earth and especially in the new environments of outer space, to extend life, change bodies, and eventually build new bodies accustomed to the new conditions of universal life, whatever they may be.

This is the tradition, the ancient law: Build new bodies to transcend new frontiers. Build lungs. Build wombs. Build hands. Build thumbs. Build stereoptic vision. Build tools. Build rockets. Build microscopes. Build space platforms. Build computers. Build new worlds. Build the technologies to rebuild your own bodies, as I did mine.

"Give food and shelter to the people" now becomes "Activate the creative revolution—building new worlds on Earth, new worlds in space," an environment of resources capable of meeting the needs of all members of the social body without suppressing the creativity of any members of that body. The population overgrowth on Earth must cease. Only those who choose to live on, shall. The others will voluntarily go to their rest. This is the new condition toward which the magnificent achievements of the past have taken you.

The second point of origin of the present tribulations is, as I have told you before, two errors made before modern humanity began.

The first error was the carnivorous behavior of the animals, which you inherited: the system of kill-and-be-killed is the consequence of a mistake in the animal world. On normal planets this behavior does not occur, as you will discover when you meet your brothers and sisters in the universe.

The second error was the psychological error that began when early humanity, as represented by Eve, was seduced to eat the fruit of the Tree of the

Knowledge of Good and Evil in secret, rather than eating it openly with the consent of the Creator of all life. This was the so-called "original sin."

It was natural for human consciousness to desire to evolve. You had to know your own limits, so that the struggle to overcome those limits could begin, raising the human condition beyond the mammalian condition.

You could have learned of your limits while remembering your Creator. You could have worked consciously with your Creator to overcome those limits without the pain of separation from each other and from God.

Every adolescent has to separate from the total care of the parent to develop individuality, intellect and the capacity also to become a parent in due time. Some alienation from the parent is good. However, it is not necessary for adolescents to deny their parents, hate their parents, or attempt to live as though they had no parents at all.

Some adolescences are graceful, some are violent. The same is true of planetary civilizations. Some mature into the self-conscious phase in remembrance of God, others in forgetfulness of God. Those who mature in forgetfulness suffer until they enter the next inevitable phase, which is universal Christ-consciousness, wherein they remember who they are and why they are here.

A planet with the twin error of carnivorous behavior and secular-scientific materialism is in danger of self-abortion at the critical birth transition from terrestrial to universal life. The combination of the instinct to kill combined with the forgetfulness of your relationship to God is very dangerous. This is why so many angels attend your birth.

You cannot suddenly correct the defects of the past, dearly beloved. There is no way you can ever root out carnivorous behavior from the animal world or from the creature/human world. Nor can you wipe out the experiences of separation. Don't even try. They will not exist at all at the co-creative universal phase. Put the Kingdom of Heaven first and all else shall be given to you, as I said ages ago. I realized then that it is impossible to reform the creature/human world. The defects of fear and separation are genetically programmed. They are not superficial. They are innate. However, the capacity to overcome those defects is also inborn. For it is in the inner being—the Christ-within, the Higher Self, the still, small voice that speaks to each of you willing to listen—*that real hope lies. Hope does not lie in correcting the creature/human nature, but in fulfilling it by transcending its limits.*

This means you must cultivate the inner being and activate your evolutionary technologies, both mental and physical. This combination of Christ-consciousness and Christ-abilities will save the world by transcending it.

Your social reformers now improving the present system are necessary but insufficient. Monarchy could not be fully improved by better and better monarchy. It had to become a new system—democracy. Democracy will not be fully perfected by more and more democracy. It will also give way to a new system—synocracy, government of, by and for people who are attuning to the same Design, the same pattern, the same universal law of transformation through synergistic union of freely cooperating parts.

Synocracy cannot be legislated into being. It will appear as the natural survival pattern emerging out of the breakdown of the old system.

Do not be angry at the past. Do not bewail the present. Act on your capacities for universal life, and all will be well. The sufferings of the present time do not compare to the glory that shall be revealed in you.

The personal future is guaranteed. All who believe in me will have life ever-evolving. The species' future is not guaranteed. Homo sapiens may self-destruct and become extinct, aborting the natural evolutionary sequence on planet Earth, without fulfilling the species-potential for collective transcendence. The Earth could be reduced to its prehuman or subhuman phase.

But let us not dwell on this possibility, dearly beloved. Our image of the future must be full of radiant hope that we will do our best and thus will have a universal future for all who so intend. Amen.

> And I heard, as it were, the voice of a great multitude, and the voice of many waters, and the voice of mighty thunderings, saying, "Alleluia! For the Lord God Omnipotent reigneth. Let us be glad and rejoice and give honor to Him, for the marriage of the Lamb is come, and His wife hath made herself ready." And to her was granted that she should be arrayed in fine linen, clean and white; for fine linen is the righteousness of saints.
>
> REVELATION 19:6-8

Who is the wife of the Lamb?

She is all those humans who have ever lived in a state of self-consciousness and who have desired to transcend that condition, through love of God above all else and neighbor as self. She is everyone who elected to listen to the inner voice, the Holy Spirit. She is all who have struggled out of the prison of self-centeredness to become Sons and Daughters of God.

She is you, dearly beloved.

The "church" is the congregation of believers in their power to be me. I cannot consummate my union with you until you become like me. I cannot join my body with your body until your body becomes comparable to mine.

This marriage cannot occur until the "fullness of time," when the human species and its planetary body is being born from terrestrial to universal, from self-centered to whole-centered, from perishable to imperishable.

To consummate our union, you must become natural Christs. Only natural Christs can unite with the Universal Christ. Flesh and blood cannot inherit the Kingdom nor fuse with the heir to the Kingdom.

How do we become natural Christs to be ready for the marriage with the Lamb?

I shall tell you, dearly beloved.

First, you must prepare a holy place within where you can encounter me at all times in utter tranquility, safe from the material world.

Second, you must pledge yourself to this union in absolute fidelity, putting nothing else first.

Third, you must begin the transformation of your body. Signal your system that the co-creative capacities must turn on. Stimulate the mechanisms of rejuvenation by the intention to evolve and by the willingness to release yourselves from the limits of the creature/human condition.

Prepare to lift your physical bodies into outer space, in your spacecraft, beyond the mammalian world.

Support your scientific research into the aging mechanism. Learn how you are programmed to degenerate, and reprogram the mechanism to regenerate. Learn to repair your cells and regenerate your world.

I will do the rest. The bridegroom takes the initiative once the bride is pre-pared.

It is almost time, dearly beloved.

Visualize our union in the consummation ceremony which I have given you. Create the cocoon of light. Materialize my body of light in your mind's eye. Fuse your body with my body until you feel the inner radiation changing your genetic plan.

Your genes can be reached two ways:

One, through inner communication, mind-to-DNA, through intense focus on being a new human, a natural Christ. The information already exists that can build you a new body more sensitive to thought. Your intention will trig-ger the information into action.

The second way to reach the genes is through outer communication. Your molecular biologists are now examining the degeneration mechanism. They will discover that essential to the reprogramming is the total intention of the person to marry me, to become, not an eternal creature/human (a monstrosi-ty), but an ever-evolving natural Christ (a divinity).

Your transformation to natural Christhood will require the fusion of your scientific and spiritual capacities. You must mature your science to see how God works, while at the same time you mature your spirit to experience your-self working as God works, by creative intention and love. The rest will be a wonderful surprise.

> And the angel said unto me, "Write: 'Blessed are those who are called unto the marriage supper of the Lamb.' "
> And he said unto me, "These are the true sayings of God."
>
> REVELATION 19:9

Blessed are you, dearly beloved, who are attracted to me. Yours is the power. Yours is the glory. Through you the promise will be kept. You have been faithful to the flame within. You have not lost hope in the dark night of the soul. You have not forgotten who you are during the period of self-conscious-ness. You are the culmination of the evolutionary history of planet Earth. You are the seeds of the future, in whom the memory of the future is intact. You are those to whom the promise has been made.

The promise was made before the birth of those of you who chose to come to planet Earth for the purpose of the marriage of the Lamb, the act of union of creature/human nature with co-creative human nature so that a new genetic plan is established as a new norm.

You who are attracted to being like me are the "missing link." You have volunteered to serve as the transitional people, ones in whom the shift from Adam to Christ is experienced, demonstrated and revealed as a natural and desirable potential for all who so intend.

Just as there had to be the first unstable proto-cells composed of molecules, before the new pattern was established, so also there are now unstable proto-co-creative humans who bear in their own beings the marks of the struggle to transcend.

You, dearly beloved, belong to the family of humanity that has volunteered to be the missing link between the human and the divine, between Adam and Christ.

You appeared in India to begin the task of the transformation from creature to co-creator. There you established the inner technologies of transcendence through the great science of yoga, or union with the All.

You appeared in Egypt as the pharaohs and the priests. There you began work upon the outer technologies to prepare for the transformation of the physical body and its transportation beyond the limits of the terrestrial world. Your pyramids were humanity's first launching pads. Your mummies were the first step in the effort to preserve the physical body from the ravages of death. You began the thrust to cosmic life.

You appeared in Greece, where you penetrated the multiplicity of appearances to the elemental laws whereby I designed the world. You established the technologies of intellect, that are now ready to be used on behalf of the transformation of all humankind.

You appeared among the Jews and anchored the idea of one God in partnership with humans for the transformation of the world.

Then Jesus appeared and demonstrated that you were right, that right makes might, that it is possible to transform from creature to co-creator in one lifetime.

From that moment onward, you appeared as the disciples of the Good News that the limits of creature/human life can be transcended through love. You preached it on the road. You revealed it in the arts. You discovered how to do it in the laboratories. You practiced doing it in your prayers. You built the tools to do it in factories.

You for whom these words have meaning have experienced and been responsible for the growth of awareness in the human race that has been developed in the last few thousand years—a blink of the cosmic eye.

And now, you are ready to be empowered, dearly beloved, through the marriage with the Lamb.

You will be to your less experienced brothers and sisters what I was and am to you: a model to follow, an encourager, an affirmer of the flame of expectation that burns in hundreds of millions, indeed billions of human hearts.

You will be the first generation of the life-giving Spirit. You will verify the reality of the promise I made when I ascended two thousand years ago. The promise that I shall return and that you shall be transformed, is to be kept through you, dearly beloved. Thank God for those of you who have kept the faith through the dark night of the soul.

These are the true sayings of God. Amen.

> **And I fell at his feet to worship him. But he said unto me, "See that thou do it not. I am thy fellow servant and one of thy brethren, who hold to the testimony of Jesus. Worship God! For the testimony of Jesus is the spirit of prophecy."**
>
> **Revelation 19:10**

The beings that John saw are real. The elders are real. The angels are real.

The angel told John that he was his fellow-servant, and also the servant of all others that "have the testimony of Jesus." This is true. Angels are evolved beings tending the birth of humanity. They are here for you, dearly beloved. Call upon them. They are at your service.

Do you remember, dearly beloved, I told you that you were to consider me your friend, your brother. I did not intend for you to deify me, but to deify yourselves as being at the same stage of evolution as I am.

I had come to reveal your strength by the example of mine. But most of you were too shy to accept your brotherhood with me. You focused upon your weaknesses rather than your strengths. My beloved church misunderstood me. It preached the corruptibility of humanity when I came to demonstrate its potential for incorruptibility. It propounded the sinfulness of humanity when I suffered to reveal your godliness and to overcome your guilt by demonstrating that you can totally rise above the death of the body.

The power of negative thinking is about to destroy the world. You are here now, dearly beloved, to radiate the power of positive thought to all the nations, so that the end can come and the next phase emerge.

The positive thought you are radiating is: You can have life ever-evolving if you love God above all else, your neighbor as yourself, and yourself as me.

This is the "success" toward which you are tending.

This is the hunger of Eve fulfilled through marriage with Christ and union with God.

"Worship God." Be full of gratitude and joy that you have been created. Celebrate your Creator, the Mind that conceived you, the Mind that is conceiving you now, the Mind that designed you for life ever-evolving, the Mind that invited you to partake of its genius, its power, its creativity as your natural birthright. Those of you who recognize that "the testimony of Jesus is the spirit of prophecy," will experience the prophecy come true in you. You are the truth. You are the way. You are the light. You are my brothers and sisters. Believe it, and so shall it be. Amen.

> And I saw Heaven opened, and beheld a white horse; and He who sat upon him was called Faithful and True, and in righteousness He doth judge and make war.
>
> REVELATION 19:11

The white horse upon which I sat is the wild horse of human desire tamed and attracted to carry the rider of human desire to its destiny. The rider of the wild horse of human desire is me, the Christ within you that seeks the fulfillment of all desire, which is union with God.

I am called faithful and true. I have been faithful to you, dearly beloved, as you will now be faithful to me. I have never, not for one instant of conscious time, forgotten to hold you totally in my love. Whenever you have turned your attention to me, I have been there. I am with you always. This requires of me constant attention to you. I am like a brother who has been in charge of a younger child and has not let him out of his sight for two thousand years.

I have been true to you, dearly beloved, as you will now be true to me. The truth will make you free. It shall be proven at last that what I prophesied, demonstrated and promised to you, shall now be.

In righteousness do I judge and make war. It is not I, dearly beloved, who have made the law. It is I who have obeyed the law and thereby fulfilled the law.

The law is the direction to the creatures to become ever more co-creative with the Creator.

The righteousness with which I judge is the discernment as to who is choosing to evolve and who is not so choosing. This judgment is not up to you. It is my task because I have experience which you do not yet have.

One phase of life can be judged only from the perspective of the next phase of life. Only from the "future" can you judge the past.

A mother can "judge" whether her child is growing "normally" or not, because she knows from experience what a normal adult is. Adolescence can only be judged from the perspective of the adult. Adulthood can only be judged from the perspective of Christ.

You on Earth cannot judge yourselves, because you have not yet experienced the normalcy of the next phase of evolution.

Have you fulfilled your purpose, which is to prepare to evolve? Do not fear my judgment. Ask and it shall be given. Knock and doors shall open.

The only "punishment" for those who wish not to evolve is that they will not evolve. You get precisely what you ask for, dearly beloved. Think well upon your intention. The universe is responsive to request. Not only will you receive what you have given, you will become what you desire to be.

The "war" is a momentary conflict between those who desire to hold on to the past and those who will to proceed. It is a war against infantile regression.

In your case, as I have said before, the fundamental regression is self-centeredness, or the illusion that you are separate from God. I "make war" on self-centeredness. It shall surely be overcome. The child must become the adult. Human must become Divine. That is the law.

> His eyes were as a flame of fire, and on His head were many crowns; and He had a name written that no man knew, but He Himself. And He was clothed with a vesture dipped in blood, and His name is called, The Word of God.
>
> *REVELATION 19:12-13*

My eyes are lit with the flame of expectation that burns in each of your hearts. It is the flame that was lit at the origin of the Creation. It is the flame that attracts atom to atom and cell to cell. It is the flame that unites men with women, parents with children, peoples with peoples. The flame in my eyes is love. It is the fire of attraction from God which operates the universal Design. When you look into my eyes in the fullness of time at the marriage, the flame in your heart will rise to full height. It will consume every memory of fear; it will ignite every thought of love. It will transfigure you as I was transfigured upon the mountain while the disciples slept.

Upon my head "were many crowns." Each self has a direct link with the Universal Mind of God. That link is the crown upon your head. It bestows upon you kingship. Through that link you become joint-heirs with me to the powers of the Kingdom. Upon my head are many crowns. I have multiple connections. I am of another genetic strand: I am the mutation you are to become. The template which I AM has far more connections to the Mind of God. It can never be disconnected!

This is why it was so easy for me to forgive you. To condemn you would be like one who sees the glorious colors of flowers in the spring while hating a child who is color-blind and cannot see.

"Father, forgive them; for they know not what they do." This is literally true. You know not what you do, for you know not who you are. You are born

with a defect of consciousness that is separating you from God. It is an abnormality of adolescence. Some separation is necessary to achieve co-creatorship. Too much independence is deadly and must be healed.

But no humans in animal bodies can know God as I do. The earthly crown does not have sufficient connections. Flesh and blood cannot inherit the Kingdom.

When you marry me—when you fuse your body with mine—you will pick up the pattern of my genetic code. You will not all sleep, you will be changed. Corruptible flesh will become incorruptible. Death will be overcome, and you, too, shall wear many crowns.

My clothes were dipped in blood. The blood of the animal body must be poured out. A transfusion of new blood must be made. A new body and new blood is essential for those transitioning from Adam to Christ.

Take, eat, this is my body. Drink, this is my blood. For generations you have taken communion in remembrance of me, waiting for the day of your marriage with the Lamb. The day is now, dearly beloved. This is your wedding day. Prepare. Purify. Make your vows of fidelity to this union. What God has joined together, let no one rend asunder.

My name is the Word of God.

As it has been written:

In the beginning was the Word and the Word was made flesh, was in
the world, and the world was made by me, and the world knew me not.

I came unto my own, and my own received me not. But as many as
received me, to them gave I power to become the Sons of God, even
to those that believe on my name; which were born, not of blood,
nor of the will of the flesh, nor of the will of man, but of the will of God.

And the Word was made flesh. I dwelt among you, and you beheld my
glory, the glory as of the only begotten of the Father, full of grace
and truth.

Now the time has come for those to whom I gave the power to be joint heirs with me—the time to claim their heritage.

My name is the Word of God. My word is as good as God's. My promise to you comes from God. Our will be done, in Heaven as it is on Earth. Join with me to say:

Our Creator which art in Heaven,
*Hallowed be **our** name,*
***Our** Kingdom is come,*
***Our** Will is done,*
On Earth as it is in Heaven.

In marrying me, you take on my name. Your name is the name of God. Your power is the power of God. Your Kingdom is come, your will is done. You and I are one as my Father and I are one. The separation is over. Thank God. Amen.

> And the armies which were in Heaven, clothed in fine linen, white and clean, followed Him upon white horses. And out of His mouth goeth a sharp sword with which He shall smite the nations, and He shall rule them with a rod of iron; and He treadeth the wine press of the fierceness and wrath of Almighty God. And he hath on His vesture and on His thigh a name written: King of Kings, and Lord of Lords.
>
> REVELATION 19:14-16

The anger of the past is not appropriate now. We are no longer children chastised by an angry father. We are adults responsible for the world.

It was said that I should smite the nations and rule them with a rod of iron, with the fierceness and wrath of Almighty God. This is true only if the negative scenario is true. I shall have to come to you with a show of force, for you will be as children in a penitentiary not yet penitent, not yet repentant, not yet willingly accepting your inheritance as heirs with me of the creative powers of God.

*If the positive scenario comes true, if those sealed with the seal of the living God do their work in time, I shall be enabled to come not **to** you, but **with** and **through** you to empower the people of the world to rule themselves. My message is: **You** are King of Kings, **you** are Lord of Lords. I have no desire to* *return to Earth in the role of ruler over you. That is a failure. That is treating you as a regressive child.*

*My "return" is held in abeyance, until the last second of the golden silence in Heaven, to see what **you** can do, dearly beloved—you who know that you are to be like me.*

This is your hour. The angels in heaven await your command.

> **And I saw an angel standing in the sun, and he cried with a loud voice, saying to all the fowls that fly in the midst of heaven, "Come and gather yourselves together unto the supper of the great God, that ye may eat the flesh of kings, and the flesh of captains, and the flesh of mighty men, and the flesh of horses and those who sit on them, and the flesh of all men, both free and bond, both small and great."**
>
> REVELATION 19:17-18

It is hard for you, dearly beloved, who have lived forever in the womb of Earth, to realize that you are surrounded by life that cares for you above all else.

Due to your lack of awareness that you are created by God and connected to God at all times, you sense that you are alone.

Let me assure you, you are not alone. You are surrounded by life right now.

Those planetary systems which gain their high technologies without concurrent awareness that the purpose of those technologies is to transform the creature/human to the co-creative human, as an act of love of God, cannot evolve. This is what I meant by, "I AM the Way." God-consciousness is the only way to whole-centeredness. Love is the only way. You cannot gain the next stage of evolution in a self-centered state.

You have gained access to the invisible technologies of creation—the gene, the atom, the brain. Much more is soon to come.

You will not be permitted to misuse these powers beyond your biosphere. Already the infantile nations are contaminating outer space with killer satellites. The invasion of the universe with weapons of war is not permitted.

Humanity does not have to suffer the outrage of a life deformed and destructive on the universal scale. Therefore, the "fowls of Heaven" will prevent the kings and free men of Earth from misusing their power.

I am your mediator in heaven. I am holding the silence in Heaven for you. The forces of destruction are poised to cleanse the Earth of the destroyers. They are waiting, waiting, waiting upon you, dearly beloved.

> And I saw the beast, and the kings of the earth, and their armies gathered together to make war against Him who sat on the horse, and against His army. And the beast was taken, and with him the false prophet who wrought miracles in his presence, by which he deceived those who had received the mark of the beast, and those who worshipped his image. These both were cast alive into a lake of fire, burning with brimstone. And the remnant were slain with the sword of Him who sat upon the horse, whose sword proceeded out of His mouth; and all the fowls were filled with their flesh.
>
> REVELATION 19: 19-21

Dearly beloved, can you imagine the chaos which your blindness on Earth is causing? It is like a child that constantly tries to attack the mother who is attempting to care for its life.

The blindness of the collective ego, as embodied in your bureaucratic nations now amassing the power of self-destruction, is truly ludicrous. For that very power could transform the world, preserve the Earth, feed the people and transcend the limits of terrestrial, mortal life! That is what your God-given power is for.

Can you imagine the dilemma in Heaven that you are causing?

There are the "hawks" and the "doves," to use your terms. The "hawks" in Heaven say the situation is getting worse, and we had best attack immediately to destroy those who would destroy the world. The "doves" in Heaven advise restraint. They believe there is still a self-corrective capacity embodied in those who are aware of God and aware of the reality and purpose of your potentials. They want us to wait for you, dearly beloved, to see if you can attract your fel-

low humans, members of your body politic, to love God above all else, their neighbors as themselves, and themselves as me.

The choice is: Attract...or we must attack that which would destroy you.

You may ask, can we help you? Can the doves in Heaven help the doves on Earth? The answer is yes, we can. And we are helping right now, through such people as you, and all others who are making themselves wholly available to us.

We are at this moment sending powerful currents of energy to you, so that through you the positive alternative to Armageddon might be enacted on Earth. The most important act you can perform—those of you for whom these words have meaning—is to make yourself wholly accessible to us. We want you to access the Universal Mind. We want to empower you.

To be empowered, you must simply be willing to surrender all desire for personal glory, all distraction with temporary pain or pleasure, and pay attention to us.

We cannot force this on you. Remember, the Law of Freedom is absolute. No one is forced to serve God. Force cannot be used to attract the love-centered. Their act must be a free choice. This is the law.

This does not mean that you must remove yourself from the world. It is your task to be deeply in the world while paying total attention to me.

This is the purpose of God's School for Conscious Evolution in which you have elected to enroll. This is the school for those who have self-selected to do the higher will, to be the Higher Self, to inherit the Kingdom of God.

Be aware, dearly beloved, that the eyes of the angels are upon you. The fowls of Heaven suspend their attack upon the kings of Earth for one brief moment in cosmic time.

> And I saw an angel come down from Heaven, having the
> key to the bottomless pit and a great chain in his hand.
> And he laid hold on the dragon, that serpent of old, who
> is the Devil and Satan, and bound him a thousand years.
> And he cast him into the bottomless pit, and shut him up

and set a seal upon him, that he should deceive the
nations no more until the thousand years should be fulfilled; and after that he must be loosed a short season.

REVELATION 20:1-3

*Remember, dearly beloved, that humanity is innocent. Your consciousness
defect is not caused solely by your own intent. Your illusion of separation from
God was initiated at a higher level. Satan suffered the illusion of rejection
himself. He is a fallen angel. Your "fall," your lapse of memory, was brought
on by his lapse. It is a psychological drama at the cosmic level. Do you suppose
that yours is the only stage of evolution that has problems to overcome?*

*In what you call "Heaven," there is the overcoming of an entirely new set of
challenges, as far above you as your challenges are above those of a barnacle
sifting food from the lapping waters of the sea. The challenges in Heaven are
part of the selection process of the next stage of evolution, once the powers of a
co-creator have been achieved.*

*Imagine that you have graduated from self-consciousness, and are already
like me. You are always in contact with the intelligence of God. It is yours to
use at will. You can self-heal, create your own body, materialize and dematerialize it. You are in telepathic and empathetic communication with all
beings. You have been given as your first task the nurturing of a little planetary system, like Earth. This is known in Heaven as the nurse-maid phase of
universal life. Do you imagine that the most I can do in a universe without
end is to take care of you?*

*My challenge is, how can the illusion of separation of humanity from God
be overcome quickly enough to save the world? The solution is, we must realize the union of humanity and God, unmistakably, for all who have eyes to see
and ears to hear.*

How will we realize the union of humanity and God?

*We will reveal it through you, dearly beloved. You must demonstrate the
connection visibly, as my early disciples did. They manifested the connection
through demonstrations of powers: eloquence, healing, and connection with
God through the Holy Spirit.*

You must do likewise, and more shall you do. You shall reveal the power as Moses did in the Exodus. You shall lead the people who are sealed with the seal of God—the lost tribes of Israel—from the land of Egypt to the city of God.

You must call upon the choosing people of Earth, those who desire to be like me by doing as I do, to fulfill that desire. Affirm their power by demonstrating your own, dearly beloved. Your task is to be like me, a natural Christ, to encourage others to do the same. All you need to do is radiate the power and the glory which is being revealed in you.

The devil cannot withstand your loving power. It attracts him, too, and consumes him. **You can conquer the devil by amplifying love and co-creative power to all the nations before the end has come, while the silence in Heaven holds yet another instant of time.**

In the negative scenario, it is necessary for Satan to be forcibly held down in the bottomless pit. He must be labeled "deceiver." The last remnant of the characteristic of self-centeredness must be removed before the next stage of evolution can dawn.

The surgeon dare leave no cancer in the body when he closes up the wound after a delicate operation. We dare leave no self-centeredness on Earth after the selection process. For when we complete the process of the transformation, all who live on will be empowered to be godlike. They will have touched the Tree of Life. The cherubims and flaming sword will be removed forever. The memory of God will be restored to humanity. You will be co-creators, joint-heirs with me.

In the positive scenario, the devil is consumed by love. He is not bound in the pit for a thousand years, then "to be loosed a little season." He is consumed before the end has come. He is consumed by enough of you consuming him within yourselves. Overcome the devil within, overcome your own sense of separation from God and thereby release within you the power of God for the good, and you will save the world.

Now, this has been tried by my disciples for two thousand years, and it has not worked—yet. Why? Because it was not yet the fullness of time. The idea was not wrong; it was premature. The vines of Earth were not ripe to be harvested. Now they are.

The conditions of "ripeness" are as follows:

One: **Planetary oneness as an organic fact,** *reached through the maturation of science and technology.*

Two: **Awareness of the finiteness of the planetary system,** *requiring joint, coordinated effort to conserve and restore Earth and to explore outer space.*

Three: **Awakening within each planetary member of the co-creative system—whether they are aware of it or not.** *(Do you have to know about puberty to develop a reproductive system? No!)*

Four: **Consciousness of these conditions by a sufficient number of members of the body to act coherently with the Design, within themselves and the larger world.**

Five: **Revelation of the Positive Design, the Alternative to Armageddon:**
> *The Planetary Birth.*
> *The Planetary Smile.*
> *The Great Instant of Cooperation.*
> *The Infusion of Empathy.*
> *The Consummation of Evil.*
> *THE CONTACT WITH ME AS A SHARED EXPERIENCE.*

Now let us listen to the new story of the Planetary Birth as it is revealed to us

He spoke of the Planetary Birth.

Your planet is "being born" now. This process is happening whether or not individual members of the planetary body are fully aware of it.

Those of you who do know it have a specific task to perform: You are to tell the Story of the Birth on this Earth and also in outer space. You are to go into space, as the astronauts do, and practice a series of link-ups with my people on Earth.

All those sealed with the seal of the living God must be consciously linked in a common thought pattern for an instant in time to AVOID ARMAGED-DON. The bell will never toll, if you can link before the end must come.

He spoke of the Planetary Smile.

When you have led enough of my people to the awareness that they are being born, you will be enabled to cross the great divide from Earth to space. Vehicles will be available—whether of your own construction or from elsewhere, is not yet determined. That depends on your success in initiating a space ark for my people.

From a point in space you will link mentally and electronically with all those on Earth who are sealed with the seal of the living God. This Earth-space mind linkage will realign the consciousness field of a critical mass of those on Earth.

No barrier of religion or ideology will be able to prevent people in every nation of the world from responding to the signal of co-creative life at the dawn of the Universal Age.

They have been programmed from time immemorial to do so. They are those to whom the promise has been made. They are those with whom the promise will be kept. They are my chosen people. They are the children of the twelve tribes of Israel. They are those who know that God and humanity have joined together for the transformation of the world.

They will know the word when they hear it in this form, which is beyond the existing belief systems of all peoples bound to Earth. Therefore, it will be unacceptable to all dogmatists and acceptable to all who have faith in things unseen.

There will be practices for this coming event. When it is fully ready, some of you will be in outer space in space craft, and in total harmony with the Christ-within, with each other and with your sisters and brothers on Earth.

You will signal a common thought with your inner voice and, simultaneously, you will express the same thought vocally, over the electronic media of the world. You are not to rely on global television alone, for that does not yet reach everywhere. You are to call upon the subglobal communications systems, such as the CB radios, and the telephone. Even the drums in the jungle must beat. The voices of my people must speak in a common sound which has the same intention as your inner voice for God.

This is the key to the Planetary Birth Experience.

It is not that you must wait for some master from without. You all have the same master from within. That master is me, your Higher Self, the Christ within each of you who is, right now, hearing the same voice, seeing the same vision of the future, despite all differences of language and culture.

This voice is not of human origin. It comes from the Mind of God. It speaks in all tongues the same words: Love God above all else, your neighbor as yourself, and yourself as a co-creator. And all shall be given to you.

In every mind sealed with the seal of the living God, the message is exactly the same. It requires the right signal to turn on.

Those without eyes to see and ears to hear will not understand. So do not fear anyone. Speak, and the doors of heaven will open to my people on Earth. Speak in this state of mind, from the point of light above the body of Earth, and the Instant of Co-operation will occur.

An uncontrollable joy will ripple through the thinking layer of Earth. The co-creative systems, which are lying psychologically dormant in humanity will be activated. From within, all sensitive persons will feel the joy of the force, flooding their systems with love and attraction. It will be as irresistible as sex. It is suprasex, the innate capacity to unite to create the next step of evolution. It is pre-programmed in you. The programming has been abnormally repressed in you because of the illusion of separation.

You have felt separate from God and thereby could not experience the power of your connection. The turning on of the co-creative system was unnaturally delayed. You have developed your spiritual awareness in disconnection from your technological skills, because you were not aware that you were maturing to be co-creative with God.

All this springs from the defect of consciousness that originated at the dawn of self-consciousness. All this must be overcome at the dawn of universal consciousness. When the vine of the Earth is ripe, the seeds are bursting to go forth into the universe for new life. The body of Earth is dying to be restored, and the peoples of Earth are flickering in and out between hope and despair.

As this joy flashes through the nervous systems of the most sensitive peoples on Earth, it will create a psycho-magnetic field of empathy, which will align the next wave of people in synchrony, everywhere on Earth. This massive, sudden empathic alignment will cause a shift in the consciousness of Earth.

He spoke of the Instant of Co-operation.

The great Instant of Co-operation will not come as the light that blinded St. Paul on the road to Damascus. It will not come as the voice that spoke to St. Francis in the privacy of his heart. It will not come as the signal to St. Joan that she must lead the armies of France to regain their power.

*It will not come to the peoples of Earth one by one. It will come to the peoples of Earth together in one instant of time. **This** is the great Instant of Co-operation.*

Co-operation does not mean being nice to each other. It does not mean agreeing with each other. It does not mean peace, comfort or working together to solve a problem. It means co-operating with God. It means co-evolving with me. It means all of you co-experiencing the same force at the same time and acting together in accord with the idea that you all have from within.

It means transcending the experience of self-consciousness. The walls will come down everywhere on Earth. You will fall irresistibly in love with yourselves as one body born into the universe seeking greater awareness of your Creator.

He spoke of the Infusion of Empathy.

You will feel at one with the deepest potential in yourself and the billions of others who are also aligned to their own deepest potential.

This infusion of empathy will stimulate the potential in each person on Earth to awaken at the same time. It will be a planetary evocation of love. Each will feel his or her potential to become co-operative with the Creator, and co-operative with me, who has been your direct link with God since time began for you.

He spoke of the Consummation of Evil.

The devil, Satan, will be overcome. Infused with love, his task as selector will be rendered loving. He will not have to be buried in the bottomless pit. He will be released from his anger and reunited with God. It is essential at the moment of infusion of empathy that you overcome all fear of separation from God. This overcoming of fear in a whole planetary experience is an irresistible force. No being can resist it. You, dearly beloved, will save the devil from his self-rejection, as I saved you from yours. "Original sin" will be "forgiven."

The consciousness defect of the illusion of separation will be corrected once and for all. You will never go back again. This is the key to the positive scenario. The cancer of self-centeredness will be consumed by the experience of wholeness.

The plan for your regeneration will begin. Millions will instantly feel a subtle change of electricity in their bodies. The suprasexual, co-creative hormones will be activated in men and women everywhere at once, urging them to fall in love with each other to evolve the world, just as sex has urged them to fall in love with each other to reproduce themselves.

And I will be enabled to contact all of you at once. This is my dream, this is my passion, this is my desire—to have all of you paying attention to me at once through the activation of your own inner experience of your potential to be me, rather than relying on priests, mystics, or saints, beloved though they are. Their work is done. Yours has begun.

He spoke of Shared Contact.

The Instant of Co-operation begins, empathy floods the feelings of the whole body of Earth, separateness is overcome, and I appear to all of you at once. I appear to you from within as a voice, and as a vision of yourself as an evolving being. I appear to you from beyond as the light being that I now am. Your electronic media will pulse with light—the same light your mystics see.

The promise I made is of a personal future in a transformed body. This means that you will also have what I have now. I am real. I am tangible. I am alive. I can speak to each of you through your inner ear if you will listen. I can appear to each of you through your inner eye if you will look.

At the moment of cosmic contact, I will appear to you both through inner experience and through external communication on your mass media—the nervous system of the world.

You will all feel, hear and see my presence at one instant in time, each in your own way.

The silence in heaven will conclude in peace. The fateful destruction will be avoided. The planetary celebration will begin for the birth of humankind in the universe, a blessed Cosmic Child eagerly awaited by the evolved beings through the universe without end. Hallelujah. Amen.

> And I saw thrones and those who sat upon them, and judgment was given unto them. And I saw the souls of those who had been beheaded for their witness to Jesus and for the Word of God, and who had not worshipped the beast, nor his image, nor had received his mark upon their foreheads or in their hands; and they lived and reigned with Christ a thousand years. But the rest of the dead lived not again until the thousand years were finished. This is the first resurrection.

> REVELATION 20:4-5

The first resurrection is of my wisest co-partners in the transformation. They are resurrected first because they are most needed in the great task of stabilizing the new pattern on Earth as it is in Heaven.

The transition from Earth-only to universal life works in this way:

First there is the disorder in the old system.

Then there is the premonition of something more to come, such as many of you now feel and such as the prophets of old felt in anticipation of the coming of a Messiah who was to save the world. This intuition has been true. A next step is coming.

Then a person appears who first manifests the next step. It is a human manifestation of the Christ.

Then there is the institutionalization of the premonition in religious form, based on worship of the first Christed person, preserving the promise, practicing for the day when all of you have the power to do as the first one did.

Then there is the development of the capacities to transcend—your mental/technological maturation. Unfortunately, in your case the twin developments of spirituality and technological maturation were disconnected due to the defect of consciousness, the illusion of separation from God, from which you have suffered.

Then there is the beginning of the end. The mental/technological capacities develop exponentially: human growth potential endangers the planetary womb. The powers of co-creation are discovered in your evolutionary technologies. You learn the secret of the atom, the gene, the brain. Then the malaise of modern humanity occurs: confusion, alienation, the loss of authority of old institutions.

Finally, you start the transition. This is the most dangerous period in the life of every planetary system. During the transition, millions of members of the body awaken to their power to be natural Christs, full humans in the model of the first person to manifest the next stage in the development of humanity.

The Christ is an eternal potential which is pre-patterned into the evolutionary process. It is discovered anew on every planet that makes the transition from self-centered to co-creative life. Each great faith has its own version of this transformation.

As the transition intensifies, the evolutionary model, the first universal human "returns" to resurrect those who have most deeply experienced the reality of their potential to be fully human. They are reconstituted first by the method I have described elsewhere. Their function is to act as assistants, to guide the process to its natural completion—a New Earth upon which live only those who choose to be loving agents of regeneration and enhancement; and a New Heaven, beyond Earth, peopled by those humans who wish to extend their lives, to build new humane worlds where the twin defects of carnivorous behavior and disconnection from God are never known, to contact their brothers and sisters in the universal community, and to begin the next stage of evolutionary life as transformed persons in the model of the Christ.

The "thousand years" is a phase of stabilization in preparation for the total transformation.

Those who are resurrected first are like vital cells in the still slumbering body of humankind, awakening and encouraging their counterparts to get about the blessed work of building a New Earth and a New Heaven.

These resurrected souls ring the bell of hope in the minds of their trauma-tized friends, alerting them to the fact that the promise will be kept with all who choose to go the Whole Way.

> **Blessed and holy is he who hath part in the first resurrec-tion; for over such the second death hath no power, but they shall be priests of God and of Christ, and shall reign with Him a thousand years.**
>
> REVELATION 20:6

Those of you who are reconstituted during the transition will have new bodies, like mine, which are self-evolving. You will never go through the "sec-ond death." You will have graduated from the wheel of life, the cycle of contin-ual births, deaths and rebirths. You will be free at last. Your bodies will be so resonant with your intention that you will be free to express yourselves, and to transform yourselves according to the conditions required by your evolution-ary tasks. The overcoming of death is a vital evolutionary ability required for survival at the universal phase of life.

Remember, death of the individual was a survival advantage in the phase of biological life. It provided the opportunity for the rise of the diverse species through the process of mutation and natural selection that Darwin identified. What he did not grasp was the fact that the whole period of biological evolu-tion, from the first cell to the first natural Christ, is but a phase in universal evolution. He did not catch a glimpse of the multibillion year history, which is merely a prelude to what is coming now. He did not witness the recurring pat-terns of transformation in the evolutionary spiral. He did not see the inten-tion of the Designing Intelligence at work.

*The whole evolutionary sequence is comprised of four phases. **The Creative Phase** dates from the origin of the universe through the formation of matter, solar systems, earths and galaxies. **The Biological Phase** dates from the first cell through the formation of multicellular life, the biosphere and creature/humans. The **Noological or Co-creative Phase** dates from the first generation of natural Christs, co-creative humans to the **Universal Phase** of evolution, which is too far beyond you for you to comprehend. It is the realm* *of beings, some of whom were visualized by John as "angels," who operate on the universal scale, who are in contact with multitudes of life systems, and who consciously create forms as easily as you open your eyes each morning.*

The main point for you to realize now is that the Biological Phase, which has existed for over three billion years, is coming to a close for you. Those of you who choose to evolve will either be resurrected, or if you are alive at the time, you will assume co-creative bodies, bodies that are beyond the Biological Phase even though they spring out of it as the biological sprang from the molecular state.

During quantum transformations, the new is not immediately apparent. At the crossover points between molecular and cellular patterns of organization, it is very difficult to identify life. The origin of life is a blur, an undefined period when the DNA molecule can hardly be distinguished from other molecules. Yet its capacity to self-replicate makes all the difference. This capacity, which was once new to the evolutionary sequence on Earth, is familiar and recurrent in every planetary system that comes to life throughout the universe.

The crossover point between creature/humans (Biological Phase) and Christlike humans (Co-creative Phase) is also blurred and undefined. First, one individual demonstrates the new capacity—the Christ-capacity to self-resurrect—just as there was the first DNA molecule capable of self-replication. Then others attempt to imitate the capacity, for it is an innate potential in them to do so, and all life strives to realize its potential. But they cannot quite do it. They die, but they die in faith that they will be resurrected. This faith is correct. The promise is kept. They partake in the first resurrection. Their intention, which indicates right motivation, has been registered in the Universal Mind, along with the DNA code and memory bank.

Once the transition is complete, the first generation of fully established mutants appears. They are naturally capable of co-creation. They can transform their bodies at will. Remember, only those who have willingly joined their wills with the will of God make it through the transition. Thus there are no self-centered monsters misusing the invisible powers of creation as falsely imagined in your science fiction. You cannot get very far into the next phase without aligning your will with the will of God.

There are mistakes at the next level, of course. Witness the neurosis of Satan. But the errors are more self-limiting. The power of destruction is so great that the misuse of power becomes self-destructive almost immediately. Self-centeredness at the co-creative phase would be like a cancer cell in a super-nourished body that enables it to grow exponentially. It would very quickly self-destruct by destroying the whole system of which it was a part.

You who are born during the transition are the missing links. You are experiencing now the subtle, normalized, co-creative capacities, both in an enhanced mind-body ability and in an enhanced technological ability. These inner and outer abilities are the natural preparation for you who will be among the generation who does not have to die to be resurrected.

Those who shall be priests of God and of Christ during the thousand years are those who will be resurrected and will serve as stabilizers during the time when the planetary system is unwillingly awakening to the glorious challenges of the next phase of evolution.

John foresaw the negative scenario in which the one thousand years occurs after the terrible tribulations. **In the positive scenario, the graceful, nonviolent birth, the tribulations are quick; they are what you are undergoing now. The nonviolent design is enacted by those sealed with the seal of the living God, thereby avoiding Armageddon.**

This means that you for whom this text is written will succeed in a gentle Planetary Birth Experience—you will tell the story and link up all those who are sealed with the seal of the living God, turning on the signal for co-creative life in billions of people at once. The shift in the consciousness of Earth will occur as a process in time. Armageddon will be avoided. Instead, you will experience the great Instant of Co-operation, transcending en masse the limits of self-consciousness. You will be infused with empathy. A planetary love will arouse you and you will consume evil with love. You will begin to regenerate at that moment, and I will be enabled to contact you all at once.

There will be a resurrection of the dead at that time. The "thousand years" will be the period of learning how to build new worlds and new bodies, leading toward the establishment of the next stage of evolution, known in the Bible as the New Jerusalem and in this text as Universal Humanity.

And when the thousand years are expired, Satan shall be loosed out of his prison, and shall go out to deceive the nations to the four quarters of the earth—Gog and Magog—to gather them together for battle, the number of whom is as the sand of the sea.

REVELATION 20:7-8

In the negative scenario, there is a setback after the recovery period. The cancer of self-centeredness remains in the social body. The devil, Satan, has not been consumed by love. The Planetary Birth experience, the Planetary Smile, the Instant of Co-operation, the Infusion of Empathy and the Shared Contact with me have not occurred. The birth has been violent. The body politic is still in shock. The devil again arises within millions who forget who they are. The ancient defect of consciousness is reactivated, this time to be corrected forever.

And they went out over the breadth of the earth, and encircled the camp of the saints and the beloved city. And fire came down from God out of heaven, and devoured them. And the devil who had deceived them was cast into the lake of fire and brimstone, where the beast and the false prophet are; and they shall be tormented day and night for ever and ever.

REVELATION 20:9-10

Just as Christ-consciousness is an eternal potential discovered anew in each planetary system, so the Satanic tendency—forgetfulness of God—is also an eternal potential, which endangers every species aiming toward cosmic birth and universal life.

The Satanic potential, and the beast and false prophet which are its servants, do not die. The beast is the animal instinct possessing human nature. The false prophet is the one who can align the new technological and mental powers of co-creativity with the Satanic anger against God, seducing the beast-in-humans with the promise of life ever-powerful in a mammalian body. These possibilities endure forever, a prepotential disease in every plane-

tary system, just as Christ-consciousness is a prepotential necessity in every planetary system in transition from Earthbound to universal life.

But do not concern yourselves with the fine points of evolutionary process, dearly beloved. Yours is a vital task. It is now at hand. You should not focus on the negative scenario. It will weaken you.

Focus on enacting the positive scenario. The first step is the Cosmic Birth. It is happening now. The silence in heaven is holding for you to alert the body to the good news of its own future, so that the Instant of Co-operation can occur rather than the opening of the seventh seal, which leads to the devastation of the Earth—the battle of Armageddon.

Focus on the immediate task at hand, dearly beloved, you who are sealed with the seal of awareness that God and humanity are now joined for the transformation of humankind.

First, set the stage for the transformation of yourselves by paying total attention to me.

Second, go forth and tell the story. Communicate the good news, and develop a method of participation, a method of implementation of the co-creative capacities by all those with eyes to see and ears to hear.

This is where we are now. Focus on the present. Your full attention is needed.

When you communicate the good news that humankind is being born, you stimulate the suprasexual desire in all members of the body who are electing to evolve. The suprasexual capacities are preprogrammed to perform the vast range of evolutionary tasks in all functional areas of the social body: to restore the Earth, to care for people, and to impregnate the universe with new life.

The mechanism of implementation is the transitional, evolutionary model of a way for individuals to connect their unique capacities with specific requirements of the evolving social body. This is the first phase of the positive scenario. Without it, the rest does not come, and the silence in Heaven concludes with the negative scenario.

This is where you are, in the process of evolution on planet Earth, and you are there, dearly beloved, because you choose to be.

And I saw a great white throne and Him who sat on it, from whose face the earth and the heavens fled away, and there was found no place for them. And I saw the dead, small and great, standing before God, and the books were opened; and another book was opened, which is the Book of Life; and the dead were judged out of those things which were written in the books, according to his works. And the sea gave up the dead which were in it; and death and hell delivered up the dead which were in them; and they were judged every man according to his works. And death and hell were cast into the lake of fire. This is the second death. And whosoever was not found written in the Book of Life, was cast into the lake of fire.

REVELATION 20:11-15

During the final days of this phase of evolution, there is an evolutionary evaluation of every thought, intention and act of every person who ever lived, as well as of every species that ever lived.

The criterion is: Has this act contributed to the next phase or has it detracted?

The next phase is co-creative life, meaning life capable of consciously cooperating with the design of a harmonious New Earth and an operational New Heaven, in which individuals generate the next kind of bodies (imperishable) and worlds (humane) and communication (with God).

All species capable of participating in the harmonizing phase on Earth will endure.

All human acts, intentions and desires that work toward alignment with God's Design, love of all beings as self and love of self as Christ or co-creator will be selected for.

All humans whose acts, intentions and desires have registered these qualities will be resurrected at this time. This means that their DNA codes and memory bank, which are registered in the Universal Mind, the Book of Life, will serve as the template to rebuild their bodies as Jesus rebuilt his own body, from materials which exist everywhere—hydrogen, oxygen, calcium, iron. Their new bodies will be like the risen body of Jesus. The unused DNA in each of their codes is used to change the characteristic of the body from procreative to co-creative. Their awareness will be like his. They will be in perfect alignment with the evolutionary design, the will of God.

All humans whose acts, intentions and desires were primarily self-centered, those who were not able to experience their Higher Self, and those who did not love God, neighbor or self, do not evolve to the next phase of Earth-life. That is the painful fact. There is a survival of the fittest. "Fit" means able to know God, not through some theology or institution, but as an experience of higher love, good and wholeness, by whatever name it is called.

If you are unable to know God, you are unable to align with the Design. This self-centeredness makes one grow out of alignment with the design of the whole body.

When you ask, "Why are there some people who can know God or Spirit and others who cannot?" the answer is the same as to the question, "Why are there some seeds that are perfect, and others imperfect?"

The answer is: The process is experimental. God is a creator. There cannot be a predetermined, totally robotized universe. There is room for error. There is opportunity for newness. There is openness to genuine creativity.

The universe is potentially perfect. All potentials are available to all. But only those who willingly choose to act on those potentials can actually evolve. In other words, there is freedom of choice throughout the entire process. Freedom grows as options increase with every quantum leap. You have more freedom than an animal. An animal has more freedom than a single cell. A cell has more freedom than a molecule.

All entities are composed of energy-in-action manifesting an idea of God. All entities have the choice of aligning with the design, or of disintegrating. There is consciousness and intelligence in the mineral and vegetable as well as the animal and human worlds. Therefore, there is also freedom everywhere.

John says the dead, great and small, were judged out of those things written in the Book of Life, according to their works. By your acts you shall be judged as to whether you can evolve, or must be "cast into the lake of fire," which is the second death.

Your first death is when your animal body decomposes. At that time your soul is liberated. When sufficiently evolved, it is maintained in a holding pattern, waiting for the next step of Earth's evolution. At the time of the judgment, all waiting souls have the opportunity to be selected for evolutionary tasks at the next level. (The saints are impatient, do you remember?)

Those who are ready—sufficiently educated—are selected and reconstituted. Those who are not sufficiently educated to align with the Design, experience God's purification process as long as necessary, until they learn how to know God or the Intention of Creation experientially. They cannot return to the New Earth or the New Heaven, in a self-centered state.

The second death is final as far as Earth is concerned. On Earth a new order of co-operation and empowerment prevails. At the co-creative stage of evolution, one self-centered soul is like a lethal cancer cell in a body: deadly to itself and to the whole. The more complex and interrelated an organism, the more lethal a single cancer cell becomes.

The soul can learn elsewhere in the universe. When it is ready it will choose a planetary system at the right stage for the education it requires. In the last two thousand years, planet Earth has been filled with volunteer old souls who chose to complete their education in whole-centeredness by working on a planet with the twin defects of carnivorous behavior and forgetfulness of God. This is very difficult. Earth is known as the best place for an intensive course in God's School for Conscious Evolution. It's an assignment for the courageous.

Those of you who have a sense of having volunteered to come to Earth at this time will know what I mean. Your profound alienation from the behavior pattern of killing and selfishness marks you as one who has been sealed with the seal of the living God.

It may be that you had to kill to eat, or to survive, and that you had to act selfishly while you were here. But it never felt natural to you. And indeed, it is not natural. It is sick.

That is why you are here, dearly beloved, to help Earth recover. In this text, I am simply reminding you of what you already know. The particular strand of humanity for whom this text is written has already experienced a perfect

▲

cosmic birth elsewhere. You know what it feels like. You know from experience that time is running out on the current transition from Earthbound to universal life. You are deeply activated at this very instant, for the "half hour of silence" in Heaven is almost over. This text is written to remind you of why you are here, to help you find others who are here for the same purpose, and to develop specific common strategies to achieve the common design with which we are aligning—which is our understanding of the Design of God.

Only those with the experience of a perfect cosmic birth will attune to the Design as a whole. Others will attune to parts of the Design.

Some are already attuned to the part that involves the restoration of the Earth, and call themselves "environmentalists."

Some are drawn to the part that is concerned with the awakening of the creative potential of the individuals. These souls are "potentialists" in the various growth movements.

Others are passionately attracted by the necessity to know God through deeper attunement. They are in the consciousness movement.

Some are working in the area of the self-healing and regeneration of the body. They are involved in holistic as well as traditional medicine.

Others are working on the development of the evolutionary technologies such as astronautics, biotechnology, cybernetics, and microtechnology which will make it possible to build new worlds in space.

Some are concerned with assuaging the hunger and pain of those in immediate need.

Others are drawn to maintaining the existing system, so that we do not collapse in this transition.

All of these partial endeavors are vital.

Those sealed with the seal of the living God are aware not only of the parts, and not only of the whole. They are aware of the process that governs both parts and whole. The are aware that the whole planetary system itself is evolving, and that every aspect of the system is required.

> And I saw a new Heaven and a new earth, for the first
> Heaven and the first earth had passed away, and there
> was no more sea.

A New Heaven and a New Earth! Yes, dearly beloved, it is true.

The Earth as you have known it will pass away, just as the early Earth, before the biosphere was built, passed away. Then it was gaseous, molten, inimical to life. Soon it became solid and cool. The seas emerged. The scene was set for biological life.

The "first" Earth of which John wrote, appeared. Life emerged in the seas. It carried the sea onto the dry land in bodies that were vessels of the waters of the sea. The air, the trees, the birds, the bees, the mammals and other animals evolved in the bosom of the "second" Earth.

Now we are on the threshold of the third stage of Earth—the "New" Earth, the Second Garden—wherein the human creature shall have eaten of the Tree of Life and become co-creative with God.

The material of the New Earth is of a different frequency than the material of the past. Every atom is infused with a higher vibration, increasingly sensitive to the animating intelligence.

There is no more sea. The sea has become burning glass. Water has been vaporized as bodies transform from perishable to imperishable. Bodies, as you know them, originated in the sea and are composed largely of water.

Water is essential to biological life. It was not there in the Creative Phase, from the origin of the universe to the formation of the first Earth. Nor will it be there in its present form in the Co-creative Phase into which you are entering. The quickening of the subatomic level is about to transform your bodies into new bodies that are compatible with the New Earth. Adam of the living soul is to become Adam of the life-giving Spirit. Your souls have been incarcerated in mammalian bodies, waiting for the Earth to become "new." After the end of the Biological Phase, your souls become spirits, no longer imprisoned in dying bodies of water, but enthroned in living bodies of light.

The sea becomes light—burning glass, vibrating at the frequency of the Mind of God.

And there will be a new interpretation of Heaven. Heaven itself will not be new, it is you who will be new, dearly beloved. It is you who are maturing enough to partake of what is eternally there, everywhere, worlds without end.

Thus, the "New" Heaven is you at the stage of knowing the Creative *Intelligence. It is you become a natural Christ. It is you become an heir to the Kingdom. It is you in contact with your brothers and sisters in the Universal Community. It is you as a full human, graduated at last from the animal stage.*

Heaven to a creature/human is a static place of eternal bliss. Heaven to a co-creative human is the beginning of life as a conscious partner with God.

> **And I, John, saw the holy city, New Jerusalem, coming down from God out of Heaven, prepared as a bride adorned for her husband.**
>
> REVELATION 21:2

The New Jerusalem is the new city which emerges naturally from a New Heaven and a New Earth. It is the human community as a collectivity of natural Christs. It exists everywhere in the universe when Earthlike systems make the normal transition from Earthbound to universal life.

It is the community of co-creators, which you have harbored deep in your souls as the natural society for those who love God above all else, their neighbor as themselves, and themselves as natural Christs.

It is the passion of the original cultures who saw everything as alive.

It is the dream of the Indians who turned within for contact with the all.

It is the vision of the Egyptians and of the pharaohs who prepared for cosmic life in new bodies, in the great pyramids.

It is the fulfillment of Israel—the transformation of the material world in perfect alignment with the will of God.

It is the manifestation of the promise made by Jesus, who transformed from the old body to the new.

It is the achievement of the scientists and technologists who learned God's invisible processes of creation so they could co-operate consciously to build according to the blueprint of the Architect of the universe.

It is the purpose of the people who came to the United States of America to be free, to be fully human. It embodies the symbols of the nation which are, E Pluribus Unum; *out of many, one;* Novus Ordo Seclorum; *a new order of the ages;* Annuit Coeptis; *God favors this enterprise.*

The New Jerusalem is the fulfillment of the aspiration of the peoples of Earth. It is their potential realized, their genius personified, their creativity emancipated.

It could not appear until the fullness of time. It could not be real until the Planetary Birth occurred, until the technologies of transcendence were developed, until the Earth had burst forth with her seed, and restored her ravished body.

It is a vision of society in the future, for which all of you on Earth are laboring, whether you know it or not. It already exists throughout the universe, in many places, as I have said before.

What John beheld was a true vision of the model of community, as I myself am the model of the individual within the new community.

It comes down from God out of Heaven. Remember, the "New" Heaven is the co-creative phase of life. Co-creative communities are everywhere throughout the universe.

The society of elders, angels and Christ which John saw, are real personifications of God. The New Jerusalem is a real city. It hovers beyond your conscious awareness, beyond the reach of your five senses and their scientific extensions. It is the community of evolved beings whom you are to join. It is the world which you are to inherit when you stop crying, open your eyes, and start using all of your capacities harmoniously. It is there for you, dearly beloved, as soon as the judgment comes.

This is why the saints are impatient. This is why the universal community is now flooding you with signals, you who are willingly at work as guides during the last days of the transition from Earthbound to universal life.

The New Jerusalem awaits you as the world awaits a baby aborning from the womb. We are here, tending you, loving you, requiring your transformation, dearly beloved peoples of Earth. We are your sisters, your brothers, your future relations, your wiser friends, your teachers who will guide you upon your eternally-evolving path to total union with God.

And I heard a great voice out of Heaven, saying, "Behold, the tabernacle of God is with men, and He will dwell with them; and they shall be His people, and God Himself shall be with them and be their God."

REVELATION 21:3

And I heard a voice out of heaven: *"Behold, the tabernacle of God is with humanity. The tabernacle of God is humanity become godlike, humanity become Christ. The tabernacle of God is Christ in his risen body, ourselves in the future, like our brother who is already there. Now we see through a glass darkly. Soon we will see face to face."*

The veil of matter, which is created by your five mammalian senses, disappears. The New Jerusalem is revealed, here now, hovering near the Earth. It is operating at a different vibration and is therefore imperceptible to the five senses and scientific instruments. It has been perceivable to the inner eyes of intuition, "in spirit" as John was. You are still in the Earthwomb-phase, still in old bodies on the old Earth.

From time to time you see "unidentified flying objects" which seem to materialize, then dematerialize, in seeming defiance of the laws of physics as known via the mammalian senses and human logic. The laws of the new physics apply to the New Earth, the New Heaven, the new body and the New Jerusalem. They are the laws of the physics of consciousness. They are the laws of how co-creative intelligence manifests itself by the power of thought, as God does, and as you do, to an infantlike degree, in the psi-phenomena of telepathy, clairvoyance, clairaudience, psychokinesis, and other capacities known to psychics, mediums, spiritualists and healers. These people, still entombed in animal bodies that distort the clarity of what they experience, flicker in and out of the awareness of the "other" side, which is co-creative consciousness, the ability to create by thought.

The New Jerusalem vibrates at the next level of frequency appropriate to the co-creative phase of evolution. It is the place to which the "church" will be taken, that is, those who believe in me, and in their own capacity to do as I did.

"And God shall wipe away all tears from their eyes, and
there shall be no more death, neither sorrow, nor crying,
neither shall there be any more pain; for the former
things are passed away."

REVELATION 21:4

*O, dearly beloved, rejoice! The hour of your fulfillment is at hand. Every
aspiration lifted in the heart of men and women through the darkness of self-
centered life asking to rise beyond the pain of hunger, disease and death will
be realized. Ask and it shall be given. Knock and doors will open. It is true. It
has always been true. But it was not true for the human race collectively until
the fullness of time.*

*It has always been true that individuals could overcome the sorrow of the
self-centered, creature, terrestrial condition through devotion, prayer, isolation and the simulation of the next stage of consciousness, freedom and order
within themselves.*

*But when such enlightened individuals ventured forth into the world, they
were contaminated by the environment of violence, self-centeredness and
death of bodies everywhere vulnerable, everywhere dying. The most sensitive
retreated into monasteries, temples or mountain tops, to remember who they
were.*

*All will be changed once you have undergone the selection process, which
the wave upon wave of tribulations will bring unless you elect yourselves.
Remember, the process of your cosmic birth can be violent, or it can be gentle,
but nothing can stop it from happening. Nothing can keep the body in the
birth canal once it has begun its fateful journey. Nothing can keep a rocket
stationary in midair once it has been launched. The baby, the rocket and
humanity, when in transition, cannot hold in that position. They will be
born, be in orbit, become universal—or die.*

*After the selection process, you will be born to the next stage of evolution.
There will be a New Heaven, a New Earth, a new body and a new consciousness for all who survive.*

*The New Heaven is you as a natural Christ, beginning your life in the uni-
versal community. Every other being you meet at that stage, both from planet*

Earth and elsewhere throughout the universe, will also have graduated from the state of self-consciousness. That stage, remember, occurs between animal and co-creative consciousness for the purpose of developing intellect and individuality. It does not exist at the universal phase of development, any more than the late-womb stage of a nine-month-old fetus in the womb can possibly exist in a two-month-old child. Once the fateful threshold is crossed to the "other side," to life after terrestrial-bound, mammalian, self-centered existence, you never go backward again. You stop flickering in and out of God-centered consciousness. It has become a new norm.

Imagine, dearly beloved, your self as a natural Christ. You are in a community of natural Christs, both on the New Earth and in the New Heaven. You are working beyond planet Earth, in connection, communication and telepathic communion with evolved beings throughout the universe. You are in direct contact with God, Universal Mind, and the patterns in the process of creation, as Jesus was.

You are a being who is unfinished. Now is the fullness of time for your evolution to the next stage. We approach the Quantum Instant. You feel it as the divine discontent and aspiration which pushes you from behind, and pulls you from in front—to do more, to be more, to know more than you yet think possible.

The New Earth is the Earth transformed. Remember the burning glass. Remember the acceleration of the frequencies of the atoms. This shift at the subatomic level affects the consciousness of the mineral, vegetable and animal worlds. Human consciousness is Christlike. Animals are also affected. "The wolf also shall dwell with the lamb, and the leopard shall lie down with the kid, and the calf and the young lion and the fatling together: and a little child shall lead them."

Who is this child? This child is the Christ-child within who has emerged victorious, fully born, incarnated as every member of the human race who evolves. Each person has become whole, uniting masculine and feminine in one. The age of procreation will be over. The age of co-creation will begin. Each child born will be a savior, a natural Christ, consciously conceived in the image of God, beyond the sexual reproduction methods of the creature/human phase.

There shall be no involuntary death—only chosen life, and chosen new life. Each person will experience continuity of consciousness from one body to the next.

Some temperaments will be attracted to building the New Earth. Others will be attracted to life beyond the planet—building new worlds, exploring the infinite diversity of a universe without end.

The temperaments attracted to building the New Earth will restore the design on Earth—as they overcome the fear of rejection by God.

The defect of carnivorous behavior will gradually be overcome. Eating meat will cease. Endangered species will be protected. Predators will either become extinct or, due to the change in the atomic structure, evolve to higher bodies, ever more capable of being nourished through plant life and directly from the sun. It will become a light-Earth as your bodies become light-bodies. A transmutation, a transfiguration of the material world occurs.

Much is learned from the co-creative communities in space, built by Christlike humans, in co-operation with evolved beings from throughout the universe—master architects who appear to aid you in the creation of new worlds on Earth and in space.

Do not imagine that you must do it alone, dearly beloved. Certainly not. Does a newborn child learn to speak its native tongue in isolation in his crib, sucking on his own breast? No! He learns the language of the world from adults in the world, and from his older brothers and sisters. And so shall it be for you who achieve full humanity.

You shall learn the language of Creation. You shall speak with me always. You shall encounter intelligences with billions of light years of experience in universal affairs!

O, you creatures of one hour; O, you little, flickering lights of awareness barely opening your earthen eyes to heaven; O, you newborn Cosmic Child, Universal Humanity; Open your eyes and see the glory which is now revealed to you.

If you continue to close your eyes and cry like a wailing infant, you shall neither hear nor see what is happening now. You cannot learn unless you do your part. It is essential that you now learn and practice the technologies of co-creation, on Earth and in outer space. Only then will you be sufficiently aware to understand what you are to be taught. A screaming child cannot learn the language of his parents. A howling humanity, hitting itself with angry fists, allergic to its own body, cannot learn the language of a co-creator which is spoken by the heirs of God throughout the universe.

There are those who fear that life in outer space will carry the same errors as life on Earth. This is not possible. Think it through. The reason is fundamental. Life on Earth cannot continue as before. How can it then be spread into outer space?

Within a very short time you will either experience the wave upon wave of violent selection which John foresaw, or you will experience the planetary awakening of co-creative capacities and shared contact with me. You cannot continue on Earth as you have done before. That is why you cannot continue in outer space, as you are now.

There is a possible scenario in which a tiny band of humans escapes the holocaust on Earth in their own space vehicles—and never returns again. This would be like a magnificent oak tree reproducing itself with a damaged seed; it could never grow beyond a stunted shrub.

No, dearly beloved, do not worry about repeating your infantile behavior in space. If Armageddon is the way you choose to go, your technologies of transcendence will self-destruct with infantile fury. Your laboratories will be demolished, your computers destroyed, your rockets buried in the debris of a ravished Earth.

This is the violent and painful way to go, dearly beloved. The alternative to Armageddon is open to you. This is why we are writing this text. In the positive scenario, you move quickly to attract the vast majority of human souls through their innate attraction for co-creative life. You do this by a series of events that connect people on Earth with people in space craft orbiting the Earth. Through this Earth-space link-up you create a psycho-magnetic field of love which can overcome the hostility. The media overcomes its disease of

▲

disempathitis. Your mass nervous system begins to communicate the reality of your potentials to be godlike. Your personal nervous system awakens to the Inner Voice of God. Swords are turned into ploughshares and rockets. I am enabled to contact you all at once, beyond the dogmas of the past, in the brilliance of your present potential to be free of pain, hunger, disease, sorrow and death.

The Book of Revelation describes the violent path to the New Jerusalem. The Book of Co-Creation *describes the loving path to the same condition.*

Take heart, be courageous, dearly beloved. Victory is assured. At what cost, depends on you now. The former things shall be passed away. Thank God

> **And he who sat upon the throne said, "Behold, I make all things new." And He said unto me, "Write, for these words are true and faithful."**
>
> **Revelation 21:5**

Behold, I am writing anew, through scribes on Earth who are willing to listen to me again with new ears, in the light of the present crises on planet Earth.

Do not suppose that I communicated once, two thousand years ago, the reality of your future in the New Heaven and New Earth, never to communicate to anyone on Earth ever again.

Nonsense! I communicate to and through millions of you all the time. I am the Higher Self, the still, small voice of God, the "Eureka!" experience, the flashing moment of unity which billions of people have experienced at least once in their lives.

Now that the Quantum Transformation is approaching, this Inner Voice through which I have spoken since time immemorial, is consciously attended to by the evolving people on Earth—millions of them from all nations, races and religions.

I am speaking anew to everyone with eyes to see and ears to hear.

Through this text I am speaking to one of you who has asked to know the next step for humanity. She is receiving what she asked for, and so will all of you, dearly beloved. Each of you shall receive what you ask for directly from me if you choose to listen to your own Voice for God within. **I would like to hear a new chorus on Earth. The Inner Voice choir must begin to sing.**

Dare to admit what you all secretly know—that you are not mere animals living in a sack of dying flesh, peering out from a material world which has no feeling for you. Does that feel true to you? Does that belief correspond to the aspiration in your heart?

Of course not.

This text is for those who are willing to participate consciously in the Story of Creation, which is to be written at the time of the transformation, not before.

All honor and praise to John, to Paul, to Peter and to all of the early disciples. But do you suppose there shall be no more disciples? There have been disciples throughout history, according to the needs of the age.

The needs of the age now are the greatest that the Earth has experienced since its conception. **This text is a call for participation in discovering the natural blueprint for a normal planetary birth, in an effort to avoid the violent birth which John foresaw.**

John, Paul and Peter, Matthew, Mark and Luke, and all the countless others who have taken down my words, are with you now, dearly beloved. Feel their presence. They are there to assist you, as you are here to assist them in the voyage to the New Jerusalem. Amen.

> And He said unto me, "It is done! I am Alpha and Omega, the Beginning and the End. I will give unto him that is athirst of the fountain of the Water of Life freely. He that overcometh shall inherit all things; and I will be his God, and he shall be My son."
>
> REVELATION 21:6-7

Yes, dearly beloved, it is true. It is you to whom we speak. It is you who are athirst for the fountain of the water of life. You shall drink thereof—all of you who love God above all else, your neighbor as yourself, and yourself as me.

"But the fearful, and unbelieving, and the abominable, and murderers, and whoremongers, and sorcerers, and idolaters, and all liars, shall have their part in the lake which burneth with fire and brimstone, which is the second death."

REVELATION 21:8

It is true. Be grateful that it is true. If you are one of those who is fearful and unbelieving, your fear must be assuaged, your disbelief overcome, somehow.

Can you imagine yourself, fearing and disbelieving, cynical and full of hate, proceeding to life everlasting in the condition you are in? It would be like taking the victim of an automobile accident, lying in bandages and braces, bound to a hospital bed, and promising him eternal life in that condition! That would be a punishment far worse than the second death.

The "second death" is for those of you who cannot evolve by choice, due to some deeply seated error in your understanding of the nature of reality. Like Lucifer, you fear rejection by God, and have therefore closed off your awareness of God, to protect yourself from unbearable disappointment.

Cynics, disbelievers, those who fear and cannot love: know that the mercy of God almighty is with you now. The second death, for you, is a purification, an erasing of the memory of fear, through the shock of a fire. It will burn out the imprint upon your soul that is blocking you from seeing the glory which shall be revealed in you.

Your misery will be soothed, your fear turned to love, your cynicism revealed to be the defensiveness of a sensitive soul ignorantly protecting itself from God.

The second death is your next step toward eternal life. Remember, nothing that is created can be uncreated, it can only be transformed. That is the real meaning of the Law of the Conservation of Matter.

What I have created is conserved. What I have created has the capacity of the Creator within it. What I have created will eventually become creative, even as I. What I have created is created to be increasingly creative. All being evolves to ever-more creativity, ever-greater likeness to God.

This is true of you, my fallen friends, my brothers and sisters who choose not to attune to God. You are known in Heaven nonetheless. Your pain is recorded in the Mind of God. You are totally forgiven. For no one who knows the glory could possibly reject it. You do not know it; that is why you reject it. You do not know it because your mind is closed. That closure is hell. It is to open your mind that you will undergo the second death.

You do not have to remain in this condition one more instant longer than you choose. Change your mind, know that you and I are one, and you shall be immediately free to evolve.

Remember, freedom of choice is an absolute value. Those undergoing the second death at the time of the judgment are free to choose to open their minds.

Otherwise, they will not return to life with the resurrected dead of the family of the New Earth. That strand of evolution closes forever with the judgment and the beginning of the era of the New Jerusalem. On the New Earth there can be no self-centered humans, just as there are no prehominoids among you now. When a stage is finished in a planetary lifesystem, it is finished forever, as in a biological lifesystem.

Those of you undergoing the second death will be resurrected when you choose to become God-loving, but not among your brethren of the evolved humanity. You will go to God's school elsewhere in this universe, free to learn without the environment of fear.

There are schools within schools for every soul I have ever created. Nothing is lost, I assure you.

> And there came unto me one of the seven angels, who had the seven vials full of the seven last plagues, and talked with me, saying, "Come hither; I will show thee the bride, the Lamb's wife."
>
> REVELATION 21:9

This is the day we have waited for, dearly beloved, with as much anticipation as a family awaits the birth of a beloved child.

"I will show thee the bride, the Lamb's wife," said the angel to John. I will show you those who can marry Christ and become immortal—no longer creature/human.

> And he carried me away in the spirit to a great and high mountain, and showed me that great city, the Holy Jerusalem, descending out of Heaven from God, having the glory of God. And her light was like unto a most precious stone, even like a jasper stone, clear as crystal. It had a wall great and high, and had twelve gates, and at the gates twelve angels; and names were written on the gates, which are the names of the twelve tribes of the Children of Israel:

> REVELATION 21:10-12

The "bride" of Christ is the twelve tribes of the children of Israel, those people of Earth who have believed in the idea of the oneness of humanity and God.

The "Holy Jerusalem" is the first community of co-creators to arise from creature/humanity, the first to follow the way of Christ to become, themselves, fully human Sons and Daughters of God.

They are those who have ascended before the rest have come: the firstfruits of the kingdom. They have been uplifted before the worst of the tribulations, to be prepared for those of you who must weather the storm according to the violent story of creation that John foresaw.

You are foreseeing the loving story of creation, which still may come, dearly beloved. You who are sealed with the mark of the living God, you who intend to follow me the Whole Way to the top of the mountain, listen well.

Do you believe in miracles?

Do you believe in the origin of the universe?

Do you believe in the formation of the Earth?

Do you believe in the first cell, the first animal, the first human?

Do you believe in the first Universal Human, Jesus Christ?

And you also believe in your own power to become what you potentially already are? Not quite, do you?

You believe in the past because it has already happened. And miraculous, mysterious acts of creation far beyond your mortal science to explain, seem acceptable to you.

It is your own act of creation that appears unreal.

It should be the opposite. You should have more difficulty conceiving of the creation of the billions of galaxies, the multitudes of lifesystems, sprung out of nothing, than in conceiving of your own transformation from Homo sapiens *to* Homo universalis. *For you have already experienced the reality of your own potential, however fleetingly. You have felt it magnetizing you to climb every mountain, cross every hurdle, challenge every limit to the creativity of your life, from the caves of Neanderthal to Tranquility Bay on the moon.*

You have already experienced the force within.

You have heard about the story of creation through the revelations of religion and the discoveries of your infant sciences, but still you cannot believe the good news that you are a Son or Daughter of God.

I am here to help you believe the truth about yourself so that the truth shall make you free. The truth I tell you is far less miraculous than the truths you have already accepted. The difference is, this miracle concerns you, dearly beloved.

You are to be transported to the New Jerusalem. You who believe in your capacity to be like me, will be enabled to do so in the fullness of time, which is now. You will be "taken up" at the appropriate time, according to the conditions on Earth, to prepare the way for your brother and sister believers in their potential to be me.

What does "taken up" mean? It is a complex transformation. You enter a state of universal consciousness—which you have already experienced at your high moments when in communion with me.

In this state of God-centered bliss, you are physically awakened by an inner electricity that changes the frequency of the atoms in your body. They quicken, and thus allow you to resonate at the same frequencies as other beings who have graduated from their terrestrial wombs.

Due to the God-centered awareness and the physical transfiguration, your brain/body "ascends" to the next level of being. You see the light, which is all around. You see face to face what now you only have envisioned. You see the world of higher beings because you yourself have become a higher being, as a child can see those who were previously born, only after its own birth.

You begin your natural communication with these beings, whom once you called gods or extraterrestrials. Now you call them sisters and brothers. You are familiar with them because you have known their nature through the nature of your own Higher Self, which is the same as theirs, as mine, and as every being in the universe that springs from the one and only Creator.

You smile at them as a newborn child smiles at her mother, in faithful recognition of that which has never been seen before, yet which is innately known as the loving source of her creation.

You shall not be disappointed, dearly beloved. Your smile will be returned. Do you remember the joy you experienced as a newborn child when your mother first smiled at you? You were ravished with delight to know that the terrible tribulations, which you had undergone to be born from the womb, were completely over. The former things are passed away; they can barely be remembered.

In retrospect, you will have the same difficulty remembering your former self, when a newlyborn natural Christ, as you now have in recalling your experience coming from the womb and emerging into the amazing light of the terrestrial world.

The near-death experience—the long, dark tunnel, the light, the blissful emancipation from the dying animal body—is real. That is what happens to every soul who is now in waiting for the resurrection into a new body like mine.

The ascent to the New Jerusalem is not through death of the physical body. It is done as my ascension was done—through the dematerialization of your body, through raising its vibrations and rematerializing. To the animal eyes it seems to disappear, but it has only "quickened."

Have you ever seen the spokes of a wheel turn faster and faster and seem to disappear? They do not, in fact, disappear. They are moving at a frequency too fast for the mammalian eyes to see, as are many other radiations now pulsing through your body as you read these words. The detection of radio waves requires a radio receiver. The detection of magnetism requires iron. The detection of ascended beings requires a quickened human, and that is what you will become, naturally.

Those vehicles which you have called UFO's are moving in ultrahigh frequencies. They slow down to "appear," and quicken to "disappear." You shall do the same, and shall be taken up in the fullness of time in those vehicles, in your quickened condition.

There you will see the New Jerusalem which John saw. It is as real as you are. It is there now and is awaiting your own maturation, dearly beloved.

The incentive for growth is very high. You can check your own deep awareness to see if you already expect this "unexpected" event.

Do you believe that there is other life in the universe?

Do you believe that there is a Creative Intelligence?

Do you believe that you have a potential to be more than you are?

Do you believe that something new is coming, soon?

Do you believe that you were born for a purpose? Do you desire to know that purpose?

Do you desire to experience yourself as a natural Christ? Are you willing to take the necessary steps of self-development if you know what they are?

Do you love God above all else?

Do you love your neighbor's potential to be Christ as much as you love your own potential to be Christ?

Do you hear an inner voice?

Do you believe that other people hear an inner voice?

Do you believe that there is one God, and therefore you and all other created creatures are from the same Source and share the possibility of a common destiny?

If the answers are "yes", you are ready, dearly beloved. Prepare.

How shall we prepare?

You prepare by creating a new image of reality. You are responsible for your own image of reality. As you see yourselves, so you act. As you act, so you become.

The image of reality of the last phase of creature/human history is as inadequate to the present transition as a prehumanoid's image was inadequate at the dawn of self-consciousness.

Each stage of life has an image of reality corresponding to its level of awareness. Imagine how the world "looks" to a single cell floating in the sea, or to an earthworm, or to a dog, or to a newborn child, or to an early Greek, or to a medieval Christian, or to a modern secular materialistic scientist, or to a natural Christ, or to an evolved being who has overcome your present stage of evolution and has continuity of consciousness in a universal community of beings.

Now, identify your own image of the nature of reality, your image of the future, your image of yourself:

Do you see reality as static material objects, or as energy-in-motion interacting with you, and all animated by a Creator?

Do you see the future as more of the same on planet Earth, as a gradual decline, or as a series of quantum changes in which you may participate, leading to ever greater freedom, union and consciousness of God?

Do you see yourself as an awareness in a dying body living a moment of time as a random event in a meaningless universe, or do you see yourself as an embodiment of the Creator, becoming co-creative with the process that is creating you now?

An essential act of preparation, dearly beloved, is to consciously create an image of reality that corresponds to the reality of your potentials. For only thus will you enable yourself to enact those potentials.

Fashion an image of God as the Creator, now creating with you, a natural Christ, the New Heaven and the New Earth. Imagine yourself in a universe full of life comparable to your own. Imagine yourself being born into this larger community of life. Image your co-creative capacities turning on: universal consciousness, Earth/space development, synergistic co-operation, mind-body resonance—overcoming disease, aging and unchosen death.

Image yourself in the image of God.

Image yourself as Christlike.

Create this image for yourself consciously, deliberately and clearly. Carry this picture in your head at all times. Share it with all those who have eyes to see and ears to hear in every way you possibly can.

Image-making is a technology of creation which the Creator uses to create. You begin to practice now. It is the key to your transformation.

Image yourself as Sons and Daughters of God in a community of universal beings engaged in the thrilling process of building a New Heaven and a New Earth, at the beginning of your life as a co-creator.

The holy city of the New Jerusalem is waiting for those capable of imagining themselves as joint-heirs with me. The Kingdom of Heaven is your innate, potential capacity to exist at the next stage.

The city John saw is built by others who have gone before, who have already evolved. It is the model of what you will build yourselves, for those who are to come.

On Earth you used models from nature and the animal world. You saw trees and built treelike buildings. You saw fur, and you took it for your own skin. You saw fish swimming beneath the sea, and you built boats and submarines. You saw birds fly and you built airplanes. You saw flowers bloom and you designed fabrics and works of art to imitate nature's beauty, which was given to you as your inheritance.

What models will you use to build new bodies, new worlds beyond the biosphere? You have no models from the mineral-vegetable-animal womb of Earth, for none of them have gone beyond the planet. I am the model for the individual, as the New Jerusalem is the model for the community. I was conceived consciously; I was born conscious; I was aware that I was a son of God from childhood; I practiced love; and I chose to be crucified, to demonstrate the potential to materialize a new body more receptive to my intention. I told you that you would do the same in the fullness of time, which is now. I resurrected my body and changed it. I ascended, as you will. I now exist in total Christ-consciousness, which is a frequency band of awareness open to all who image themselves as me, whatever name they use.

The New Jerusalem is the model for new worlds to be built and inhabited by natural Christs. It is built by those who have gone before, for you who are yet to come. The children of the twelve tribes, the believers in their own poten-tial to be like me, will be the first to ascend. They will use what they see as a model for that which is to be built by Universal Humanity.

The first new worlds in space will be little replicas of the biosphere designed for survival. They will be awkward and nonaesthetic, as all new bodies are. Remember that the first fish to flop onto dry land were marinelike; only grad-ually did they transform.

So, gradually, your new worlds will refine as your collective capacities increase. Remember, none but the whole-centered survive for long. You will not be dealing with humanity as it is now. This is a key point for the builders of new worlds to remember. It will help you welcome the selection process brought on by the tribulations. You cannot build new worlds beyond your Earth as self-centered humans. **You will not have to. You will not have "close encounters of a third kind," but rather direct encounters with your own kind, at the next stage of evolution.**

Do not fear "aliens." You have learned on Earth, after much suffering, that there are no "foreign" nations because there are no foreigners. You are all cre-ated from one model, with each individual unique and each culture unique, but none foreign. You are living within one body. You are all members of one body.

You should know now that there are no aliens in the universe. They are Sons and Daughters of God at various stages of evolution. Yes, they are differ-ent—diverse beyond your present capacity to imagine—but they are not alien.

The word "alien" is a product of the state of self-centered, fearful con-sciousness in which each individual feels separate. It does not apply to the co-creative, universal phase.

The New Jerusalem is a model city at the next phase of evolution, which is co-creative life. It is peopled with co-creators, all of whom have graduated from the phase of self-consciousness. It is a community of co-creators, who have continuity of consciousness from one body to the next.

They are in direct communication with the Universal Mind through their awakened inner organs of perception, now still dormant in most Earthbound humans. They are in direct communication with other evolved master builders throughout the universe, many with billions of years of experience in co-creation. They have all the abilities I had. The works I did, they do, and far greater works.

You are preparing now for ascension to the New Jerusalem, dearly beloved. You are preparing as individuals by imaging yourselves as me. You are preparing as a collective of individuals by discovering who you are, connecting with each other, and probing even deeper for the details of the loving path to universal life.

This is the key purpose of this text: to act as a context for discovery of the specifics of the greatest mission on planet Earth. This is the mission of heroes and heroines, for which you have volunteered, dearly beloved. All those who read this text and feel called from within to act out the loving birth of humankind, have a prepatterned element of this design in their unused DNA.

This text serves as a context for individuals who are activated by this awareness, to discover their specific task within the whole activity. This is not easy, for all the tasks are new, unnamed, unheralded, unrewarded and unknown, except to those with eyes to see and ears to hear.

The New Jerusalem is hovering here, at the next frequency, right now. It is peopled with more fully-evolved beings, your teachers, waiting for you to grow up and start using your full potentials harmoniously, so they can begin the next stage of your education as godlike co-creators, which is the exercise of building new worlds after the model of the New Jerusalem.

The time and manner of your ascent is open. The details of any planetary birth process are as unique as the birth process of a biological organism. We know the general sequence of events. We know the inevitable outcome. No one knows the timing and the specific functions of individuals, due to the fact of freedom within the system.

Each individual called from within to participate in this task may or may not respond. Each has personal hurdles to overcome. No one is forced to act on behalf of the whole. Thus the wide variability among planetary births throughout the universe.

Your planetary process is happening now. The response of each actor in the play is critical. The angels of creation and the angels of destruction await your actions, dearly beloved. Think upon it with all your hearts, minds and souls.

The New Jerusalem appeared to John to "descend" because, from his perspective "in the spirit," the city materialized from a higher frequency. No one in the spirit can perceive the full reality of the new city.

The city was designed for you, dearly beloved. It is your new home, your new community, your new school.

> [O]n the east three gates, on the north three gates, on the
> south three gates, and on the west three gates.

> REVELATION 21:13

The New Jerusalem has twelve gates, and at the gates twelve angels. The gates have the names of the twelve tribes of the children of Israel written upon them. These tribes come from every quadrant of the globe. Remember, Israel is not a blood-type nor a geographical location. Israel is the idea that God and humanity are joined together for the transformation of this world, and new worlds beyond. The "holy people" who believe in this idea are scattered throughout the Earth.

God chose a particular group to communicate this idea because he had to start somewhere. The Jewish people have faithfully and magnificently preserved this idea through their arduous history. But they do not own the idea. The idea is universal. It is known throughout the universe because it is true.

Just so, the idea of Christ does not belong to the Christians. It also is universal; it, too, is known throughout the universe. It is the model of the phase of co-creative life which all beings everywhere in the universe go through after "birth" from their planetary wombs. It has to be embodied for the first time on every planet with evolving life. The first embodiment on planet Earth was me.

The children of the twelve tribes of Israel are the next to go into the co-creative phase.

> And the wall of the city had twelve foundations, and on
> them the names of the twelve apostles of the Lamb.

> REVELATION 21: 14

▲

The foundations of the New Jerusalem were laid by the twelve men who first carried the Word to the world. The children of the twelve tribes are those who will be last to carry the Word to the world. The end of the two thousand years of evangelism is approaching. When the Word has been heard by all the nations, the end shall come, as I have proclaimed before.

You, dearly beloved, are direct descendants of the twelve apostles of the Lamb. Yours is the task to complete what they began.

Your work is to extend and fill in and help act out the gospel concerning the end times, the tribulations and the New Jerusalem.

The apostles thought the end would come in their time. It did not. It is coming in yours.

You are the bridge over the abyss. You are the riders of the tidal wave of change, surfing the crest, then leaping upward, from the waters of the Earth to the fountain of life in the Kingdom of God.

From the mineral kingdom you grew, from the vegetable kingdom you enlivened, from the animal kingdom you arose, from the human kingdom you are now born to the Kingdom of Heaven, which is you-in-the-future as a natural Christ.

> And he who talked with me had a golden measuring rod to measure the city, and the gates thereof and the walls thereof. And the city lieth foursquare, and the length is as great as the breadth; and he measured the city with the rod: twelve thousand furlongs; the length and the breadth and the height of it are equal. And he measured the walls thereof: a hundred and forty and four cubits. According to the measure of a man, so also the angel measured.
>
> REVELATION 21:15-17

This is a clear instruction to you, dearly beloved, as was the building plan Noah received ages ago.

> The length of the ark shall be three hundred cubits, the breadth of it fifty cubits, and the height of it thirty cubits.
>
> GENESIS 6:15

The purpose of Noah's ark was to preserve the best specimen of the seed of the human family, and of each of the species, from an early selection device, the flood. It was an attempt to purify the Earth of self-centered humans, but it failed because, "the imagination of man's heart is evil from his youth." That is, there was the innate twin defect of carnivorous behavior and the forgetfulness of God, which reappeared in Noah's sons.

The purpose of the New Jerusalem is to provide an interim abode for those who are capable of evolving to the next stage of evolution, where they can remain during the tribulations if the negative scenario occurs; or, if the positive scenario occurs, where they can experience the reality of co-creatorship during the Quantum Transformation, to act as loving teachers of their brothers and sisters who are also evolving on Earth.

In the case of the negative scenario, the New Jerusalem is the essential salvation of the whole human seeds of Earth. In the case of the positive scenario, it is the essential training ground and model for the building of the New Earth and the New Heaven.

How do you suppose you will be able to build new worlds on Earth and new worlds in space without a blueprint, a manual, a guideline, a school of social architecture for co-creators? You cannot. That is why your experts are currently in such an inner panic. They don't know how to manage a planetary ecology, or develop synergetic self-government, or maintain a steady-state economy, or build self-sustaining, self-evolving worlds. Their panic is justified. They do not know how to do it. It cannot be done by empirical, materialistic means alone. The suprasensory channels of cognition must be open to knowledge by identity, and co-operation by attraction, as well as to scientific methods.

This is the purpose of the New Jerusalem. It is the first school for co-creative humans in the great discipline of conscious evolution.

*Let it be clear: I am not advocating passive repentance as my churches used to in the past. I am advocating active creativity, the use of all your faculties, and the power of all your initiatives, **combined** with the planetary shift now occurring at a metasystem level beyond human will alone.*

It is when you align your will with the will of God, with the patterns in the process of evolution, that all Heaven rather than all hell will break loose.

The New Jerusalem is large, large enough for millions of people, "according to the measure of a man," as the angel measured.

The angel was teaching John what to expect, what to report back to the people in Earthbound consciousness. Here is the point, dearly beloved. Listen well. John reported on the vision of the human condition at the next stage of evolution. It was the most hopeful vision ever stated, and hope attracts the heart. This vision activated a flame of expectation in the hearts of hundreds of millions of human beings. There will be a time and place beyond the creature/human terrestrial, self-conscious world for a personal future and a joint reward. This vision aroused an interest in the future. This interest in the future focused at first on life after death and on other-worldy realms totally beyond the capacity of prescientific humans to imagine building themselves.

However, out of the interest in a personal future in a transformed material condition, attention was paid to the material world and to the potential of the individual. Science and democracy emerged among those who held the vision of the New Jerusalem, however vaguely.

Remember my suggestion that you practice imagining and envisioning the New Jerusalem yourselves.

Here is the fact: The vision has activated the capacity to build not only one New Jerusalem, but as many as are required to carry the seed of higher human life into the universe.

If you examine the reality of your potentials now, at the dawn of the universal age, you will discover that you will be able to do it yourselves in the fullness of time, which is now. Life after death becomes life everlasting after this stage of evolution.

The New Jerusalem that John saw was not built by humans. It was built for humans by more evolved beings in the universe who have long since mastered the building of new worlds.

It will be your model.

However, you already have the capacities to begin. Like a newborn baby, you will not develop in isolation—and you are not in isolation, you are surrounded. You will encounter and learn from those others.

However, you must do a great deal for yourselves to be prepared for that encounter. Like a newborn child, you must manifest the will to live beyond the womb, in order to do so.

Let us examine your capacities to build a New Jerusalem.

Your healers are working to give you faith in your self-healing powers, using the power of positive imagery and personal responsibility to convince a drug-dependent society that you can be optimally well, better than you have ever felt before, with no clear limits to human wellness yet defined.

Your highest spiritual beings, even now, are telling you that each of you has access to an inner teacher, an inner healer, through which you can attune to God. They tell you that through a process called "initiation," you can transform yourself into an "ascended master." They speak of the hierarchy of evolved beings.

Your energy specialists, who study the full range of renewable resources on Earth and in space, even now, indicate a sufficient resource base in the immediate universe for the evolution of humanity for millions of years.

Your productivity specialists, who understand the resources of an Earth/space environment, even now speak of the possibility of total sufficiency for everyone.

Your researchers into human potential tell you that your mind-body is far more complex an instrument than you have yet used. Some indicate that your nervous system is still evolving, promising a natural capacity for enlightenment, dormant at the self-conscious stage of development. They speak of superlearning, superperformance, superbeings in the making even now.

Your researchers into meta-normal abilities tell you, even now, that extraordinary capabilities such as remote sensing, psychokinesis, levitation, clairaudience and clairvoyance are latent in many, suppressed by cultural disapproval and scientific disbelief.

There are those on Earth who say you can build new worlds in space, even now. You will begin with little worlds, then replicate and enlarge. You will use nonterrestrial resources from the moon and the asteroids to fabricate immense cities in free space. You have the materials of a thousand Earths right at hand. You are at the dawn of astroculture now, learning how to process lunar materials, farm the celestial bodies, capture solar energy, travel, work, live and explore the infinite environment beyond the confines of your mother Earth. Soon you could be established in the universe, free to grow.

Some of your imaginative architects weave miraculous images of gossamerlike materials, lighter than the gravity-bound structures of Earth, which will compose your cities in space.

Your sociologists and psychologists even now are designing models for synergistic self-government for humans living in total interdependence in space, where co-operation is as vital as the oxygen you share.

Your environmentalists, even now, are simulating total, closed-system, recycled, steady-state ecologies for your communities in space.

Your cyberneticians and builders of intelligent machines, even now, speak of "silicon based life" and self-replicating machines, robots capable of exploring and building in space, at human command.

Your biologists and aging specialists are probing into the genetic code, the building plan of your bodies, ferreting out the mechanisms of degeneration and disease, to alter and correct them, aiming to create for you a body free of disease, capable of self-regeneration and renewal.

Your UFO researchers inform you that entities of another dimension are interpenetrating your own.

Let the reality of your potentials, even now, pervade your being.

Now imagine these capabilities, and others, consciously activated as a conscious decision by the body politic of planet Earth.

You see the picture of a newborn cosmic civilization, eagerly and joyfully restoring the Earth, meeting the deficiency needs of all people, controlling unwanted pregnancy, procreating chosen children, each whole and normal and desired, and emancipating individual creativity in co-operative endeavor to fulfill the unlimited opportunities for creative work.

You see the people listening within, aligning with the same pattern in the process of evolution, breaking the barriers of pre-universal nationalism, ide-

ologies, creeds and dogmas, as they join together to explore the universe, within and without.

You see yourself living either on the planet or beyond the planet. You are regenerating, not dying. You know you are a natural Christ; you have met your older brother. And you have met all the others who have been selected for ongoing evolution at the time of judgment of the quick and the dead. Your community is graced by the presence of evolved beings, the saints and seers of the human race; you are illuminated with the presence not only of Christ, but of all other great spiritual leaders who have desired to exist as a person in a transformed body in a transformed world.

You are also in contact with beings throughout the galaxies who travel by thought, materializing and dematerializing like the consciously created holographic images already conceived by your scientists when the tribulations had barely begun.

There are no self-centered beings there. No crime. No criminals. No rape. No murder. No killing to eat. No lusting to kill. No need to kill. No sexual reproduction, only conscious conceptions: suprasexual union, chosen families, empathetic relations in attunement with each other and the plan of creation. No involuntary death, only transformation with continuity of consciousness. No fear. No hatred. No greed. None of the problems of mortal life. You have new challenges, new struggles, new joys, but, thank God, not the endless repetition of the ancient plagues of humanity.

> **And the wall was built of jasper; and the city was pure gold, like unto clear glass.**
>
> REVELATION 21:18

The New Jerusalem is a city of light. The materials that compose it are lighter than the materials you have known on Earth. Its atomic structure is accelerated. It shines like a prism through which the sun pours. It glows like the stained glass windows of Chartres. It is an environment of total beauty. It is designed by human nature at its highest.

Aesthetics is inherent in the nature of reality. Only the beautiful endures. Every work of mineral, vegetable and animal nature that we have inherited is beautiful.

The works of humanity, in the self-conscious or early phase, are not uniformly beautiful, except in instances of artistry, craftsmanship and loving care. This is because humanity in the self-conscious phase is unfinished and incomplete. So are its works.

We cannot judge ourselves until we fully become ourselves. "Ourselves" are not fulfilled as living souls in dying bodies. "Ourselves" will be fulfilled only as life-giving Spirits animating co-creative bodies that transform and do not die.

The environment that will be created by us-in-the-future will be as beautiful as the works of nature. They will be the glorious works of "human nature" in its fulfillment as joint-heirs of the Kingdom of God, builders of the co-creative communities on Earth and in the universe beyond.

God is an artist. We are created in the image of God. Our artistry has yet to be emancipated. The innate creative capacity of humans at the stage of natural Christs would seem godlike to us now. We have seen glimpses of it in our transcendent art, architecture, design and technologies. We see the dim outlines of our artistic ability in our cathedrals, our temples, our ceremonies and in our exquisite early instruments of co-creation—the microchip, the rocket, the radio telescope. The root of the word art is artus. It means "to join together, to fit." The root of the word religion is religare, "to bind back and make whole." At the next stage, art and religion will fuse in a common act of co-creation. We will attune to the Design of the Architect of the universe, and use our skills to build what we envision.

The New Jerusalem is an example of the architecture of the future, built by Sons and Daughters of God.

> **And the twelve gates were twelve pearls; each separate gate was of one pearl, and the street of the city was pure gold, as it were transparent glass.**
>
> REVELATION 21:21

The streets of the city were pure gold! Are you aware, dearly beloved, of how many people, mired in the mud of poverty, ugliness and disease, have taken those words to heart in the past two thousand years? Millions of them. Countless millions of living souls in dying bodies have lifted their eyes to heaven and prayed to be sent to the New Jerusalem.

And so shall it be, dearly beloved, so shall it be. They shall be there. Their desire has been registered in the Universal Mind. Their memories and experiences and acts are recorded in the Book of Life.

It is said by some of your so-called pragmatists that people are not concerned about the future, that they will only act on behalf of their immediate needs. This view is false. The essential human characteristic that distinguishes self-consciousness from animal consciousness is the awareness of potentialities to be realized.

People must attend to immediate needs to survive, just as animals do. But people are activated at the level of co-creativity by the opportunity to realize their potential to be more, do more, know more than their animal selves.

Religions have been formed around the rare experiences of God-centered life by the spiritual geniuses of the human race. All these religions have pointed to a future state of being, potentially here now, but not as yet realized due to the limits of human self-consciousness. These preserved experiences of enlightenment have lifted human civilization from the rudiments of survival to the threshold of life ever-evolving in a universe without end.

Those souls who believed that the New Jerusalem was paved with gold were right. It is. Gold is a metal used by the alchemist architects who build the co-creative communities of evolved humanity. Its beauty, dearly beloved, will lift your hearts with joy everlasting.

Visualize the most beautiful day on Earth. The sun is out. The trees are shimmering green. The seas are glistening blue. The birds are singing. The children are playing. The flowers are growing. All of that is energy-in-action, according to ideas of God.

Now visualize yourself as a natural Christ in a community of Christs, free from hunger, fear, death and disease, emancipated, aligned with the knowl-

edge of creation taught by ancient creators of worlds without end in the universe without end. Imagine what you will create when you are fully human.

John the Divine was a first child of humanity to catch a glimpse of the
works of art built by more evolved beings than you. You shall do as they, and
even more shall you do.

> **And I saw no temple therein, for the Lord God Almighty
> and the Lamb are the temple of it.**
>
> R<small>EVELATION</small> 21:22

The purpose of the temples of this world has been to preserve the seed of
hope for new worlds. When the new worlds come, the temples will be fulfilled.
They have been beacons of light in the wombs of our minds, reminding us of
our relationship to God. When that relationship is secure, the temples will disappear.

In the New Jerusalem, humanity and God are one. There is no need for
intermediary priests or buildings to house the reminders of God. The whole
city is a demonstration of God-in-action.

The separation of church, state, science and art is overcome in the cities of
the future. Every act is a conscious manifestation of divine intent. Every
human will is freely aligned with the will of God.

"The Lord God Almighty and the Lamb are the temple of it." People love
God above all else. They love their neighbors and themselves as natural
Christs. Their bodies are like the body of the risen Christ. In the New
Jerusalem the material world is a perfect manifestation of the spiritual ideas
that are its source, sustainer and evolver.

There has been much criticism of the conflict religion has caused on Earth
in your self-conscious phase. It has been terrible indeed, because religion
touches the deepest nerve in the person. Deeper than self-preservation, deeper
than self-reproduction, is the desire for self-transcendence.

It is deepest because, ultimately, it is the only desire that can be wholly fulfilled. The desire for self-preservation in the dying body is doomed to defeat.
Flesh and blood bodies will surely die. The desire for self-reproduction
through offspring is doomed to defeat. Each child is unique and evolves his or
her own self, not yours.

*The desire for self-transcendence **can** be fulfilled. For it is the Law of Self-Transcendence that every being can overcome its limits and continue evolving toward ever higher consciousness, freedom and co-operation with God. Not all beings do so choose. But all beings are free thus to choose.*

Of all the species on planet Earth now, humanity has chosen to self-transcend. The magnificent sea mammals with brains as large as yours have chosen to self-perpetuate in a steady state, rather than self-transcend in a new state. They are perfectly adapted to planet Earth, as it is now. But planet Earth will change. Eventually it will be consumed in the fires of its mother sun. Those creatures who have chosen to be co-creative, capable of building new worlds like the New Jerusalem and new bodies like my risen body, will prevail.

Thus the conflict over religion is deep. The various religions on planet Earth have been expressions of methods of self-transcendence. When members of religions disagree with each other, they are arguing over the most significant subject on Earth—the ever-evolving reality.

The choices you make through your religions are of ultimate significance. If you choose a religion that trains you not to desire a personal future in a transformed body, you will not have one. If you choose a religion that tells you that only your kind are loved by God, training you to exclude others due to religion, you shall be excluded from a future available only to those who love their neighbors as themselves. If you choose a religion that teaches you to worship the past and not the future, you shall receive what you have requested.

The universe is responsive to request. You receive what you ask for. The religious views of the future, when prayed for by their adherents, dictate precisely what the adherents will receive at their next stage. As you believe, so it shall be done unto you.

Cast your mind's eye over the religions of the world. Discover their idea of the future. And, believe it or not, dearly beloved, you will see the scenarios that will be acted out by those people.

Culture is now global. We are no longer individuals bound to the ideas of our ancient ancestors. Each of us on Earth is capable of choosing our image of the future and working with all our hearts, minds and spirits to achieve it.

We are no longer cultural slaves dictated to by the prevailing consensus. We are cultural creators, conscious that as we see our selves, so we act, and as we act, so we tend to become. Those who choose to become a natural Christ, building a New Heaven and a New Earth, learning the way to the future in the New Jerusalem, shall be fulfilled.

> **And the city had no need of the sun, neither of the moon to shine in it: for the glory of God gave it light, and the Lamb is the light thereof.**
>
> REVELATION 21:23

How do you experience yourself? Is it what you see in the mirror? Or is it the seer, looking outward at your mirror image, who is you? Is it the knower, or the known that is you?

It is the knower. It is the seer. At the next stage of reality you, as the knower, will know by identity the knower that is also every other. For all of you are one. This does not mean that you are the same. You are each unique. You are one in that each is a unique manifestation of one God. You are one because you are created by one God.

When you "see" the sun with your co-creative eyes, you will see it as an intelligent being radiating light to serve a purpose of God's. You will be in communication with that intention.

Remember, everything that is created shares the creative intention of the Creator—which is to know and act like God. When you see the moon, you will not see with creature eyes a "lifeless" ball circling the Earth. You will experience it as intentional energy-in-action serving an idea of God—and providing an inspiration for humans to fly, to orbit, to inhabit worlds beyond worlds beyond worlds.

The New Jerusalem will need no sun or moon to shine upon it, although the physical bodies of sun and moon will still be there, still providing the light now seen by the creature eyes and their extended instruments. But you and I will be seeing with the eyes of Christ, by the light of the God-within. The glory of this sight is that you see God-in-action everywhere.

> And the nations of those who are saved shall walk in the
> light of it, and the kings of the earth bring their glory and
> honor into it.

REVELATION 21:24

Those who choose this version of the future will be there. Those who do not choose it will not be there. Choose well, dearly beloved, choose well.

The end shall not come until "this Gospel of the Kingdom shall be preached in all the world for a witness unto all nations." We are holding the silence in heaven until everyone on Earth has a chance to choose life-everlasting.

What, you may ask, of all those souls born before I came to Earth? How could they choose a personal future if they did not know?

Those to whom the promise was made have always known it. Their souls transcend in time. They will be there. It is for the sake of the less-evolved souls on Earth now that we wait, so that the birth can include all souls capable and desirous of evolving toward universal life.

> And the gates of it shall not be shut at all by day, for there
> shall be no night there.

REVELATION 21:25

Co-creators do not depend on the light of the sun to see. They see by experiencing the God-force in action.

Do you suppose God requires light from the stars to see you? Do you suppose you will require light from the sun to see God? No, dearly beloved. It is insight that enables you to see the source of all being.

> [A]nd they shall bring the glory and honor of the nations
> into it. And there shall in no way enter into it anything
> that defileth, neither whatsoever worketh abomination,
> or maketh a lie, but only those who are written in the
> Lamb's Book of Life.

REVELATION 21 26-27

What is the honor and glory of the nations, dearly beloved? What is truly honorable and glorious in our lives?

To honor is to respect the intrinsic, inalienable value of another being, without qualifications.

What is the inalienable value that we honor in each other?

It is that which is sacred, that which cannot be violated. The nations that honor the sacredness of the individual are those which believe that each is created by God, and that each has a personal future of ultimate value. Those who shall be brought into the city of the future are those who honor the sacredness of the person. This value springs from the sense of the ultimate value of the individual connected with God.

The political system that affirms this, the sacredness of the person, is the natural form of self-government.

Can you imagine the creative energy that will be liberated in a society where all the energy is invested in transforming, growing, learning, exploring?

Let us face this concept directly. It is essential for you to understand. Evolution constantly selects for those who elect higher manifestations of freedom, complexity, order, union, love, co-creativity and co-operation.

In every stage there are innumerable contenders for evolutionary advance. Everything is tried. Not everything succeeds. What does succeed in the long run, is that which facilitates the progress of the whole system.

You will find in the New Jerusalem the characteristic of love of God, self and all being. The terrible burdens of creature/human government—coercion, defense, conflict and lack of understanding among factions—will not exist, for only those who understand and love will be there.

Fortunately, it is not your task to judge. You will benefit from the selection process. It is written in the Book of Life. Only the beautiful endures. Only the good prevails. This is the essence of progress, as well as the essence of pain. This is the result of freedom to choose to follow the will of God, or to negate it with a lesser purpose of your own.

The stakes are high, dearly beloved. Choose well.

> **And he showed me a pure river of the Water of Life, clear as crystal, proceeding out of the throne of God and of the Lamb.**
>
> Revelation 22: 1

The source that animates your being is pure, clear, uncontaminated life, proceeding from the Mind of God, enacted through the flesh of Christ.

The idea became flesh. The perfect idea became perfect manifestation. At the stage of the New Jerusalem, the word becomes flesh, perfectly. The translation from word to act, from idea to reality, from potential to actual, is perfect. Nothing is lost in the translation. For there is no corruption, no disconnection, between the Creator and the co-creator. When we are consciously connected to God at all times, the Water of Life will run through us with no interruption, forever and ever.

Imagine a community of universal, co-creative humans who are connected consciously at all times to the Universal Mind, acting always out of pure love, in alignment with the progressive will of God for ever-deepening, higher, greater participation in the act of creation. It is escalating ecstasy, dearly beloved, ever-rising joy.

You have followed the compass of joy, guided by the flame of expectation within you, to the threshold of the New Jerusalem. You seek entrance at the pearly gates. You knock, and doors will open; you ask, and it shall be given.

Dearly beloved, do you know that God has waited eternities for you to ask to enter the Kingdom? When you ask for entrance into Heaven, there is a celebration throughout the universe. Another being has joined the universal community of co-creation. Thank God.

Dearly beloved, you who are reading this text, and you who are aligning with the Design through other descriptions of it, rejoice. Ask for entrance to the New Jerusalem now.

This will seem unbelievable to your rational intellect, for it can only know reality from without, not from within. You are not to discard your intellect. It is a precious instrument to carry out the Intention of Creation. You are to hold it in abeyance long enough for your intuition to experience Heaven.

Dearly beloved, to "go" to the New Jerusalem now, you must do the following:

Desire the Kingdom of Heaven above all else;
Put the Kingdom first.

Will your entrance into the Kingdom with absolute certainty that God wills it for you. By so willing, you are at last doing what God really wants of you. It is not simply that you stop hating and start forgiving. That is a negative goal—like saying your goal in life is not to be sick. Not to be sick is a goal for the sick. To be in Heaven is the goal for the well. Those of you who are well, who have overcome your sickness of body, emotions, ego—which is the sickness of the illusion of separation from God—must now affirm that the purpose of wellness is not more wellness, but transformation. You are to will your transformation into a natural Christ, transported to the first universal community open to you, known as the New Jerusalem.

This community exists now throughout the universe. There are more New Jerusalems in the universe than there are grains of sand in the sea.

Think how many villages, towns and cities there are on planet Earth. Think how incredible they would seem to the first human who awoke with self-consciousness: a miracle beyond belief—cities of humans, who look like him! Humans with similar biological apparatus doing the miraculous things you now do—talking across the world, living in environments conceived by humans, responsive to their request. You want light—you flick the switch, and there is light. You want to speak to China—you pick up the phone and call, and there is China on the line. You want to fly—you step into a plane, and there is flight. You want to learn how many years ago God created the universe—you pick up a book on cosmology, and there is the answer.

Imagine yourself as the first humans at the dawn of self-consciousness, viewing the life of people in the great cities of planet Earth in the third quarter of the 20th century. Incredible! **The next stage of evolution always seems incredible to the one that came before.**

Now, imagine yourself as a first co-creative human at the dawn of universal consciousness—which you are. You are viewing the image of the next stage of your evolution, in community with other co-creative humans from planet Earth, in communication with a multitude of evolved beings from other star systems throughout the universe, in direct contact with the Mind of the Creator.

The Earth as you now know it will soon pass away. Self-centeredness will die out. The Earth will be renewed. Whole-centered humans will be renewing it. They will also be transcending it by participation in building new worlds in space. By these twin acts of renewal and co-creation, they will attain the status of citizens of the universe, and gain access to the millions of communities of godlike beings, recorded in the Book of the Gods, which the angel refused to let John read.

You alive now, before the judgment of the quick and the dead, are in an evolutionary speed-up which only occurs at quantum transformations.

Those of you whose task it is to act as guides to your fellow humans through cataclysmic shifts that are to come, must catch a deeper glimpse of the new model of community, in order to help the confused millions see ahead to a light at the end of the tunnel.

Without that light, panic will ensue. Without that hope, the people will perish, en masse. *But with that light, people will be empowered* en masse *to continue, continue, continue until they reach the promised land.*

Therefore, dearly beloved, hold your intellect aside. Let your imaginations go free. Envision yourselves as a more mature species in a community of evolved beings. Now ask that you be taken there to see with your eyes what John the divine saw with his.

Ask with total faith, and it shall be done. Do you remember when I performed the healings in the early days? I always said, it is your faith which made you whole, your faith and the will of God for your wellness.

The same principle applies to your ability, not to cure yourselves of illness, but to evolve yourselves to the next degree of wellness. Have absolute faith and consciously will yourself to see and experience the universal community that surrounds you now.

I will do the rest. You cannot transcend by human will alone. You cannot transcend by God's will alone. It is the union of your active will with God's active will that shall provide for you the preview of coming attractions that you must have to activate your potentials now.

The goal of this phase of evolution is natural Christhood for the individual, and the New Jerusalem for the community.

My New Order of the Future must experience this state of being in advance of others, to arouse them to self-evolve.

*As Moses led the children of Israel out of the land of Egypt, you are to lead the children of humanity out of self-consciousness to the promised land of co-creation—which was the goal of Moses, too. He lived before the fullness of time. You live **in** the fullness of time. Thank God. Amen.*

> **In the midst of the street of it, and on either side of the river, there was the Tree of Life, which bore twelve kinds of fruit and yielded her fruit every month; and the leaves of the tree were for the healing of the nations.**
>
> REVELATION 22:2

On either side of the river of the Water of Life grows the Tree of Life. This tree bears fruit whose taste brings union with God. It is nourished by the river of the Water of Life, which is the animating spirit of the Creator that flows through the Creation. You and I meet there, dearly beloved.

The New Jerusalem is the city wherein the Tree of Life grows.

Adam and Eve reached the first Tree of the Knowledge of Good and Evil. They separated out from the animal world and began the arduous phase of self-consciousness. They suffered the error of the illusion of separation and carnivorous behavior, caused by suprahuman and nonhuman error: Lucifer's self-rejection, and the animal's self-consumption.

I came to planet Earth to correct the error and point the way to the Tree of Life through my demonstration of the crucifixion, the resurrection, the ascension, the promise that you also shall do the works that I do, and even greater works shall you do.

Now we approach the time of the Second Eve, the Second Adam, the Second Couple, the Second Tree and the Second Coming. All occur at the same marvelous period in history, which we are now entering.

The Second Eve is human consciousness transformed through union with Christ. It is transformed intellect discovering God's invisible technologies of creation, now joining with God to co-create a New Heaven and a New Earth. It is human intellect and individuality desiring union with God at sufficient intensity to consummate the marriage of Christ and Eve. The marriage of human nature with suprahuman nature is the mystical marriage for which you have prepared since time immemorial. It is the initiation of suprasexual co-creation.

This wedding takes place between me—Christ—and all humans who are willing it with their whole being now. Through this marriage you experience the ecstasy of union with me. The union ceremony, wherein you place your dense body in my light body, transforms your mind-body systems to resonate at higher frequencies, rendering you capable of seeing face to face that which you now see through a glass darkly.

The Second Adam is Adam of the life-giving Spirit, the Adam who follows Eve to the Second Tree and thereby transforms. Eve-consciousness leads at points of Quantum Transformation. The feminine aspect of human consciousness expresses pure desire for life. When life has reached an impassable limit, from the perspective of the old, Eve-consciousness reaches beyond the old limit to the new opportunity for life. Eve-consciousness is the pure desire for the evolution of life towards union with God. She rises at every point of radical change.

Adam-consciousness, the masculine aspect of human consciousness, has a pure desire to know how the creation works, to be partners with God in the universal enterprise. When Eve-consciousness takes the first step in the discovery of the next stage of life, Adam follows to consolidate the new condition and improve it through incremental change.

At the Tree of Life each person unites feminine and masculine consciousness within his or her own being. Feminine desire for union with God and masculine desire for partnership with God fuse in each person at the threshold to the Tree of Life.

Each whole being then unites with me. I AM the potential within each of you to evolve beyond creature/human life. I AM the potential beyond you which has already been actualized in countless beings throughout the universe.

As your co-creative potential is aroused, you unite with me, who is a real being beyond you. This is the part that is difficult for creature/humans to believe. It was difficult for Moses. I had to persuade him with miracles. It was difficult for the first disciples. The resurrection was not enough. I provided the Pentecost. I provided the Holy Spirit to awaken their co-creative systems and arouse them to acts of genius—healing, materializing and communicating directly with me.

I will do the same with you. We shall demonstrate the powers of co-creation through you, at the threshold of the Tree of Life, so that you will be empowered to lead the children of Earth to the promised land.

What shall these demonstrations be? What miracles shall be performed that we might be empowered to lead the children of Earth to the promised land?

The demonstrations will be of your capacity to be a natural Christ, to regenerate your body, to communicate directly with me and to lift up into space in spacecraft and there connect with your brothers and sisters on Earth, in such a deep alignment that I can contact you all at one moment in time, which is now. "Now" in cosmic time is whatever length of time it takes to complete this idea, which has already been conceived and therefore already is.

This shared contact is known as the Second Coming. It is available as soon as the conditions have been met.

The Second Eve and the Second Adam unite masculine and feminine within each, making a whole being. Then each whole being marries me, the Christ, making each a co-creative being. Then each co-creative being unites with another co-creative being in a partnership to create unique acts to fulfill the Design of God. This union of co-creative human with co-creative human is called the Second Couple.

The Second Couple reaches the Second Tree, the Tree of Life. The first couple cannot do it. Man and woman, joined together to procreate flesh and blood, cannot achieve life everlasting. They cannot inherit the powers of gods. Their emotions are tainted with the twin defects of killing to eat and the illusion of separation. They are possessive and incomplete. Their judgment is clouded by fear. They cannot be entrusted with the evolutionary capacities of longevity, nuclear power, microtechnology, antigravity, limitless energy, whole new worlds.

Co-creative couples inherit the Kingdom. In Noah's ark, the species went in two by two. The union of opposites is the way to transcendence. That is the law.

In universal communities, couples are united in a degree of union that you have glimpsed at the peaks of human love. The peak is but the footstool to the mountain of creative love that you shall climb together, two by two, dearly beloved, when the Kingdom comes.

Those of you who are now practicing co-creative couplehood are paving the way for humanity. As you become whole and unite with each other, awakening the co-creative power within each, emancipating untapped human potential, you have direct encounters with me and with your brothers and sisters in the universe.

We are as real as you. We are more real than you are now. For we are connected to the mind of God, and have been partaking of the Water of Life for countless eons of your time. We have been eating the fruits of the Tree of Life. We no longer consume animal flesh. We no longer have animal bodies. We are immortal.

The leaves of the Tree of Life will heal you of the remaining scars of self-centeredness, as they heal us of moments of disconnection. Remember, Satan is either consumed by fire or by love. In the New Jerusalem, there is no illusion of separation. The function of so-called evil is to select the whole from the imperfect. In the New Jerusalem this function is voluntary. Individuals test for weakness, and they self-correct. It is not done by coercion but by attraction to the continuation of life. Self-correction occurs through the knowledge of conscious evolution in alignment with the will of God.

> **And there shall be no more curse, but the throne of God and of the Lamb shall be in it, and His servants shall serve Him.**
>
> REVELATION 22:3

The curse of the fall is over. The suprahuman struggle between Lucifer and God has been resolved. In the violent path to the New Jerusalem, Satan is finally buried forever in the "lake of fire and brimstone," the place of eternal purification. No one emerges imperfect. The lake of fire and brimstone is the

great purification process in the universe. It is the universal therapeutic healing ground. Remember, nothing that is created can be uncreated. Everything
that is created continues in some form.

The throne of God and of the Lamb are All in All. God-consciousness and
its manifestation in acts of creative service is the way of life in the New
Jerusalem.

Only the good endures. Only the beautiful continues. Only the whole
evolves. So be it. Amen.

**And they shall see His face, and His name shall be be on
their foreheads.**

REVELATION 22:4

You shall see God face to face, and you shall know that God is your name.
Our Creator, who art in Heaven, has given God's name to the Sons and
Daughters of God. If God is our parent, we inherit God's name. We are God's
children. God and we are one. That is the meaning of this story, dearly
beloved—as you have always known.

You shall see God's face with the inner eyes of awareness that you and God
are one. Only they who know they are of God, at one with God, see God face
to face. That is the law. Its purpose is to protect those who do not know God
from gaining godlike power. This power in the hands of those who do not
know the laws of God is destruction on the universal scale. It cannot be. This
is why the Tree of Life was protected by cherubims and a flaming sword when
you were driven out of the first Garden of Eden.

To reach the Tree of Life you have two paths before you, dearly beloved: the
path of violence laid forth to John wherein the destructive are destroyed by the
angels; and the path of love laid forth in the Planetary Birth Experience,
wherein the constructive are attracted by the angels to communication, communion and fusion in a psychomagnetic field sufficiently powerful to align the
majority of humanity with the will of God.

The violent path is an abnormal birth. The loving path is a normal birth.
Which shall it be? We shall see, according to your acts now, dearly beloved.

If you do your part, we in heaven shall be empowered to do ours. It is a cosmic drama in which you now are the key actors—those of you who know what is happening now. The rest are still asleep in the womb of self-centeredness, nursing their wounds and crying in pain.

The children of God are on the stage of history ready to act out the drama of the last days. You for whom this text is written are keepers of the script, readers of the blueprint, discoverers of the Design.

> **And the angel said unto me, "These sayings are faithful and true, and the Lord God of the holy prophets sent His angel to show unto His servants the things which must shortly be done."**

REVELATION 22 6

Dearly beloved, you who have eyes to see and ears to hear, you who believe in your capacity to follow me by being me, listen well.

The angel of God is speaking to you. Here is what he says:

Dearly beloved on planet Earth, harken to my words. The silence in heaven is about to end. The doorway to the New Jerusalem is about to open. The tribulations are about to start. The Quantum Instant is near.

I call upon you to activate the capacities to save the world from self-destruction. I call upon you to undertake a mission comparable to the first disciples of Jesus. They were the first to carry the message of the reality of our potentials to the nations. You are to be the last to carry the message.

They lived at the beginning of the change. You live at the "end times," when the old shall pass away and the new shall appear.

This text is a call to action to the new disciples of Christ to manifest their own capacity to do as I did, and more. This text is for the avant-garde of humanity who awaken with love in their hearts and joy in the spirit at the glory which shall be revealed in us.

I call upon Homo universalis, *those in whom the flame of expectation burns high, to set about the double task of self-transformation and the activation of the world's capacity to achieve the goal of its history.*

You are to become natural Christs. You are to communicate to the world its potentials to restore the Earth, free the people, and impregnate the universe with new life. *You are to participate in the Instant of Co-operation, the Planetary Birth, the Second Coming.*

You are to bring on the shared contact with me. You are to ascend to the New Jerusalem. You are to overcome physical death. You are to be in touch with your universal brothers and sisters. You are the first sons and daughters of humanity to become the Sons and Daughters of God, as a new norm.

So be it. Amen.

> "Behold, I come quickly." Blessed is he who keepeth the sayings of the prophecy of this book.
>
> REVELATION 22:7

*Blessed are you, dearly beloved, who know I am with you always. Blessed are you who will **do** the sayings of the prophecy of this book.*

In the time of John it was necessary to keep the sayings to preserve them for the fullness of time, when they can be done. Now is that time.

Behold, I come quickly to those of you who will ask me to come by choosing to become like me. What I require of you, dearly beloved, is not the prayers of children. I require your maturity. I require co-equals capable of being joint-heirs.

> And I, John, saw these things and heard them. And when I had heard and seen, I fell down to worship before the feet of the angel who showed me these things. But he said unto me, "See that thou do it not, for I am thy fellow ser-vant, and of thy brethren the prophets, and of those who keep the sayings of this book. Worship God!"
>
> REVELATION 22:8-9

I, Jesus, am a Son of God. You, humanity, are also Sons and Daughters of God. My message to you is: Join me. Be me. Together we will worship God through becoming one with the Divine.

You are no longer to worship me as a God. You are to become godlike. Together we will worship the Creator of the whole.

My mission was to demonstrate that humanity has the capacity to act like God. Your mission is to prove me right by demonstrating your capacity to do as I did, and even more.

O dearly beloved, if you knew how eagerly your willingness to be me is awaited in Heaven, you would hasten to throw off the shackles of self-limits this instant.

Listen well: the sayings in this book are true. They were prophesied by John and will be acted out by you.

> And he said unto me, "Seal not the sayings of the prophecy of this book, for the time is at hand. He who is unjust, let him be unjust still; and he who is filthy, let him be filthy still; and he who is righteous, let him be righteous still; and he who is holy, let him be holy still."
>
> REVELATION 22:10-11

*Seal not the sayings of **this** book. The time for them to happen is at hand. It has been a long time, dearly beloved, and it still continues, to give you time to save the world from the violent path to universal life.*

The selection has not yet been made. We are in a holding pattern, circling, circling, circling the destination, waiting for the word to be heard so that the choice can be made by all peoples of Earth.

Yours is the feather that tilts the scale. Yours is the grain of salt that crystallizes the solution. Yours is the flame that makes the steaming water boil.

Yours is the most marvelous moment in the history of humanity. Put forth the word. Sound the trumpet. Heaven awaits your act.

> "And behold, I come quickly, and My reward is with Me, to give to every man according as his work shall be."
>
> REVELATION 22:12

We are circling, circling, circling a hair's breadth from your awareness, waiting, waiting, waiting for every member of the planetary body to be included in the selection.

Every person on Earth must know that he or she has the freedom to choose life-everlasting, through love of God, and of their neighbor and self as me. Then the end shall come.

The word you are to put forth is that every person on Earth has the choice of life-ever-evolving through the activation of the full individual potential. The word you are to put forth is that every person on Earth has the innate capacity to be a co-creator. The word you are to put out is that the time for decision is ending.

You are to provide the opportunity for a planetary signal wherein each person who chooses life over death can register that decision visibly—a coming to witness before the world.

The lights must go on everywhere in the world at once to signify the rising of the flame of expectation in the hearts of the members of the body of Earth.

In every country there is a sound which means "yes." In every culture there is a gesture which means "yes."

The sounds and the gestures of "yes" must now rise from the body of Earth so we may know that the danger of the violent path has been avoided by the free choice of humankind.

Who chooses "yes" shall evolve. Who chooses "no" shall not evolve. Then behold, I will come quickly, my reward with me.

> **"I am Alpha and Omega, the Beginning and the End, the First and the Last."**
>
> REVELATION 22:13

I, Jesus Christ, am humanity fulfilled. Humanity fulfilled is inheritor of the Kingdom. The Kingdom is the awareness that all is one. When all is one, each is the beginning and the end, the first and the last.

You are Alpha and Omega. You are the beginning and end. You are the first and the last. You are me.

> **Blessed are they that do His commandments, that they may have right to the Tree of Life, and may enter in through the gates into the City.**
>
> REVELATION 22:14

The commandments in this text are coded instructions for universal life. They could not be fully understood until the capacity to act upon them had matured. They were lodged deep in the human mind as aspirations to be fulfilled in the fullness of time.

The people who have lived before the scientific age could understand the personal, ethical and spiritual aspects of the commandments. They could not understand those aspects which depend upon evolutionary technologies that are as yet barely one generation old. These are the technologies of co-creation—nuclear, genetics, electronics, astronautics, robotics, microtechnology, cybernetics and noetics.

Only one generation of humans, your own, has known of the existence of these capacities combined; they are the essential components of your access to the Tree of Life.

The commandments of love have been acted out by the good people of Earth. They shall be rewarded. But the commandment to act like me and to do as I did, including the resurrection and the ascension, could not have been acted out by any except a few, in the secret mystery schools of Earth, until the maturation of your scientific capacities.

Here is the double-edged sword. The capacities necessary for life everlasting are those capable of total destruction. Thus the dilemma in Heaven. Can a still self-centered species inherit the Tree of Life? No. Yet your species stands at the threshold of the Tree of Life.

Either the good will prevail, connect, link and magnetize the majority of humanity to act with love for life everlasting, or the violent selection of the self-centered will begin.

> **For outside are dogs and sorcerers, and whore-mongers and murderers and idolaters, and whosoever loveth and liveth a lie.**
>
> REVELATION 22:15

The selection process will exclude all who are exclusive. The selection process assures that only the loving will evolve to the stage of co-creator.

"I, Jesus, have sent my angel to testify unto you these things in the churches. I am the Root and the Offspring of David, and the Bright and Morning star."

REVELATION 22:16

I, Jesus, have sent mine angel to testify unto you these things in the churches of the world, wherever two or three are gathered in the name of their potential to be me.

I am the root and the offspring of David. I spring from the root idea that God and humanity are one, united for the transformation of the world to a New Heaven and a New Earth. I am the offspring of this idea. I was the first on Earth to demonstrate its reality.

I come from the bright morning star. I come from afar. I am he who materializes in every planetary system undergoing its birth. I am everywhere there is a world aborning. I am the beginning of universal life everywhere. I am the way through which every species must graduate to become co-creative with God.

This cannot be done without love. Nowhere is this done without love. Amen.

And the Spirit and the bride say, "Come." And let him who heareth say, "Come." And let him who is thirsty come; and whosoever will, let him take the Water of Life freely.

REVELATION 22:17

The spirit which is sent unto each person in the world, says, "Come, you are beloved, you are wanted, you are welcomed. Come."

The bride, which are all those who have already chosen to unite with God by becoming like the Christ, says, "Come, you can do as I do, and even more shall you do."

Whoever feels a longing in the heart for love everfulfilling, whosoever hungers for union with God, whosoever thrills to the morning of life everlasting, come, drink of the Water of Life.

It is free to all who desire to become heirs of God. It can only be received by your free choice to desire it. Everyone is equal in this respect. Everyone is sacred in this regard. Everyone is his or her own judge in this regard. All who choose life everlasting have judged themselves worthy to be me.

> For I testify unto every man who heareth the words of the prophecy of this book: If any man shall add unto these things, God shall add unto him the plagues that are written in this book. And if any man shall take away from the words of the book of this prophecy, God shall take away his part out of the Book of Life and out of the Holy City, and from the things which are written in this book.
>
> *REVELATION 22:18-19*

This is true. If humans behave as they are now behaving, the prophecy of John will surely be fulfilled. Humanity will take the violent path to Heaven. However, if humans change their behavior, the prophecy of John will be avoided. It will have served as a magnificent warning that has helped us change our course in time.

Its description of the fulfillment is true. Birth is inevitable. Some will live to see it. The question is, how many? That is up to you, just as John prophesied.

This text was written not to add or subtract from the divine book of Revelation. It was written to inform you of the alternative to Armageddon.

Remember, the Law of Freedom is absolute. You shall have the future you choose.

> He who testifieth these things saith, "Surely I come quickly." Amen. Even so, come, Lord Jesus. The grace of our Lord Jesus Christ be with you all. Amen.
>
> *REVELAT ION 22:20-21*

I who testify these things two thousand years later also say, surely do come quickly. We are ready. The potential is within us to be like Christ.

I ask that you, with the force of the will of God, become what you are. Amen. So be it. Thank God.

A Call to a New Order of the Future

The next thirty years is the period of the great transition from one phase of human evolution to the next. "We shall all be changed," either violently with great pain, or gracefully with love.

The Planetary Birth—the emergence of the Universal Human—is one description of a widely intuited potential for the human race to shift its collective consciousness from fear and separation to unity and love.

This work is a call for us to work together to catalyze this blessed process in our life time. It is to help those of us who experience ourselves as a Universal Human to recognize each other and to fulfill our destiny now.

Together—
We can see what none of us can see alone.
We can do what none of us can do alone.
We can celebrate what none of us can appreciate alone.

The pages that follow provide opportunities for you to participate in this great evolutionary adventure:

✦ A letter inviting you to assist in understanding and envisioning a New Order of the Future;

✦ An invitation to a spiritual practice;

✦ Instructions for celebrating the most powerful sacrament I have ever experienced, the Planetary Birth Communion;

✦ Information about Symposia and Teachings for Conscious Evolution, and *The Rings of Empowerment* manual that will guide you in forming co-creative circles and teams;

✦ A Core Library for Conscious Evolution;

✦ An Idea Index;

✦ Additional materials available from the Foundation for Conscious Evolution.

A LETTER OF INVITATION

Dear Companion on the Way:

As you know, my life has been guided by key questions: What is the meaning of our power? What is our story? What is the future of humanity? Now I have a question for you: What is this "New Order of the Future?" In the writings the Christ voice constantly calls this Order to take initiatives vital to evolution now. If this work has resonated with a truth in your own heart, it means you **know** something, it means that you have an important part to play. At the end of this Section 3, we invite your reponse, so this Order can serve its true purpose. Here is the guidance I received, which may be a stimulus to your own intuition.

At the very beginning of the writings, at the Mount Calvary Monastery, I was asked to found this New Order in myself, and to find other founders. I recorded in my journal the following paragraph, which has already been quoted...and more:

> *You, all of you who are desirous and ready, are the Way. Be a beacon unto yourselves. This tiny band, this brave congregation of souls attracted to the future of the world are my avant-garde—the New Order of the Future.*
>
> *Barbara, form this Order quietly, peacefully with no fanfare and consecrate it to God at Mount Calvary as soon as you gracefully can. These are self-selected souls who have come to Earth to carry the miracle of the resurrection into action as the transformation of humanity from* Homo sapiens *to* Homo universalis.
>
> *This Order of the Future is dedicated to the intuitive and intellectual discovery and implementation of my Design in perfect faith that it is there and it is good. Its purpose is to provide deep communion for the pioneering souls of Earth with each other, with me and with the whole world.*
>
> *This Order is to develop an unsung ministry, communicating potentials, encouraging creative action, celebrating triumphs large and small, seeking no power for itself, only the empowering of life itself.*

Members of this Order are to pledge themselves to love, honor and support each other in whatever tasks are given to them. They are to become members of my new family of universal humanity, humans becoming fully human, in humility and faith accepting their place as participants in the process of creation, partners with God.

There is to be no proselytizing, no propaganda, no quest for worldly power as it is now known.

Each member of the New Order will be involved in work in the world. When the Order comes together each will share aspiration, vision, inspiration and needs. There will be a natural, spontaneous synergy, a matching of needs and resources, a support which does not need to be planned by human will.

The Order will learn to listen to each other, to the voice within each, and to the higher self, Christ-consciousness, or whatever new names emerge.

You will be guided as to the ceremonies and celebrations of the New Order of the Future.

Form evolutionary circles [circles of evolutionary consciousness], remembering that wherever two or more are gathered in my name, there I am. These circles will link and connect, like tiny replicating cells of light and life and strength and vision...."

What is this community of pioneering souls to do and be? How can we best serve to evolve ourselves and our world?

My own understanding is that those of us who identify ourselves as founders of a New Order of the Future are a vital, future-oriented strand of humanity. People in this state of consciousness have reassembled under many different names at evolutionary epochs in human history, such as the time of the early disciples or the founding of the United States of America. Its principles are encoded on the Great Seal on the dollar bill: *Novus Ordo Seclorum:* A New Order of the Ages; *E Pluribus Unum:* Out of Many One; *Annuit Coeptis;* God Favors this Enterprise.

The roots of this New Order reach back to the first flicker of consciouness that humanity is to evolve beyond the creature/human condition. It began in Egypt, India, Greece and Israel, where great individuals experienced their connection with all being beyond the limits of the self-centered mind. This New Order is to become a synthesis of the teachings of all the great avatars, seers, saints and visionaries of the human race. Each wisdom tradition brings its own gifts for the evolution of the world.

The Book of Co-Creation calls to a New Order of the Future in the context of the birth, teachings, death, resurrection, ascension and promise of Jesus Christ for life everlasting. He provides the template of the Universal Human, our potential self, and the pattern of the next stage of evolution: the New Jerusalem, beyond sorrow, beyond pain, beyond planet-boundedness and death.

Now, as Sidney Lanier says:

> We gather together, not to worship one Messiah, but to recognize that all of us are to be messiah. We are at the time prophesied by the prophet Joel, when the Lord will pour Spirit upon **all** flesh. Now we have to grow up and become responsible for the birth of messiah in each of us. Through that inner birth we also will participate in the resurrection, which we now call "the transformation." The new story we have to tell is the story of all of us. The story of our cosmogenesis. This story includes all past stories. They all converge in the birth of the Universal Human, the sovereign person.

This is an Order of universal consciousness of love and truth, an Order of "partnership with God." It transcends all past divisions. It is for those who experience themselves as universal beings, and who identify with the whole story of creation.

I received the call to this New Order through the Universal Christ. Each of us may receive it in our own way. All paths, all faiths have a vision of a higher state of being. All are essential to the "ecology of souls." The call may come to each of us according to our own tradition. However, when we **respond** to the call, we step beyond our prejudices and divisions, beyond labels and self-imposed restrictions. We enter the Circle of the Whole as universal beings in love and service.

The Christ voice advised:

Use the name Christ sparingly to describe the Inner Teacher. The better phrase is co-creator, our potential self, the future human. Every human being on Earth can identify with this potential self.

I, Jesus Christ, was simply a first example of what you all can be. Since very few could actualize their full potential during the last two thousand years, I was deified and put above you. People worshipped me instead of actualizing themselves.

Ultimately I envision that this Order will become a global community for conscious evolution, a spiritual communion across race, nation and religion, acting as leavening in the loaf of society, attracting individuals, institutions and organizations to see and act upon our collective potential for a positive future.

I received this guidance, recorded in my journal after finishing the writings:

All evolutionary initiates are at the same stage of evolutionary initiation—attempting to stabilize and normalize their natural Christ abilities while replunging into the world-in-action.

*Everyone of you who makes it through this critical period will find each other and meet within the next phase, for you **are an order of the future.***

This New Order is undergoing its test. Each person has been given his or her assignments. All the assignments are connected. The test is effectiveness. Can you make it work enough for it to grow? You will meet everyone else capable of doing the same.

This New Order of the Future, at its outset, is not to shepherd the beginner, but to strengthen the co-evolutionary initiates. Their union is essential now. SEEK AND YOU WILL FIND, dearly beloved...

The Order is composed of members of a "transition team." The old team has preserved the expectation of the promise which has been made. They have built the means of transcendence.

The churches and other institutions, scientific and democratic, have maintained awareness of the evolutionary goal of human history. This goal is a personal future in a transformed body in a transformed world in a universe without end, heirs of God, co-creators, at the dawn of the Universal Age.

The transition team is to act as a guide through the transformation from the first Adam of the living soul, to the last Adam of the life-giving spirit.

This is the time of the cosmic "twinkling of an eye" when you shall all be changed. This Order of the Future is composed of all souls on Earth who now know they are here for this purpose.

The "new team" will be those who are the second fruits of Homo Sapiens, the sons and daughters of Man, who are born as divine-humans not creature humans. The new team is not here yet. It is not time. The new team is composed of fully matured humans, who will appear after the judgment of the quick and the dead—the post-mammalian generation of whom Jesus Christ was a first model.

The old team preserved the seed of hope. They planted it in the ground. It grew in the coldness of the soil, slowly, until the spring rains came and warmed the Earth.

The transition team is here to grow the flower, to open the bud, to BE THE BLOOM so all the budding beings in the whole garden of Earth can know they too can grow. The transition team is not to organize a permanent institution. Its purpose is to act and dissolve.

This Order is neither religious, nor political, nor social, nor scientific. It is a synthesis. Its purpose is to identify the pattern in the process of evolution through scientific investigation and spiritual intuition. As the pattern is identified the Order finds the way to help facilitate the pattern through action. It communicates the pattern through all media for maximum participation and co-creation worldwide.

Clearly, this New Order is not an organization, church or religion. It is a state of consciousness. It lives in the hearts of those who recognize it in themselves and others. The goal is for those who have this awareness to achieve planetwide recognition of universal consciousness in all of us.

WHAT DOES A NEW ORDER OF THE FUTURE MEAN TO YOU?

We would like to know of your response to this work. What does it mean to you? From your deepest wisdom, what do you know of this New Order of the Future? What is your founding and ongoing contribution to this work? Your response to these questions (see "Declaration of Intention" on p. 319) will form the foundation for the growth of this New Order and its work in the world. Among the responses we have already received concerning the nature of a New Order of the Future are the following:

✦ An invisible mystery that goes beyond the traditional walls of my church or religious denomination.

✦ The Body of those who accept and live within whole-system consciousness, in effect becoming cosmic persons.

✦ A core of people who realize and affirm identity with and participation in universal consciousness, forming an all-inclusive transcendent community.

We will study readers' responses to these questions and report on their overall pattern in a forthcoming newsletter.

To support a New Order for the Future, we have established The Foundation for Conscious Evolution as a center of communication for the movement for conscious evolution.

By its very nature, The Foundation for Conscious Evolution is co-creative! It is through your participation, inspiration and support that we will evolve. Accordingly, we look forward to your response, and greet you with joy and anticipation of the next phase of the evolutionary journey.

Barbara Marx Hubbard

INVITATION TO PRACTICES

If you are moved by this work it is very likely that the "Inner Teacher," the still small voice of God, is active within you, or about to be activated. When the Christ experience occurred to me in 1980 I heard the words:

*BE ME. I want demonstrations **now, Barbara.***

I responded: "I choose it, but I don't know how to do it."

The reply was: *You choose it, **I'll** do it.*

I understand this to mean that the Christ self, the universal self, is potential in each of us. It is brought forth by our choice, our attention, our love, our discipline and practice. This commitment evokes partnership with the Universal Christ. We do not do this alone!

For the last thirteen years I have done my best to follow this commandment, as I know millions are doing, each in our own way. It is my intuition that there is a critical mass of people just a veil away from Christ consciousness. The veil is thinning daily as the "noosphere," the thinking layer of Earth, matures and the "global brain" (and heart) links us up throughout the world. The Planetary Birth Experience is one way of describing a change in our souls' frequency to be simultaneously resonant with Christ-consciousness on a planetary scale.

This Sunday morning, March 6, 1993, as I put the final touches on the manuscript before taking it to the printer, I received the following guidance for the reader of this book from the Inner Teacher:

For those of you who know that I AM within you, here is my word:

This work is to be used as a signal to you who are ready to evolve as natural Christs, universal humans.

Be Me. Put this purpose first. Be your full Potential Self. I AM within each of you now. There is a simple act you can perform:

Each day arise at dawn.

Sit in your private place.

Visualize me as your Potential Self.

Let me appear before your inner eye.

Notice all my characteristics—

how I see, how I love, how I create.

Now see yourself manifesting as the God within you.

As I AM, YOU ARE.

Notice all of your characteristics.

Love yourself as you love me.

Now contemplate yourself in your full glory.

Allow your divinity to rise up within you.

Be transfigured as I was.

Your attention is like sunlight upon the seed in Spring.

Ask questions of your universal self.

Record your responses in your journal.

Then join in evolutionary circles of two or more.

Place me at the center of the circle.

Allow me to be the nucleus

of the new life form which you are.

Meditate upon the risen Christ.

Let me activate you at the cellular level.

Speak from within to one another.

Reveal the truth of who you are.

Receive yourselves as Universal Humans.

Read your journals to one another.

If you are so attracted

offer the Communion to one another.

It will accelerate your transformation

as the living expression of the Christ.

I offer here a beautiful affirmation which can be used in conclusion. It is called "The Seven Spirits of God."

I am love.
I love God above all else,
my neighbor as myself
and myself as a natural Christ.

I am wisdom.
I distinguish what is breaking through
from what is breaking down.
I identify with what is breaking through
and I release what is breaking down.

I am faith.
I know there is a perfect Design of creation.
Each of us is a vital element in that design.
I know I am now acting
in perfect harmony with that Design.

I am courage.
I know that I am not working alone.
I am surrounded by mighty companions
on this Earth and in the universe beyond.
Together we work toward the inevitable victory.

I am patience.
The timing is not in my hands.
I live in eternity.
I act in the present.
I am fulfilled.
I surrender my need to know the timing
and act in joy.

I am power.
To the degree that I empower others
I am now empowered.

I am surrender.
Not my will but thy will be done
on Earth as it is in heaven.

I would be glad to offer to you more of these teachings of the Inner Christ. I suggest that you follow a similar path of inner listening, speaking and recording. (Reading *"The Revelation,"* Section Two, aloud in your group will stimulate your inner voice.) I believe that out of such meditative dialogues an extraordinary set of events will unfold.

I have included on the following pages key practices that have made the difference in my own evolution.

If you would like to receive "Teachings from the Inner Christ" please let me know by checking the appropriate item on page 365 and you will be notified when they are available.

THE PLANETARY BIRTH COMMUNION

In 1990 I was deeply guided to offer the communion to myself and colleagues on a daily basis. I had checked into a little abbey in Boulder, Colorado, for a silent retreat. The Christ voice spoke again:

You have come home to me. The bread and wine hold within them the substance of my new body. The key for you now each day is to breathe deeply in a "birthing experience" of the resurrected body. Then do the communion and experience my body transforming yours. Do this in prepration for the Planetary Birth which will be induced through this experience given to the new disciples of Christ who choose to work together for the Planetary Pentecost, when the Spirit of God is poured out upon all people. This is the purpose of your mission on Earth. All your projects will be reoriented, aligned and empowered as you accept this purpose and put it first...finally.

Just as your thoughts were realigned by allowing me to interpret the New Testament through you, now your actions will be aligned by the substance of the Eucharist. By entering into your body, my body can orient your actions from the source rather than from the end result or goal. Do not abandon my church. Expand my church, evolve my church, transform my church into a new vehicle for the new beings, for the Plantary Birth, for the resurrection of the Whole Body.

I have offered the communion in this manner for three years, and find that my life has been completely reoriented. It is the sacrament given to founders of a New Order. I present below, for those of you who are attracted to this celebration, the script that I have followed.

BACKGROUND

Jesus first offered the communion at the Last Supper, asking his disciples to incorporate his body and blood of the New Covenant in remembrance of him. Through their faith, the bread and the wine was experienced as a new substance. Hundreds of millions if not billions of people have since incorporated the spiritual substance of the Christ, thus establishing a powerful field of consciousness.

Whenever we offer the Planetary Birth Communion we enter that evocative field. We are lifted up by it. We forgive, nourish and evolve one another by actually incorporating the living body of Christ.

This particular form of the communion is given specifically for those who share the purpose of catalyzing the Planetary Birth. My guidance was to do it every day, alone or with colleagues. It reorients our lives from within, setting in motion an alchemical process that activates the Christ within and reorients our lives in alignment with our deepest life purposes. It takes us deeper into the mystery of our transformation as natural Christs.

The Planetary Birth Communion is a sacred and potent sacrament, an "outward and visible sign of an inward and spiritual grace." It is never to be imposed, nor offered casually. It is only for those who deeply choose it. It returns to the people the power of blessing and offering the sacrament that until now has been reserved to the clergy.

THE COMMUNION CEREMONY

Join together in circles of two or more. Each "evolutionary circle" becomes an omni-center of universal consciousness, seeding our global brain with the vital message: "We are being born!"

Although the communion can be offered alone, it is more powerful when two or more are joined, particularly if they share the great purpose of the Planetary Birth. For as Jesus told us, "Where two or three are gathered together in my name, there am I in the midst of them."

The role of celebrant or guide should be rotated, as it was with the early disciples. It was then presided over by women and men alike.

This is a sacrament-in-progress. You will bring your own inspiration and modification to it. The following is what I do.

Setting:

Establish a sacred space and time. Allow no interruptions. Use candles, flowers and other expressions of beauty.

Prepare the communion table with a sacred cup of wine or grape juice, and small pieces of bread, preferably unleavened, for each person.

Sit in a circle around the communion table as an intimate group, as close together as is comfortable.

Begin by meditating in silence.

In consciousness evoke the Presence of the living Christ. Experience this Presence, at the center of the circle, now activating the Christ within each member of the circle.

Invocation:

The celebrant leads the group in saying these words:

> *We are gathered here together as*
> *Co-founders of a new order of the future.*
> *We are a deep communion of pioneering souls*
> *from every race, nation and religion.*
> *We experience within ourselves*
> *the emergence of the Universal Human,*
> *the natural Christ,*
> *the Co-creator of new worlds without end. Amen.*

Forgiveness:

Each person takes an opportunity to ask for forgiveness and to offer forgiveness. This forgiveness can be done silently, or aloud. The main point is to release anger, grievances, fear and other distracting consciousness into the healing field of the living Christ.

Intention:

Each person may state his or her intention for the communion, such as "My intention for this communion is to experience the full emergence of myself as a divine being."

Preparation:

The celebrant says these words, which I received directly from the Christ Presence:

> *You have come home to me now.*
> *The Eucharist holds within it the substance of my new body.*
> *Breathe deeply in a birthing experience*
> *of the resurrected body.*

Take time to breathe deeply together. Experience the Christ at the center of the circle. With each breath feel every cell in your body ignite with the divine fire of the living Christ.

The celebrant continues:

> *Take this bread and this wine*
> *and experience my body transforming your body.*
> *When my substance is incorporated into your substance*
> *you are transformed by*
> *growth through identity with the divine.*
> *Do this in preparation for the Planetary Birth,*
> *which will be induced*
> *through this experience given*
> *for those new disciples of Christ*
> *who choose to work together for the*
> *Planetary Pentecost.*

Transformation:

The participants collectively bless and transform the bread and wine into the body of Christ. All members extend their hands toward the bread and wine.

The celebrant lifts the bread and the wine, saying:

> *Take, eat, this is my body.*
> *Take drink, this is my blood,*
> *given for you to transform into the living Christ,*
> *the Co-creator of new worlds without end. Amen.*

Communion:

Then the celebrant first eats the bread and drinks the wine or juice, stating in his or her own words a statement like, "I _____, do gratefully incorporate the living substance of the Divine."

The celebrant serves the bread and wine to the next person, who speaks his or her own words, takes communion, and in turn serves it to the next until the ceremony is complete.

The Great Silence:

Let the experience reach into every cell. Allow the alchemical process to work, lifting the mind-body into the Christ field of energy.

Speak from Within:

The celebrant may say the following words, which invite participants to speak spontaneously as their own inner voices:

> *Allow me to speak in your voice,*
> *from your hearts,*
> *of the mighty works*
> *which you are to do for the Planetary Birth.*
> *This is the purpose of your mission on Earth.*
> *All your projects will be reoriented, aligned and empowered*
> *when you accept this purpose and put it first.*
> *By entering your body, my body orients your actions*
> *from the source rather than from the end result or goal.*
> *I shall be unfolding as you from within.*

Here we may offer acknowledgments of our unique gifts, purposes and contributions toward the Planetary Birth. We become wise men and women bearing gifts for the Cosmic Child, humanity...ourselves as we really are.

Thanksgiving:

Give thanks for the communion. Express gratitude for those things that are working toward our birth, on the planet and in our own lives.

Closing:

The celebrant closes with a summary. "We give thanks for this event..." The words I heard were:

> *You have come home to me.*
> *Do you feel it?*
> *As you do this as a daily ritual*
> *you will be fully guided.*
> *Do not abandon my church.*
> *Evolve my church.*
> *Transform my church into a new vehicle*
> *for the new beings, for the Planetary Birth,*
> *for the resurrection of the Whole Body.*

A closing benediction may be offered.

When the communion is complete, preserve the sacred space of consciousness for as long as you can. Allow conversation to deepen and inspired insights to flow. In this field of Christ-consciousness, we ask and receive.

This sacrament serves as a direct source of guidance from the living Christ to all who ask.

The celebrant consumes any remaining bread and wine, and the vessels are cleaned as soon as possible in due respect for their sacramental service.

FURTHER OPPORTUNITIES FOR YOU TO PARTICIPATE

GATHERINGS AND TEACHINGS FOR CONSCIOUS EVOLUTION

It is very important that those of us who respond to this call gather in groups, small and large. When we come together, and join spiritually, our "genius codes" are unlocked, our creativity is expanded, our vocations are affirmed and deepened.

The Foundation for Conscious Evolution will convene periodic Symposia and Teachings for Conscious Evolution, offered to all who are attracted. These gatherings are one of many initiatives to reconvene the "diaspora," the scattered souls of Earth who have within them a "memory of the future," a sense of the evolutionary potential of the human race.

These gatherings are intended to draw together leaders at the growing edge of human endeavor to help understand and activate humanity's social, scientific and spiritual capacities to catalyze a Planetary Birth Experience in our lifetime.

The gatherings will feature a core instruction in conscious evolution, to deepen our understanding and implementation of our divine potential.

Barbara Marx Hubbard will offer a special teaching for New Order founders who seek to to actualize their evolutionary potential to be natural Christs.

THE RINGS OF EMPOWERMENT: HOW TO FORM EVOLUTIONARY CIRCLES TO DISCOVER AND FULFILL OUR LIFE PURPOSE

The core group, or support group, is essential for our evolution. As the AA groups have served millions of people in recovery from addiction, so "EA" (Evolutionaries Anonymous!) groups provide "birthing circles" for Universal Humans, co-creative families to support our personal and social self-actualization. *The Rings of Empowerment* manual presents the best practices we have discovered to bring our life purposes to manifestation in the world, modelling the change we would like to see in our relationships with one another. This manual has been edited by Carolyn Anderson of Global Family to serve a worldwide network of core groups. She writes:

The Rings of Empowerment is a manual for discovering and fulfilling your life purpose as part of a co-creative team. It contains specific tools and experiential exercises for tapping into your innate knowing, for discovering and deepening your vocation of destiny, for finding your teammates and for gaining the entrepreneurial skills required to actualize yourself in the world. It is designed to empower individuals and teams at the leading edge of transformation to co-create the world we choose. (See p. 365 to order *The Rings of Empowerment* manual.)

Please complete this and send it or a copy to the Foundation for Conscious Evolution, 336 Bon Air Center, #384, Greenbrae, CA 94904.

DECLARATION OF INTENTION

Building a Common Union of Co-creative Consciousness

I hold these truths to be self-evident:

> There is a Designing Intelligence of the universe.
> I am the creation of that Intelligence.
> I am ready to become co-creative
> with that Intelligence to bring forth within me
> the next stage of the evolution of our world.
> I recognize in all humility that I am
> an infinitesimal part of an infinite universe,
> capable, even in my infancy,
> of resonating with that Infinity
> to an ever more precise degree.

I, _____, declare my intention to become a Universal Human. I recognize that I am founding a New Order of the Future within myself and my world. I seek a planetwide recognition of all who share this awareness.

I give thanks that my intention, aligned with all others, is now activating this shift in consciousness and action.

In my deepest wisdom, this is what a New Order of the Future means to me:

(Use the back of this page or extra paper if necessary).

I would like to participate in The Foundation for Conscious Evolution and a New Order of the Future.

___I enclose $5.00 to receive first information on future Foundation activities and to be placed on the primary mailing list.

___I would like Barbara Marx Hubbard to speak at a major event. Name of event:_____Please send information.

___Recognizing that The Foundation for Conscious Evolution (a 501(c)(iii) tax exempt, nonprofit organization) requires funds to sustain its work, I enclose my check, payable to the Foundation for Conscious Evolution, for $_____.

Name:_____

Address: _____

Phone: _____

Thank you! We welcome your participation.

A CORE LIBRARY
FOR CONSCIOUS EVOLUTION

The context from which *The Book of Co-Creation* springs is the emerging meta-discipline of Conscious Evolution. This new world view takes a whole-systems perspective, and sees an implicate design of evolution that leads to ever greater freedom and consciousness through more complex order.

From the perspective of Conscious Evolution, all knowledge contributes to our understanding of how the cosmos evolves, thus enabling us to co-create a future equal to our power, aspiration and spiritual wisdom.

The high calling of a conscious evolutionary who identifies with *The Book of Co-Creation*'s purpose is:

✦ To assimilate, understand and appropriate into his or her own being the New Story of Creation;

✦ To awaken the Universal Human within, through deep choice, self-discipline and psycho-spiritual practice;

✦ To communicate the New Story of Creation to others;

✦ To fulfill his or her vocation of destiny in the great transition leading to our Planetary Birth as a universal species.

In support of this calling, we recommend for *study* the following Conscious Evolution Core Library of books in print (except as noted) as of January 1993.

PART 1: A NEW IMAGE OF REALITY
THE COSMOLOGY OF WHOLENESS

THE NEW STORY OF CREATION:
Evolution As a Purposeful Process

Elgin, Duane. *Awakening Earth: Exploring the Human Dimension of Evolution* (William Morrow, 1993).

> An overview of human evolution, from the deep past into the deep future, with an hypothesis of the evolutionary transformation to occur in the next five hundred years.

Hubbard, Barbara. *The Evolutionary Journey* (1982, available from Foundation for Conscious Evolution, address on p. 365.)

> The 15-billion-year story of creation leading to our birth, with a vision of our future as a universal species. Includes a one-year study guide for conscious evolution.

Jantsch, Erich. *The Self-Organizing Universe: Scientific and Human Implications of the Emerging Paradigm of Evolution* (Pergamon, 1981).

> A profound examination of purposeful dynamics in evolution.

Keck, L. Robert. *Sacred Eyes* (Knowledge Systems, Inc., 1992).

> An invitation to view the entire human journey and your own life from the perspective of a transformed soul, with a new deep value system and a new concept of God.

Murchie, Guy. *The Seven Mysteries of Life: An Exploration in Science and Philosophy* (Houghton Mifflin paperback, 1981).

> An imaginative description of how life came to be "the culminating celestial fact."

Roszak, Theodore. *Voice of the Earth* (Simon & Schuster, 1992).

An examination of how empirical science is confronting "mind in the cosmos," the design and tendency toward higher order in nature.

Russell, Peter. *The Global Brain: Speculations on the Evolutionary Leap to Planetary Consciousness* (J. P. Tarcher, 1983); *The White Hole in Time: Our Future Evolution and the Meaning of Now* (Harper, San Francisco, 1992).

Two seminal works on personal, social and technological evolution, which predict humankind's imminent shift from separated to shared consciousness.

Smuts, Jan. *Holism and Evolution* (Greenwood Press, 1973 reprint of 1926 edition).

A description of nature's tendency to form whole systems that increase freedom.

Swimme, Brian, and Thomas Berry. *The Universe Story: From the Primordial Flaring Forth to the Ecozoic Era* (Harper Collins, 1992).

A review of the entire 15 billion years of cosmic evolution interpreted as a "communion of subjects rather than a collection of objects," to the point where the direction of our further evolution is subject to choice.

Teilhard de Chardin, Pierre. *The Phenomenon of Man* (Harper Collins, 1975); *Christianity and Evolution* (Harcourt Brace Jovanovich, 1969).

Teilhard is a spiritual godfather of conscious evolution. His body of work lays the theoretical groundwork for our awareness of divine purpose as an operative factor in evolution, which is generating our emergence as Universal Humans in the image of Christ.

THE NEW SCIENCE

Bohm, David. *Wholeness and the Implicate Order* (Routledge and Kegan Paul, 1980—presently out of print).

A quantum physicist's fascinating theory of a metaphysical substrate to the material world.

Capra, Fritjof. *The Tao of Physics,* 3rd edition (Shambhala Publications, 1991).

An exploration of the complementarity of modern science and mysticism.

Davies, Paul. *The Mind of God: The Scientific Basis for a Rational World* (Simon & Schuster, 1992).

A thorough examination of the implications for the God-hypothesis of contemporary scientific discoveries and understandings.

Harman, Willis. *Global Mind Change: The New Age Revolution in the Way We Think;* and *A Re-examination of the Metaphysical Foundations of Modern Science* (both Institute for Noetic Science, 1990 and 1992).

Anticipations of the "new reality" implicit in the cosmology of wholeness that is now emerging in the physical, medical, psychological and neurosciences.

Prigogine, Ilya, and Stengers, Isabelle. *Order Out of Chaos: Man's New Dialogue with Nature* (Bantam, 1984).

Prigogine's description of the dynamics of phase transitions from states of lesser to greater order.

Sheldrake, Rupert, *A New Science of Life: The Hypothesis of Formative Causation* (J. P. Tarcher, 1988); *The Presence of the Past: Morphic Resonance and the Habits of Nature* (Random House/Vintage, 1989); *The Rebirth of Nature: The Greening of Science and God* (Bantam, 1992).

A radically new hypothesis of the origins, maintenance and behavior of forms, from atoms to galaxies, by means of universal, non-physical "fields."

Templeton, John M., and Robert L. Herrmann. *The God Who Would Be Known: Revelations of the Divine in Contemporary Science* (Harper & Row, 1989).

A sensitive exploration of how the divine is revealing itself in nature.

THE CONVERGENCE OF SCIENCE AND SPIRIT

Abraham, Ralph, Terence McKenna, and Rupert Sheldrake. *Trialogues At the Edge of the West: Chaos, Creativity and the Resacralization of the World* (Bear and Company, 1992).

Three perspectives on the seeming "one-mindedness" of the cosmos, which the authors discuss variously as "the divine imagination," the "world soul" and the "Cosmic Christ."

Capra, Fritjof, and David Steindl-Rast, with Thomas Matus. *Belonging to the Universe: Explorations on the Frontiers of Science and Religion* (Harper Collins, 1992).

A physicist and two priests discuss the "divinization from within" that tends to accompany our new understandings of the cosmos.

Dossey, Larry. *Recovering the Soul: A Scientific and Spiritual Search* (Bantam, 1989).

A physician's holistic view of mind and reality, proposing that mind and being are nonlocal, and thus independent of time, space and matter.

Feuerstein, Georg. *Wholeness and Transcendence: Ancient Lessons for the Emerging Global Civilization*, revised edition (Larson Publications, 1992).

A distinguished student of ancient Hinduism makes available the riches of Indian spiritual wisdom in a context truly accessible to Westerners seeking their way to universal human maturity.

Lemkow, Anna F.. *The Wholeness Principle: Dynamics of Unity Within Science, Religion and Society* (Quest/Theosophical Publishing House, 1990).

An overview of how we are regaining our sense of connectedness with the cosmos.

Talbot, Michael. *The Holographic Universe* (Harper Collins, 1992).

A tangible perspective on cosmic wholeness and the universal interconnectedness of all things, including mind and matter.

White, John. *The Meeting of Science and Spirit: Guidelines for a New Age* (Paragon House, 1990).

A lucid description of the next stage of human evolution and how we will attain it; with a fascinating analysis of the Second Coming of Christ.

OUR STORY IS A BIRTH
Shifting society from self-centered terrestrial to whole-centered universal consciousness and action.

Capra, Fritjof. *The Turning Point: Science, Society and the Rising Culture* (Bantam paperback, 1987).

An analysis of the evolutionary shift now occurring in the basic systems of society.

Ferguson, Marilyn. *The Aquarian Conspiracy*, revised edition (J. P. Tarcher paperback, 1987).

A ground-breaking survey of emerging new paradigms in politics, relationships, medicine/health, education/ learning, economics/vocation.

Henderson, Hazel. *Paradigms in Progress: Life Beyond Economics* (Knowledge Systems, Inc., 1992).

A new way of looking at economic, social and environmental systems, to bring them into harmony with the total system of life on Earth.

Stikker, Allerd. *The Transformation Factor: Towards an Ecological Consciousness* (Element, 1992).

The potential role of Taoism and Teilhard de Chardin's thought in shifting human consciousness from self-centered to symbiotic consciousness.

Vajk, Peter. *Doomsday Has Been Cancelled* (1977, available from the author, P.O. Box 8040-148, Walnut Creek, CA 94596, for $11.00 including shipping and handling).

A vision of our potential to build new worlds in space, by one of the first post-Copernican social thinkers to recognize the future of humanity as a universal species.

PART 2: EMERGENCE OF A UNIVERSAL SPECIES
The Harmonious Fulfillment of Our New Capacities

UNIVERSAL CONSCIOUSNESS
The shift from local self-centered consciousness
to nonlocal God-centered consciousness.

Aurobindo, Sri. *The Life Divine* (Auromere, 1983).

The major statement of a modern master, Teilhard de Chardin's Eastern counterpart, whose life and work demonstrates the possibility of the evolutionary transcendence of *Homo sapiens*.

Bucke, Richard M.. *Cosmic Consciousness* (Citadel Press, 1984).

A seminal work on the evolution of consciousness, from animal awareness to cosmic awareness, concluding that the human race is moving toward a transhuman, godlike state as far beyond us as we are presently beyond the animals and as animals are beyond vegetal life.

Emerson, Ralph Waldo. *Essays: First and Second Series,* especially *"Self Reliance"* (Random House/Vintage, 1990).

A call to the full emancipation of our unique genius as sovereign persons. The works of Emerson, and of other transcendentalists such as Thoreau and Whitman, are among the earliest American expressions of humankind's collective awakening to our potential for conscious evolution.

Holmes, Ernest. *The Science of Mind,* Fiftieth Anniversary Edition of 1938 publication (G.P. Putnam's Sons, 1988).

A modern articulation of the perennial philosophy of unitive consciousness, which teaches how to think, not about Jesus, but the way that Jesus himself thought. This is a pure and radical teaching, with the potential to lift humanity from victimhood and pain to natural Christhood. Its transcendent technology of "affirmative prayer," or "spiritual mind treatment," is a powerful practice to bring forth the divine human (see the volume by Jaeger and Juline, under "Practices," below). Classes are taught in churches of Religious Science throughout the world.

Wilber, Ken. *Up from Eden: A Transpersonal View of Human Evolution* (Shambhala Publications, 1981).

A survey of the stages of evolution of the human psyche, whose author is considered by many to be as pioneering in our day as was Freud in his.

Yogananda, Paramahansa. *The Autobiography of a Yogi,* revised 12th edition (Self-Realization Fellowship, 1981).

The self-revelation of a great modern master who demonstrated the further reaches of human consciousness and capacity.

UNIVERSAL ACTION
Our physical ability to live and build new worlds in space.

O'Neil, Gerard K. *The High Frontier: Human Colonies in Space* (Space Studies Institute, Princeton, 1987).

> A profound examination of the purpose and promise of space colonies.

White, Frank. *The Overview Effect: Space Exploration and Human Evolution* (Houghton Mifflin, 1987—presently out of print).

> A sweeping vision of our evolution from a terrestrial to a solar and galactic species.

UNIVERSAL LIFESPAN
Optimum wellness, self-healing, self-transformation, life extension and regeneration, conscious reproduction, overcoming death, resurrection, new bodies.

Chopra, Deepak, M.D. *Quantum Healing: Exploring the Frontiers of Mind/Body Medicine* (Bantam, 1990); *Unconditional Life: Mastering the Forces that Shape Personal Reality* (Bantam, 1992).

> Brilliant works by a Western-trained physician and student of the Vedas and Ayurvedic methods of healing, which clearly demonstrate our potential for self-healing through conscious thought.

Murphy, Michael, *The Future of the Body: Explorations into the Further Evolution of Human Nature* (J. P. Tarcher, 1992).

> The major work on meta-normal capabilities of the mind-body, dormant in us all, which lead to a third order of evolutionary transcendence, comparable to the emergence of life from nonlife and of human life from animal life.

Satprem, Mother. *The Mutation of Death* (Institute for Evolutionary Research Ltd., 1987).

A remarkable description, by her associate and assistant at the Sri Aurobindo Ashram in Pondicherry, India, of Mother's life work to transmute her cells to immortality.

UNIVERSAL CONTACT
We discover that we are not alone.

Bova, Ben, and Byron Preiss. eds. *First Contact: The Search for Extraterrestrial Intelligence* (NAL/Dutton, 1991).

The world's leading astronomers confront an ultimate question: Are we alone in the universe?

Hynek, J. Allen. *The UFO Experience* (Time-Life Books, 1990 reprint of 1972 edition).

A respected scientist's views on the significance of UFO's.

UNIVERSAL POWERS
Moving beyond brutalizing, unchosen work via a global/universal technological nervous system, an extended body of immeasurable capacity.

Clarke, Arthur C. *Profiles of the Future* (Harper & Row, 1973—presently out of print).

A glimpse of possible future technologies that would literally give us the capacity of a universal species.

Drexler, K. Eric, and Chris Peterson, with Gayle Pergamit. *Unbounding the Future: The Nanotechnology Revolution* (William Morrow, 1991).

A report on the quantum jump in technological capacity that is now leading to the routine transformation of matter through molecular engineering.

Drexler, Eric K. *Engines of Creation* (Doubleday Anchor, 1991).

> A layman's guide to nanotechnology giving us the ultimate power of co-creation with nature at the atomic level.

Fuller, R. Buckminster. *Cosmography: A Blueprint for the Science and Culture of the Future* (Macmillan, 1992).

> A comprehensive overview of Bucky's philosophy and application of "Design Science."

Fuller, R. Buckminster. *The Critical Path.* (St. Martin's Press, 1982).

> Bucky's life work and thought applied to our becoming "citizens of local universe" through understanding the design of nature.

Glenn, Jerome Clayton. *Future Mind: Artificial Intelligence—Merging the Mystical and the Technological in the 21st Century* (Acropolis Books, 1989).

> A pioneering synthesis, drawing upon two forms of mind expansion that often appear to be antagonistic yet are potentially synergistic.

Leary, Timothy. *Info-Psychology: A Manual on the Use of the Human Nervous System According to the Instructions of the Manufacturer* (New Falcon Publications, 1989).

> A manifesto to "the seven percent who we assume are DNA-designed to attain biological immortality, leave the womb-planet, become galactic citizens and fuse with superior interstellar entities."

Levy, Steven. *Artificial Life: The Quest for a New Creation* (Pantheon Books, 1992).

> A report on the potentials of computer technology for creating autonomous, self-organizing and self-reproducing artificial organisms.

Penrose, Roger. *The Emperor's New Mind: Concerning Computers, Mind and the Laws of Physics* (Viking Penguin, 1989).

A major work on the relationship between contemporary physics, the dynamics of human consciousness and the potentials for artificial intelligence.

UNIVERSAL HUMAN
The sovereign person, co-creator, natural Christ.

Grof, Stanislas, with Hal Zina Bennett. *The Holotropic Mind: The Three Levels of Human Consciousness and How They Shape Our Lives* (Harper San Fransisco, 1992).

An exploration of our potentials for transcending present limitations on human consciousness.

Maslow, Abraham H. *Toward a Psychology of Being,* 2nd edition (Van Nostrand Reinhold, 1971).

The seminal studies in human wellness and self-actualization that launched the human potential and transpersonal psychology movements.

Zohar, Danah. *The Quantum Self: Human Nature and Consciousness Defined by the New Physics* (Quill/William Morrow, 1990).

A new model of consciousness, psychology and human nature that discerns "something deeply feminine about seeing the self as part of a quantum process, about feeling in one's whole being that I and you overlap and are interwoven, both now and in the future."

CHRIST AS A LIVING PRESENCE AND
TEMPLATE FOR HUMAN EVOLUTION

Calhoun, Flo. *I Remember Union: The Story of Mary Magdalena* (All Worlds Publishing, 1992).

> An intuitive biography of Mary Magdalene, Judas and Jesus, prior to and following the resurrection, with implications for the re-emergence of Christ consciousness in our time.

Fox, Matthew. *The Coming of the Cosmic Christ* (Harper San Francisco paperback, 1991; leader's guide also available).

> A vision of the living Christ that connects us all, by a spiritual pioneer and founder of "Creation Spirituality."

Rossner, Fr. John. *In Search of The Primordial Tradition and the Cosmic Christ: Uniting World Religious Experience with a Lost Esoteric Christianity* (Llewellyn Publications, 1989).

> An examination of the relationship between modern scientific and spiritual discoveries and ancient insights into Cosmic Being.

Sparrow, G. Scott. *Witness to His Return: Personal Encounters with Christ.* (A.R.E. Press, 1991).

> A case study analysis of the nature and implications of close encounters with the actual presence of Christ.

PART 3: PRACTICES FOR THE CO-CREATOR

A Course in Miracles (Foundation for Inner Peace, 1976).

> A spiritual psychology from the Christ consciousness, with a workbook of daily practices, which teaches forgiveness and release from the illusion of separatedness. Study groups convene worldwide.

Holmes, Ernest, and Willis H. Kinnear. *How to Change Your Life* (Science of Mind Communications, 1982).

A compendium of Ernest Holmes' key writings on the practical application of spiritual principles in daily life.

Houston, Jean. *Godseed: The Journey of Christ* (Quest/Theosophical Publishing House, 1992).

A book of exercises for embodied understanding of the life and meaning of Christ.

Houston, Jean. *The Possible Human: A Course in Enhancing Your Physical, Mental and Creative Abilities* (J. P. Tarcher, 1982).

A compendium of "psychophysical and psychospiritual exercises" for tapping into our creative genius.

Jaeger, Mary, and Kathleen Juline. *You Are the One* (Science of Mind Communications, 1988).

A workbook for learning and practicing the transcendent technology of "affirmative prayer."

Zukav, Gary. *The Seat of the Soul* (Simon & Schuster, 1990).

A guide to our evolution from five-sensory to multi-sensory being, and to the achievement of authentic power by aligning our souls and our personalities.

In addition to the above are Twelve-Step programs of many kinds, which assist us in turning our lives over to the Higher Power, and recovering from the condition of separation from God and one's true self. These programs are applicable to all self-destructive syndromes.

VIDEOTAPES

The following videotapes are available from the Foundation for Conscious Evolution.

The Book of Co-Creation Video Book

An award-winning ninety-minute dramatic presentation of *The Book of Co-Creation* narrated by Barbara Marx Hubbard for small group study. Produced by David Smith.

Bucky and Barbara: Our Spiritual Experience

A one-hour dialogue between Barbara Marx Hubbard and R. Buckminster Fuller, hosted by Michael Toms of New Dimensions Radio, produced by David Smith.

A Positive Vision of the Future

An inspirational dialogue with Barbara Marx Hubbard concerning the social and spiritual revolution now taking place on Earth, taped on the Colorado River.

Call or write the Foundation for Conscious Evolution for information on the following products. (See order form at end of book).

The Global Brain
The White Hole in Time

Two inspiring video summaries of Peter Russell's books by the same names.

Twelve Canticles to the Universe

Briane Swimme, co-author of *The Universe Story*, reveals the thrilling drama of cosmogenesis and the nature of evolutionary intelligence.

APPRECIATIONS

An expression of love and gratitude for this precious
extended family of pioneering souls from whom I have
drawn my strength, inspiration, courage and love.

Members of my family: My father and mother; my sisters and brother,
especially my sister Patricia Ellsberg who has been my soul mate and eternal friend since she was six; my beloved children and their mates, Suzanne
and Sandy Brown, Woodleigh, Alexandra, Wade, Lloyd, and Gale
Whipple; and my grandchildren, Danielle, Jarret, Peter and Renee; my
husband, Earl Hubbard, with whom five children and a new image of
humanity were conceived; and my co-creative partner John Whiteside
with whom I went forth to tell the story.

Colleagues and teachers of conscious evolution: Sri Aurobindo, Winifred
Babcock, Ralph Blum, David Bohm, Ray Bradbury, Peter Caddy, Arthur
C. Clarke, Norman Cousins, John Denver, Eric Drexler, Krafft Ehricke,
Duane Elgin, Ralph Waldo Emerson, F.M. Esfandiary, Matthew Fox, R.
Buckminster Fuller, Jerome Glenn, Stanislas Grof, Willis Harman, Hazel
Henderson, Jean Houston, Gopi Krishna, George T. Lock Land, Timothy
Leary, John Mack, Abraham H. Maslow, Mother, Robert Mueller, Michael
Murphy, Brian O'Leary, Gerard K. O'Neil, Belden Paulson, Ilya Prigogine,
Sondra Ray, Gene Roddenberry, Albert Rosenfeld, John Rossner,
Theodore B. Roszak, Peter Russell, Jonas Salk, Rupert Sheldrake, Jan
Smuts, David Spangler, Lloyd Strom, Brian Swimme, Pierre Teilhard de
Chardin, Michael and Justine Toms, Thomas Troward, Peter Vajk, John
White, Terry Cole Whittaker, Lancelot Law Whyte, Gary Zukav and the
great historian and teacher of it all, Roger Weir.

Beloved friends and social innovators with whom I have worked all these
years and whose companionship has inspired me to keep up my courage
no matter what happens, including Carolyn Anderson, Sanford Anderson,

Jacqueline Baldet, Peggy Bassett, Faye Beuby, Roger Brown, Flo Calhoun, Barbara Carpenter, Kathryn Chardin, Ella Cisneros, Edward Cornish, Marion Culhane, Tovi and Gregg Daly, Lawrence de Bivort, Bill Donovan, Joe Eger, Leslie Ennis, William Galt, Kathleen Gildred, William Golden, Joseph Goldin, William Hallal, Marian and Glenn Head, Gail and Greg Hoag, Carol Hoskins, Marta Houske, Helane Jeffries, Hans Keller, Logan Kline, Eleanor LeCain, Bernard Lietaer, Layne Longfellow, Martin Lopata, Avon Mattison, Rashmi Mayur, Daniel Masiarz, Rita McInnis, Barry McWaters, Carol Rosin, Stephan and Haydan Schwartz, Judith Skutch and William Whitson, Marie Spengler, John Steiner, Jan St. John, Michael and Diane Sutton, Sylvia Timbres, Ward Phillips, Hal and Laura Uplinger, Rama Vernon and Max Lafser, Sasha White, John Zwerver and my faithful friend and inspiration in all I do, Bill Gray.

God-parents of *The Book of Co-Creation:* Dawson Church and Brenda Plowman, Georg Feuerstein, Katherine Grace, Joanna Harcourt-Smith, Bob Love and Carole Baste, the devoted and brilliant editor, Noel McInnis, Jeanne McNamara and Linda Duffy, Richard Polese, David Smith, who created the beautiful video tape, Archbishop Warren Watters, Amb. Eduardo Zuluetta, and Rev. Marcia Sutton, my minister and eternal friend, who focused me on the Christ within.

Finally, three people whose faith in this project brought it to fulfillment: Jean Lanier, whose clarity and magnaminity of soul bound us together; Laurance S. Rockefeller, founder of The Fund for the Enhancement of the Human Spirit, whose grant made the publication of this book possible, and whose intuition about the "Christ of the 21st Century" deeply inspired me; and my dearest life partner Sidney Lanier, who sees the promise of humanity, and whose love and vision oriented my life in its true direction.

TOGETHERNET

**A 21st Century Communications Network
dedicated to people and projects
in service to the Earth**

Those of us who share a passion for conscious evolution require a vehicle to communicate insights, initiatives and questions. Important information relating to how to co-create a planetary awakening must be shared as quickly and widely as possible. TOGETHERNET, a service of the Together Foundation, has set up a special computer conference for readers of *The Revelation* who choose to communicate electronically.

Created for the sole purpose of providing a communication system for those engaged in assisting the Earth in a peaceful transition to its next evolutionary phase, TOGETHERNET can be accessed by any Macintosh or IBM compatible computer that has a modem. It has the reputation for being the easiest-to-use computer network on the planet. For information call or write the Together Foundation, 130 South Willard St., Burlington, VT 05401, Phone (802) 862-2030, Fax (802) 862-1890.

If you require information on people, projects or organizations that are aligned with the purposes of this book, you can call a special toll-free number, (800) ECOLINE, staffed by the Together Foundation in connection with the University of Vermont. They can provide you with names, telephone numbers and addresses relating to projects and events.

Who Is Who in Service to the Earth is a directory of eight thousand projects (both organizations and individuals). Published by the Visionlink Education Foundation, this directory is available through the Together Foundation at the above address.

INDEX

A

Abel, 176

Adam
  first Adam, 68, 161
  as masculine aspect of human consciousness, 286
  Second Adam, 68–69, 118, 161, 173, 221, 286, 287
  See also men

address, of The Foundation for Conscious Evolution, 365

adolescence, 154–156, 216, 225

adulthood, co-creative, 156

aesthetics, 275

affirmations, 308–310

aging, 152, 172, 218. *See also* immortality; lifespan; rejuvenation

alchemy, 136, 137

alienation, 107, 131, 210, 238

aliens, inappropriateness of term, 266. *See also* extraterrestrials

Alpha and Omega, 86, 151, 293

androgyny, 56, 154

angels
  birth is attended by, 216
  co-creation and, 132, 141, 156
  described, 148–149, 221
  fallen angels, 178–179, 230
  impatience of, 189
  the Lamb and, 132, 148–149
  reality of, 250
  Satan overcome by, 178
  seven angels, 146
  Universal Phase of evolution and, 239–240

anger, 214, 217, 226

animal nature
  co-creative nature and, 118–119, 123–124, 128
  described, 118
  evolving from, 164
  failing to transcend, 201–202
  great whore and, 201–202
  in pure form (living beings), 141
  self-consciousness distinguished from, 276
  transcending, 129
  See also animals; beast

animals
  carnivorous behavior of, 143, 176, 177, 178, 215, 216, 246
  endangered species, 254
  free will of, 245
  predators, 254
  protection of, 128, 254
  self-transcendence not chosen by, 278
  transformation of, 192, 254
  See also animal nature; beast

Apocalypse, four horsemen of the, 134–136, 163, 166

apostles. *See* disciples

architecture, 210, 275

ark
  Noah's ark, 270
  symbolism of, 170, 172

Armageddon
  alternative to, 147, 162, 232–237
  avoiding, 232, 241
  described, 167–168, 194–195
  See also tribulations

armaments, 202

art
  co-creative, 155, 275
  and communicating the Story of Our Birth, 189
  existing, 168, 210, 275

artificial intelligence, 171

ascended masters, 272

ascension, 74, 187, 188, 207, 262. *See also* New Jerusalem, ascending to

aspiration, 107–108, 117

astroculture, 273

astronautics, 131, 137, 147, 294

atomic bomb, 40, 76, 131, 163

atomic power, 163, 171, 294

atomic structure, quickening vibrations of, 192, 194

attention, on God, 71–72, 236, 243

audiotapes, 363

authority, loss of, by old institutions, 238

automatic writing, 134

B

Babylon, 184, 200–203, 205, 206, 208–209, 210
  end of, 211–213

barley, symbolism of, 135, 136

BOOKS AND TAPES
BY BARBARA MARX HUBBARD

(See Order Form, page 365)

BOOKS:

The Revelation: Our Crisis Is a Birth

An extraordinary decoding of the Book of Revelation, revealing the consciousness required by the human race, not only to survive, but to blossom into full realization of its capacities. The book presents Jesus as the prototype of the future human. $16.95 paperback, $25.00 hardcover.

The Book of Co-Creation: The Gospels, Acts and Epistles

This is the remainder of the *Co-Creation* manuscript. Write or call to have your name placed on the list to be advised when it is available.

The Evolutionary Journey: Your Guide to a Positive Future

A poetic overview of the fifteen-billion-year story of creation. It provides the evolutionary perspective vital to full understanding of *The Revelation.* It projects the human race into the future, describing what it is like when "everything that we know we can do works." It is a preview of coming attractions! The book provides one idea per week for study with assigned readings, giving the reader an excellent course in conscious evolution. $7.95 paperback.

The Hunger of Eve: One Woman's Odyssey Towards the Future

Barbara Marx Hubbard's autobiography, a graphic story of her unfolding from an agnostic mother of five to a cosmic futurist. The book is an inspiration to all men and women who seek to discover their destinies. $11.95 paperback.

Connecting at the Heart

A workbook containing specific directions for starting and maintaining resonant core groups, a twelve session outline of processes, and suggested steps to reach higher levels of resonance. Published by Global Family. $14.00 paperback.

The Rings of Empowerment

A guide for discovering and fulfilling your life purpose as part of a co-creative team. It contains specific tools and experiential exercises for tapping into your innate knowing, discovering and deepening your vocation of destiny, finding your teammates and gaining the entrepreneurial skills to actualize yourself in the world. It is designed to empower individuals and teams at the leading edge of transformation to co-create the world we choose. Published by Global Family. $20.00 paperback.

VIDEOTAPES

Bucky and Barbara: Our Spiritual Experience

A one-hour dialogue between Barbara Marx Hubbard and Buckminster Fuller, hosted by Michael Toms of New Dimensions Radio. The tape offers rare glimpses into the deeper experiences of two powerful evolutionary thinkers and gives insights into the future of our global village. Produced by David Smith at Xavier University. $29.95.

The Book of Co-Creation Video Book

An award-winning ninety-minute dramatic presentation of *The Book of Co-Creation*, narrated by Barbara Marx Hubbard for group study. Readings from the book are followed by deep discussion and visualizations of an evolving planet on the brink of a shift in mass consciousness. Produced by David Smith at Xavier University. $29.95.

A Positive Vision of the Future

An inspirational dialogue with Barbara Marx Hubbard concerning the social and spiritual revolution now taking place on Earth, taped on the Colorado River. $29.95

AUDIOTAPES

Meditations from the Inner Source

Guided visualizations and daily practices to stabilize God-centered consciousness. $10.00.

The Best of Barbara Marx Hubbard

Six of Barbara's best speeches delivered at conferences around the world. Three tape set, $25.00.

THE FOUNDATION FOR CONSCIOUS EVOLUTION

BOOKS AND TAPES BY BARBARA MARX HUBBARD AND COLLEAGUES

0001 ❑ THE BOOK OF CO-CREATION: *The Revelation: Our Crisis is a Birth.*
A decoding of the biblical Book of Revelation offering an alternative to Armageddon.
Vol. 1 ($16.95 paper, $25.00 hardcover) $_____

0002 ❑ THE BOOK OF CO-CREATION: *The Promise Will Be Kept: The Gospels, Acts and Epistles.* A call to become co-creators in the image of Christ.
Vol. 2 ($30.00 spiral bound) $_____

0003 ❑ TEACHINGS OF THE INNER CHRIST. *Instructions for the Transition Team.*
Inspired guidance, meditations and practices for readers of the
Co-Creation books. ($20.00 spiral bound) $_____

0004 ❑ THE EVOLUTIONARY JOURNEY. The new story of creation, carrying us through
our birth as a universal humanity…what it will be like when everything works.
($7.95 paper) $_____

0005 ❑ THE HUNGER OF EVE: *One Woman's Odyssey Toward the Future.*
Hubbard's personal story from mother of five to cosmic futurist.
($11.95 paper) $_____

0006 ❑ RINGS OF EMPOWERMENT. Ten practical principles and practices to form
co-creative teams. By Global Family. ($20.00 paper) $_____

0007 ❑ WHO IS WHO IN SERVICE TO THE EARTH. (2nd Edition) By Hans Keller.
A directory of over 8,000 projects and organizations. ($30.00) $_____

VIDEO TAPES

0001 ❑ THE BOOK OF CO-CREATION VIDEO. An award-winning 90-minute dramatic
presentation of the book for group study. David Smith, producer. ($29.95) $_____

0002 ❑ A POSITIVE VISION OF THE FUTURE. An inspirational dialogue with Barbara on
the Colorado River presenting the "new story" with poetry and humor. ($19.95) $_____

0003 ❑ BUCKY AND BARBARA: OUR SPIRITUAL EXPERIENCE. One hour dialogue with
Barbara Marx Hubbard and Buckminster Fuller. ($29.95) $_____

0004 ❑ BARBARA MARX HUBBARD SPEAKS ON CONSCIOUS EVOLUTION (*UNITY, August '93*)
26 minutes ($19.95) $_____

AUDIO TAPES

0001 ❑ MEDITATIONS FROM THE INNER SOURCE. Guided visualizations and daily practices to
stabilize God-centered consciousness. ($10.00) $_____

0002 ❑ THE BEST OF BARBARA MARX HUBBARD. Six of Barbara's best speeches delivered
at conferences around the world. (Three tape set $25.00) $_____

0003 ❑ WOMEN'S CREATIVE ENERGY. KPFA interview. ($10.00) $_____

NEWSLETTER

NEWS ❑ The New Center Letter written by Barbara Marx Hubbard, Sidney Lanier and
colleagues reveals important insights in the field of conscious evolution and
connects us as a community of pioneering souls. ($25.00 per year) $_____

Make check payable to:
The Foundation for Conscious Evolution
336 Bon Air Center, #384, Greenbrae, CA 94904

PAYMENT METHOD:

❑ Check/Money order enclosed

❑ Visa/Mastercard Exp. Date:

Card #_____

Signature _____

To order by phone 1-800-444-7030 Fax (415) 925-1646

❑ **I wish to contribute to the non-profit Foundation for Conscious Evolution** $_____

Allow 2–3 weeks for delivery

SHIPPING AND HANDLING:

$4 first item, $2.00 ea. additional item $_____

Sales Tax – California residents only add 7.25% $_____

TOTAL DUE: $_____

Ship to: _____

_____

_____

▲

ABOUT THE AUTHOR

Barbara Marx Hubbard lives and works in Northern California. She is president and co-founder with her partner Sidney Lanier of The Foundation for Conscious Evolution. She is available for lectures on Conscious Evolution. The sequel to *The Revelation: Our Crisis is a Birth* is entitled *The Promise Will Be Kept: The Gospels, Acts and Epistles.* It is now available in spiral binder and will be published in 1994. You may write to Barbara Marx Hubbard at The Foundation for Conscious Evolution, 336 Bon Air Center, #384, Greenbrae, CA 94904. Order books by calling 1-800-444-7030.